W9-CZS-415

The Secret of M. Dulong

ALSO BY COLETTE INEZ

The Woman Who Loved Worms and Other Poems

Alive and Taking Names

Eight Minutes from the Sun

Family Life

Getting Under Way: New & Selected Poetry

Naming the Moons

For Reasons of Music

Clemency

Spinoza Doesn't Come Here Anymore

The Secret of M. Dulong

A Memoir

Colette Inez

THE UNIVERSITY OF WISCONSIN PRESS

The University of Wisconsin Press
1930 Monroe Street
Madison, Wisconsin 53711

www.wisc.edu/wisconsinpress/
3 Henrietta Street
London WC2E 8LU, England

1 3 5 4 2

Printed in the United States of America

Library of Congress Cataloging-in-Publication Data
Inez, Colette.
The secret of M. Dulong: a memoir / Colette Inez.
p. cm—(Wisconsin studies in autobiography)
ISBN 0-299-21420-6 (cloth: alk. paper)
1. Inez, Colette. 2. Poets, American—20th century—Biography.
3. Adoptees—United States—Biography.
4. Belgian Americans—Biography. 5. Birthmothers—Belgium.
I. Title. II. Series.
PS3559.N34Z475 2005
811′.54—dc22 2005005445

FOR *Saul* AND *Maurice*

Illustrations

L'Institut de Puériculture 5
Colette, age eight, in Belgium 17
The house on Bayview Avenue 39
Colette with Alex Scotti, 1950 166
Aunt Jeanne 177
Marthe in her fifties 180
Colette's father, the monsignor 192
Colette and Saul at their wedding, 1964 197
Saul, 1975 201
The Dulong family house in Nérac, 1986 203
Marthe in her early thirties 217
Cousin Maurice in Nérac, 1994 230
Jeanne and Marthe as young girls, 1908–9 236
Marie and Alfred Dulong in their seventies 255

Acknowledgments

Portions of this book, appearing here in slightly modified form, originally appeared in the following publications:

Confrontation: "Exile and the Writer" and "Visitors"
Helicon Nine Reader: "Second Visit to Nérac"
Colorado Review: "Scenes from Bayview Avenue"
The Connecticut Review: "The Homecoming?"
Thomson/Gale Contemporary Authors: "Colette Inez"
After Confession (Greywolf Press): "Family Talk"

I want to thank the National Endowment for the Arts and the New York Foundation for the Arts for grants that aided me while writing this work, and equally appreciate the valuable gift of time offered by Yaddo, Inc., the MacDowell Colony, the Virginia Center for the Arts, the U-Cross Foundation, the Blue Mountain Center, the Djerassi Foundation, the Millay Colony for the Arts, and the Medway Institute.

I am also grateful to many generous friends for their support and encouragement while I wrote this memoir.

Author's Note

The events and experiences narrated have been as faithfully given as memory permitted. A few names have been changed to protect the privacy of individuals involved.

The Secret of M. Dulong

1

I paraded my new red dress and blue coat before everyone at l'Institut de Puériculture on the rue Chant d'Oiseaux. Twirling and running on the points of my toes, I arched my arms overhead like the ballerina I had seen Anne imitate behind Sister Theodore's back. "How grand we are," my friend exclaimed, studying me with exaggerated awe. "In America you'll become a fine lady and never come back to see us."

"But I will, I promise. And we'll have tea in a hotel." I imagined being served in a splendid dining room, nibbling dainty sandwiches, dabbing our mouths with linen napkins, outfitted in frilly hats with veils and bows, gloves buttoned at the wrists like those of genteel women who appeared in popular magazines sometimes left by visitors and smuggled into our rooms. We would chat about the king and queen of Belgium, about garden parties, charity balls and talk of our families.

Yet even with my eyes shut tight in concentration, even when in thought I stretched our bodies to adult height, we remained children.

When I pictured Anne's loosened braids wound into a tight bun at the back of her neck or tiny, spidery lines around our eyes, nothing changed. We were Colette, who would soon be eight, and Anne, who was nine, in a Catholic home for orphaned and abandoned children in Belgium, 1938.

Anne and I began our good-byes in the yard behind the institute. Pale as the figurine of a saint, almost a head taller than I, Anne was one of many children parceled out to relatives after the death of her mother. She was destined to stay with the Sisters. Expectations? Taking the veil as a Bride of Christ, finding placement as a domestic servant, drudgery as a farmer's wife, or at best, employment as a shopgirl or factory hand. Boys were in greater demand, spirited away and adopted by people who reckoned their higher value. It was their beds that often emptied soon after they arrived.

I blotted Anne's eyes with my soft new handkerchief, bought the previous day in Brussels. Studying the elaborate stitching, I assumed a child like me had embroidered its flowers and leaves, a girl whose parents, like mine, had also left her as a baby with the nuns. "You were dropped on the doorstep in a bag," children teased. Was it true?

Their high voices filled the grounds. Anne and I joined Marc, Chantal, Marie, and diminutive Jean-Pierre, who threw his arms around me and kissed my cheek. We called him Petit Jean; although our age, he never outgrew his early uniform.

We had once shared an L-shaped room, but when I turned seven I was moved into a section for girls—with two facing rows of five white iron beds, a narrow aisle between them. I slept along the far wall nearest the window that opened on a spacious back court. Anne was placed in the center, and Chantal near the door would be first to escape as loud bells roused us for matins. Petit-Jean remained in our former ward.

A young, melancholy woman occasionally visited him, her spiked heels clicking down the long corridors. Purplish-blue crescents shadowed her eyes, and glossy lipstick printed red butterfly wings on Petit-Jean's face.

L'Institut de Puériculture

"She is my girlfriend," was his usual reply when we asked. With a bat of his thick eyelashes, "Yes, she has chosen only me." Next to Anne, I would most miss le Petit-Jean.

And there behind her desk was Mother Superior, who filled me with dread. Perhaps it was her deeply creased face that resembled a map of river systems, or the authority of her square, steel-rimmed glasses, or her small mouth incised with clumped lines. Most fearsome was her penetrating glance, which fixed my particulars in one daunting look. "You are a fortunate child. God has willed it that you go to America," she had said.

Only the day before, while I was attending noontime service, a novitiate whispered astonishing news in my ear. "Two men have come for you." And she escorted me to the Reverend Mother's office. They stood by the door when I entered, not priests in long black gowns as I half expected, but two civilians in dark suits and white shirts.

The weekly scattering of male visitors had made me curious about trousers and neckties, cigars and pipes, pipe cleaners and matches. I was fascinated by hirsute men with slick greasy hair, bristles on their upper lips, hair poking out of nostrils or matted and curling out of open summer shirts—males with thick or scrawny necks, heavy-boned or light in physique, their pungent odors. These men were different, smelling of cologne and dressed like office workers in Brussels.

One of the two, who was as handsome as a film star pictured in magazines, carried a briefcase. The other smiled beneath a crisp, auburn moustache and riveted me with small, bright blue eyes. Mother Superior introduced us.

"Colette, I wish you to meet Mr. Bale and Mr. Branigan from America." America, *Les États Unis?* I had marveled at that wide country spread across the class map, and had even memorized many of the names of its forty-eight states. I caught my breath, my heart pounding. Father! Which is my father? Has he come for me? But which one? My eyes leapt to the taller Bale, whose brown wavy hair and calm face pleased me.

I ignored his older friend and asked with forced composure, are you my father? No. Can you bring me to my parents? No. Are they in Africa? Africa and America sounded alike to me. No. The strangers explained they came only as companions for a long sea voyage, nothing more. I would leave with them tomorrow for America, then pass through the iron gates to unknown prospects in another continent.

What was an ocean like? Our gazetteer depicted a blue body of water far larger than the gray lake we crossed and recrossed strapped into double-bladed skates. Who were these men who had come to fetch me for a long journey across the sea?

The red one with pompoms, please." I pointed to a short-sleeved dress with embroidered flowers and a neckline that closed into a bow. Bale, Branigan, and Sister Hebert—a sharp faced nun with rimless glasses, appointed as our chaperon—stood by during my shopping trip to the center of Brussels. My first department store was a miracle of chandeliers and glass counters with glittering jars and small pots of perfume, lotions, powders, rouges, and creams.

"Don't touch what isn't yours. Stop preening." I tried to obey the Sister's stream of commands, but mirrors flashed and beckoned everywhere, some full-length and three-way, others small ovals with handles I grabbed and lifted to my face, seen before only in basin water, cups, bowls, polished cutlery and in the brass knob of Mother Superior's office door.

In the children's dress department, carousels bursting with bright clothing, I danced and curtsied deeply to a tall mirror, jubilant to meet my reflection again. I held up my coveted new dress, pressed its empty sleeves against my arms, and pretended I was a child with a private room like the upstairs boarders who would rejoin their families in the Congo.

"You will now pick another dress to take with you, and do not keep the gentlemen waiting," Sister Hebert ordered, her lips pressed tightly together. I was tempted to linger in this carnival of objects. Sensing my bewilderment, the Sister asked the men "to choose what is appropriate for her. The child has not been taught to decide for herself."

"The child may select whatever makes her happy." It was spoken slowly by Bale in an awkward accent. *Heureuse,* uttered like a soft, blurry stammer. To be happy, someone wished me happiness, an event as unusual as taking tea with a Congo girl or seeing myself whole in the looking glass, as odd as shopping in midafternoon during the early spring of my last days in Belgium.

The red plaid coatdress had pockets above and below the waist and buttons that ran from collar to hem. Next, a blue coat with brass buttons, a matching beret, and patent leather shoes with buckles. Finally, socks and underpants, divinely soft after years of scratchy muslin.

Bale and Branigan helped cart my new wardrobe in shiny boxes and paper sacks back to their rented car. They sat smoking slender American cigarettes, clearing their throats, smiling, nodding and unhurried. Red-haired Branigan took the wheel for our drive through the city's outskirts at the end of the trolley line, and to the brick building that seemed to lose its immensity as my departure neared. Even the spears of the wrought iron gates appeared less formidable on this return to the institute's first-floor hall, as I walk up two flights of stairs and take a right turn into the room holding ten identical narrow beds, mine at the far end.

The Congo girls were lodged at the institute by parents settling in Africa, who desired respectable Catholic educations for their daughters, who would eventually be reunited with their families. The girls' separate lives seemed cherished and indulged. A dozen or so, seldom seen by us, studied in a secluded distant wing in pleasantly furnished rooms; they wore personal clothing and attended chapel at different hours.

Until a few days ago, my picture of their lives was spotty and confused. More than once, I had seen girls with trunks and boxes climbing from cars parked at the institute entrance and heard their whispers and giggles on the staircase leading to the floor above our dormitories.

"They're private students and don't have to wear uniforms or follow our rules," Anne explained. "We're wards of the state. That's how we're described on papers," she said with solemn authority. Having lived on a farm and in the city, Anne was more seasoned than I in the ways of the world.

Tea with one of the Congo girls had been arranged as my departing gift. I fussed with my preparations, wetting my hair to tame obstinate curls, straightening knee socks and buffing shoes with rough textured W.C. tissue.

"One of the girls has an uncle who lives in America," Sister Bernard said, "and she will show you a picture of his house."

Following the Sister's thumping trail through corridors and up stairways, I breathlessly arrived in a parlor paneled with pastel-tinted pictures of the regents of Belgium. The room was furnished with a settee and easy chairs; a standing lamp with a silk shade was alien and dreamlike, its plush comfort a world apart from the sterility of the floors below. I sat as taught, back straight, legs crossed at the ankles, and waited for the girl with an uncle in America and parents in Africa.

She joined me and was introduced by a full name I can no longer recall. But in my universe of children on the floors below, only first names were used, and hearing a surname was exceptional. She had shoulder-length, light-colored hair, like a fairy princess in the illustrated storybooks we were not formally allowed to read but came to scan.

"Would you like to see my uncle's house in Baltimore?"

I gaped wide-eyed at a photo of a gracious house with shuttered windows and a front porch blanched in light. Uncle Luc, erect as a statue embedded in his lawn, squinted through glasses. While not as ornate as the houses I glimpsed during trolley trips to Saint Julian's for Easter services, it spoke of the prosperity granted to ordinary people, the wealth I assumed would also be mine in America.

Out of the corners of her eyes, she keenly followed my response. For the moment I was a celebrity! Someone soon to travel countless miles and be rewarded as was she with a second name. But where would I live? I struggled to recall the places mentioned by the men during their idle conversation.

"I will go to New York," I declared. She gasped: "Oh to live in such a splendid place."

Over cups of tea and vanilla biscuits, we returned to her album. Photos of palm trees and white buildings in Leopoldville. Pictures of dignified natives in white tunics and beads; others of children of our age standing in unsmiling groups beside round huts with thatched roofs. Then, at last, a photo taken by Uncle Luc of New York City's towering buildings, some with needlelike crests.

"Skyscrapers," she said. "You will live with clouds and birds while I am in Africa with lions and monkeys." Mimicking an ape, she stuck out her jaw and scratched her delicate torso. More hilarity. I wiped my eyes and sipped the last drops of sweet tea. We were soon to live in strange lands, each with its own astonishments.

A firm hand on my shoulder signaled the end of my visit. Hearing the five o'clock bell, I raced ahead of Sister Bernard through the halls and down several flights of steps. Entering the chapel, I genuflected, bobbed down on one knee, briskly made the sign of the cross, and tumbled into a pew for a moment of silent entreaty. The prayers of evensong had begun.

The rituals of my last night at the institute were like others before it. We regrouped after supper and marched in lines to vespers at dusk. Prayers intoned at bedside. Lights out at eight sharp. Patterns of a measured life. In the excitement of our short meeting I had asked little of the newcomers about my family. If their mission to take me home was a secret covenant with others, even with the glum and mysterious aunt who sometimes visited me, I was not told.

Before I stepped through the iron gate, le Petit-Jean kissed me wetly, his stubby lashes fluttering against my cheeks. "Come back when you are a fine lady," Chantal called out, waving her crumpled handkerchief.

I shook hands with Mother Superior, who interrupted her duties of office to bid me good-bye. I bade farewell to the Sisters who wished me Godspeed. Even unsmiling Sister Theodore allowed a gleam of warmth to brighten her intense dark eyes while admonishing me to behave myself in America or know the reasons why.

2

The open sea was an immense gray mirror reflecting clouds and the first gulls I had ever seen. Gull. Branigan traced the word in a French-English dictionary he consulted during talks with me and other French speakers on board. At his urging, I tried to pronounce it in English, but confused the word with "girl."

"No, no, a gull" he corrected. It was a fine distinction gone amiss in mouthing and digesting an ungainly language. "You are a girl. Here, watch me." I studied the rolled tip of his tongue as he sounded an *l*, and formed the word again without the purred *r* after the hard *g*. Success.

Only yesterday we had raced the clock to reach our ship, speeding in the Americans' rented car through rain-drenched Antwerp to collect my passport. I hurried across bustling streets under the shelter of Bale's black umbrella, followed by Branigan, who shielded his hat with a newspaper. Our goal was a drab building in the heart of a commercial district. Gone was the scent of flowers that spiced the springtime air of Brussels miles away.

We were just in time. As I waited on line for the paperwork to be done, the unfamiliar hum and buzz of office sounds and ringing telephones enveloped me. Telephones were novelties I had seen only twice before. One sat mutely on Reverend Mother's desk between her books and holy pictures. Another hung on the wall of the scullery; I would pass it during warm days when the children carried plates and cutlery from the kitchen to wooden tables placed on the grounds for outdoor suppers.

The next morning I waved farewell to Antwerp and to my country, a thumbprint on the world map. As the ship sailed west, I leaned over the rail and watched the shore recede to a gray film dwindling down into the open sea.

I pictured our ship crossing the North Sea hour by hour, the captain at its helm as much a master of our nautical fate as the Reverend Mother, who steered the course of our lives on land. We were bound for Southampton, England, there to board another liner for my family reunion in New York. Bale and Branigan were vague when pressed for details.

Although unwaveringly kind, the Mister Bs, as I thought of them, skirted all direct questions. Why did my family wait so long before sending for me? Were they rich, and how did they make their living? I had imagined them converting savage Indians in the far west of the country on reservations so remote they were lost to civilization.

The only relative I had met was an aunt. On visiting days I was usually isolated with a handful of other girls hemming and embroidering towels and ladies' handkerchiefs whose proceeds went to aid our missions in Africa. We, the stitchers, huddled away from the droning traffic of relatives on weekly calls, were resentful, knowing full well there was no one to share Sunday with us. We had given up asking why, wanting to believe ourselves as worthy as Jeanne and Marie, bounding ahead of grandmère and grandpère, Uncle Paul, or cousin so and so, skimming a forbidden hoop between them in the yard.

Patience, I told myself. Perhaps my own parents were missionaries detained in Tanganyika, Kenya, or the Congo, ragged splashes of color in the rainbow of nations depicted on our map. My parents, I imagined, were busy gathering gifts, a horde of toys they would bring me only when enough were collected to fill the cavernous refectory in which we took our meals. How astonished Jeanne and Claude would be with my truckload of spinning tops and balls, dolls and jacks, blocks and pinwheels, train sets and cars, enough to share with everyone, should the nuns allow it.

Since no one spoke of them, my parents became the couple I invented; their elegance and holiness were cut from snips and ends of fairy tales and religious parables. I embellished them; mother and father were not missionaries but people of means who slept in private berths on great ships and greeted the day in pale clothes and large hats. Illustrated magazines showed them stepping from glistening cars. Surely, they feasted on bonbons and sipped hot chocolate served to them in gold mugs.

They were noble and spoke politely to one another in hushed tones. When summoning servants, they said please and thank you very much. They never snapped their fingers or loudly blew their noses.

One strange afternoon—I may have been six or younger—my hour of reflection was interrupted. Sister Theodore entered, her eyebrows rising above dark and penetrating eyes, brushed aside my thin pile of untrimmed linen and led me briskly down a corridor to a large room furnished with benches and hardbacked chairs. In a nondescript suit, like that worn by the lay teacher who trained us to knit and crochet, was a plain woman in a snugly-fitted hat. She was seated, silently counting prayers on a rosary.

"She is your aunt come from France," the nun explained. An aunt? Excited by the introduction, I brimmed over with questions about my parents. Who and where were they? When will they take me home? Why did they leave me here as a baby? She ignored my questions and muttered something about the weather, how unusually warm it was.

A deep line cut the space between her eyes, which were large and gold-flecked and somehow familiar in the light. How could that be?

Had she come here before? The nun wagged an admonishing finger and ordered me to hold my tongue and behave. Impudence was corrected with a switch or a cane, and I had no difficulty recalling the stinging pain of my last punishment for stealing a toy rattle from the infant ward.

My aunt wore her smooth, oak-brown hair knotted in a tight bun; her clear, olive skin was unlike my pink complexion. Only her broad forehead resembled mine. She was perfectly still and unsmiling; I could not believe she ever fidgeted or squirmed when discovered in a lie or ever left damp crescents of sweat under the armpits of her dress. It was unthinkable that she might gnaw her fingernails or poke out her tongue, as I did when a nun turned her back.

Gripping a book of common prayer, she asked me to kneel and pray with her. I obeyed and mumbled an invocation by rote, distracted by the scent of strong soap clinging to her freshly laundered clothes. A pleasant odor, but I found little else to like in this morose woman, her drab wool garments, her single gold tooth flashing like the gold crucifix she wore at her throat. Our visit ended as it began with expected commands: obey the Sisters; pray to God for His compassion. Her brusque departure was as baffling as her sudden arrival.

She returned later that year, and perhaps a few times after, again asking me to implore God to forgive our sins, to have patience and faith, to trust in the Lord when I incautiously spoke of family. We knelt and prayed. To prod her for more information would be impertinent. As bidden by the nuns, guardians of propriety, I must wait to be spoken to.

When informed by Sister Bernard we were studying the lives of the saints, she tested me. How many tales had we heard of the saints and their glorious redemptions? The founder of the French Poor Clares, Colette, after whom I supposed I was named, entered a convent, and expressing extreme piety, walled herself in a cell between two buttresses of Notre Dame de Corbie. That was before she helped reform the Franciscan brotherhood, the Colettine Reforms, on orders from Saint Francis and from Saint Clare who came to her in a vision.

Saint Anne of Susanna was persecuted for rejecting a marriage arranged by the Emperor Basil. Only after her suitor's death was she allowed to enter a convent. Hers was the namesake of another Anne, Saint Anne, the patroness of seamstresses, lace makers, carpenters, stablemen and the fabricators of brooms—a saint invoked by the poor or by those searching for lost objects. "I will pray to her to find you again." My friend, Anne, assured me her patron saint would not ignore her requests.

Saint Bathilde? Captured by Corsairs and sold as a slave. Saint Eulalie? Endured tortures and was burned alive on a pyre. Saint Georgette? Fasted every day and incessantly sent prayers to God. In a ratifying message from heaven, doves hovered over her remains during her burial. Rose of Lima chiseled her bed out of rock. Eager to show off what I knew, I was equally thrilled and oppressed by these stories of devotion and sacrifice.

At one visit the aunt wore a maroon knit dress, and I stared raptly at her skin through the tiny windows of its weave. But the plainness of her brown, flat, laced-up shoes displeased me. I secretly craved a more fashionable relative who other children might admire me for having.

The one time she brought me a plaything, a stuffed dog, the nuns reminded her of the institute's inflexible rule, its prohibition against private ownership. Our clothes, issued by the commissary, were not our own. Nor were rosaries and combs, underpants and shoes, night dresses and chamber pots. We were taught it was vain and agitating to prize possessions. Nuns felt we would squabble over them.

As usual, the aunt said little. Was she as dissatisfied as was I with our visits? I wondered why she came. When the aunt spoke privately with the nuns, I imagined she was told of flaws in my character, such as my stubborn refusal to clean the last fragment of slimy mutton fat from my plate or how I sat with head in hands and spun daydreams during lessons.

I overheard a nun saying to the aunt, "She may not be pretty, but she's quick to learn." Such talk of personal appearances was rare.

I was told my aunt was not of the farm. Her soft hands with short nails were like those of the nun who later described her as a scholar of French history. Medieval history. Yes, I somewhat understood this, knew something of Charlemagne, the Song of Roland, Jeanne D'Arc, and the French kings.

During our meetings, a question or two about my studies was followed by my quick answers; I concealed my annoyance at being quizzed by a visitor who evaded my every question. We exhausted what I knew about the lives of the saints, and she appeared bothered by my excitable accounts of the torment of martyrs. "Calm yourself, child," she said, lines deepening and forming tiny pouches around her slender lips.

From the corner of my eye, I began to discern an outsider who might know nothing about my parents. I suspected she was a relative so far removed from our family that its members were strangers. That would explain her elusiveness. Who she was and why she journeyed to the institute was a story waiting to be told.

"We are not put here on earth for pleasant times," she instructed, and, "the Sisters have your best interests at heart." Absorbing these phrases, I sat demurely, ankles crossed, hands folded in my lap, and sneaked glances at her long, mournful face.

Bale said nothing of my parents or of my relatives. He admitted only to being an attorney protecting people unjustly accused of breaking the law. My complicated paperwork was also part of his job. He lived with his wife, Sue, outside New York City, where his law office was located.

"Soon," he answered when I asked if he had children, a question which braved the Sisters' warning never to press adults on personal matters. But with this abrupt dislocation, the lessons of rue Chant d'Oiseaux were fast dissolving into the mists of our passage.

Images of my friends' faces began to vanish like vapor steaming from the cabin mirror as the Mister Bs shaved, dipping razors into hot water and sculpting narrow trails on lathered cheeks.

Jolted from the dim gray light of the institute's refectory, I found myself foraging in an immense and dazzlingly lit dining room. Long buffet tables were laden with a bonanza of fruits I had never before

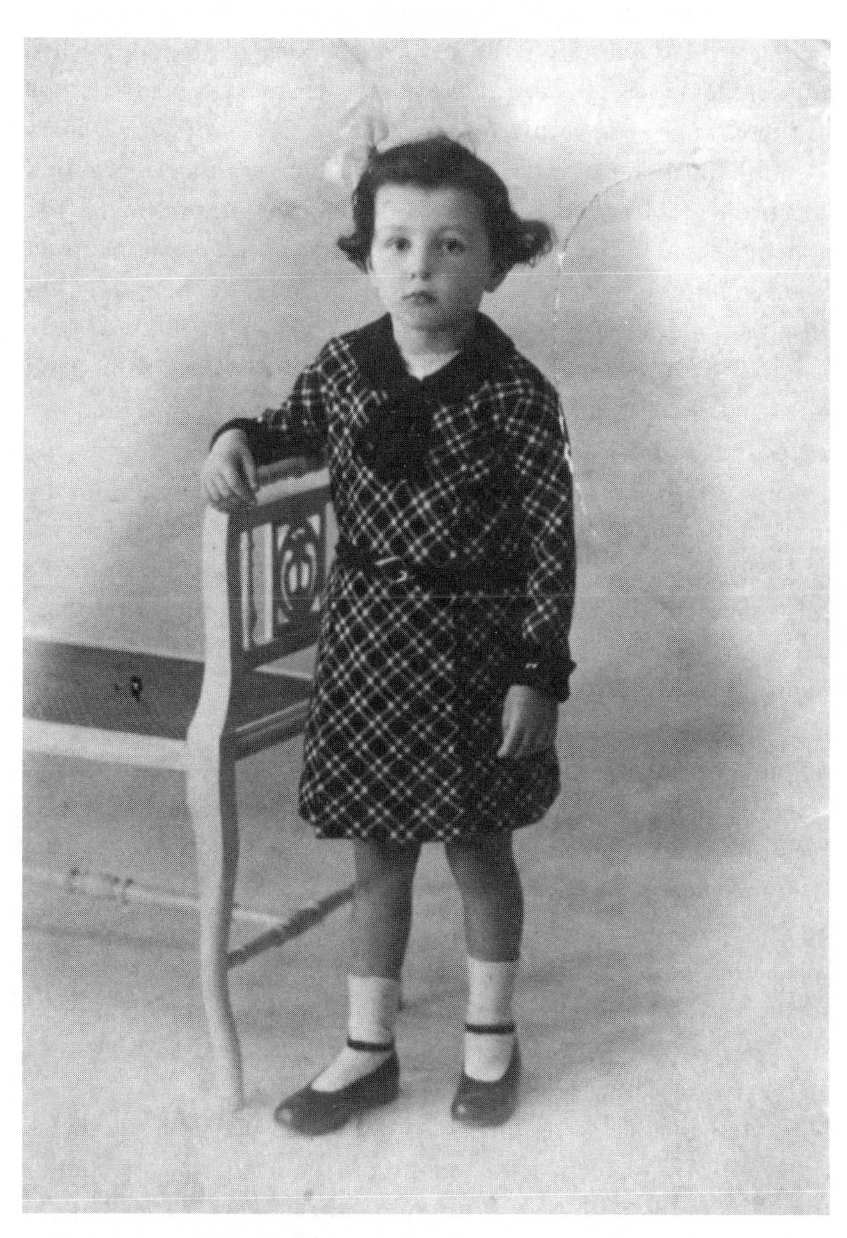

Colette, age eight, in Belgium

seen: bananas like slender boats; light green, thin-skinned melons resembling winter moons; the sheer extravagance of pineapples recalling turbans worn by Asian monarchs whose photographs I had admired in copies of *National Geographic* visitors left behind at the institute. I marveled at my good fortune.

Nibbling a slice of cake, I recalled our midday meals of pea soup and bread, cabbage and the fish bones lodged in our teeth. I was grateful Jesus allowed us to honor his miracle of fishes and loaves on Fridays, bite-by-bite. There was no meat eaten on those days, no glutinous mutton fat to swap with Anne under the table for her handful of soggy vegetables. Our desserts were baked apples and puddings served Saturday and Sunday and ravenously devoured in a concert of slurps and clicking spoons.

After dinner coffee, the Mister Bs joined other men assembling in the ship's lounge or in its smoke-filled card room. I excused myself and dashed off to the playroom or circled the decks between the ship's many levels in heady freedom. Tired and panting, I returned to say good night to the Americans, whom I began to accept as benign and lenient caretakers.

Also on board were Sisters of another order; some English children; members of the Belgian consulate, who shared our table; and several Dutch and German couples, whose languages resembled Flemish, a forbidden tongue at the children's home.

One day Bale pulled out his wallet and showed me a snapshot of Sue. "How pretty," I exclaimed, charmed by her lustrous eyes and regular features. "And my mother in America, is she pretty too? Does she have other children?" A baby brother like Petit-Jean or an older sister like Anne would do very well. But if that were so, why was I an outcast?

Bundled babies were sometimes discovered beside our entrance gate, and I wondered if I was among the foundlings whose infancy the older nuns recalled. After routine punishments, Sister Bernard pondered how the sweet baby she knew had become such a refractory child. Stout Sister Paul would chuck me under the chin and confess to favoring me, but that was years ago. I dimly remember her wide and kindly gap-toothed smile in a dream of taking her hand during my first steps in the infant ward. "The family you are to meet will tell you everything," responded Bale. Why did he use "the" and not the possessive "your" before the word "family," which took the feminine article in French? He gave it the masculine "le," but then Bale sometimes garbled his syllables. Of course, one must not correct adults. Odd that he withheld the facts; perhaps my family swore him to confidence until the instant we rang the doorbell of their stately house, sat side by side in a cozy room and were served trays of cocoa and sponge cake.

Although Bale was resolute in his silence, I liked the graceful way he pulled cigarettes from a shiny pack illustrated with a camel and pyramids. "Are they from Egypt?" I asked, marveling at the smoke rings he sometimes puffed, lazy zeros set in fragile motion.

"No, from America." His eclipsing smile again, the melancholic, turned-down brown eyes. When he granted me a sip of the tea-colored liquid both men emptied by the glassful before dinner, he laughed at my grimace. How could people relish such a drink even more distasteful than the wine served at Mass to honor our crucified Lord?

The Mister Bs slept in bunk beds, one atop of the other; I occupied the lower berth against the opposite wall. I was comforted by their nearness, especially that of Bale who touched my shoulder with a reassuring hand during a shipboard fire drill. "It's all in God's plan." Branigan left it at that.

During a genial moment welcoming personal questions, Branigan admitted to being a scholar who taught at a "great university" and described himself as someone who knew a great deal about one thing. Bale and he were classmates at Catholic University and had remained friends. Nothing more was intimated about their relationship.

Branigan's tight blue eyes were forbidding; I felt guarded under their unwavering stare. And unlike Bale's pleasant and sometimes distracted reserve, Branigan's testy manner kept me on my best behavior. He specialized in Roman history, the subject of his published articles. I nodded respectfully, smiled and asked permission to leave.

Accustomed to waking at 5 A.M., I learned to steal out of the stateroom before the late-rising Mister Bs. Days ago, at sunrise, I had tapped Branigan's limp shoulder. "It is morning," I'd chirped. Bolting upright, he struck his head on the overhead berth and groaned, his blue eyes snapping. "Never wake us unless told. *Jamais. Sans permission*. Never."

I caught a whiff of his sour breath. From the upper bunk, swaddled in striped pajamas, Bale peered down groggily. *"Exactement."* He flopped heavily back to bed in another display of the eccentric and comic ways of adult males.

After quietly dressing and slipping from the cabin, I would follow the corridors to the promenade deck whipped by briny air and foam. Racing along slick passages and up and down ladders, startling early risers, I would finally sink into a canvas sling chair to watch the sea and sky melt into the distant horizon, imagining we were sailing toward a great waterfall like that seen on the page of a geography class calendar.

Sister Jerome once spoke of an American waterfall called Niagara—an Indian name? We had learned about Indians, who taught the pilgrims to plant corn, and of Pocahontas, who saved John Smith's life in Virginia. I was told the state of Virginia was named after the Virgin Mother, as a tribute to our Catholic beliefs. Although not of our faith, the early colonists were God-fearing and devout, the Sister explained. Anne claimed that, nevertheless, non-Catholics and unbaptized babies went to Limbo, a neutral place between Purgatory and Heaven. The image of yowling pagan toddlers in a close-to-celestial infant ward seemed peculiar, but I couldn't pretend to entirely apprehend my religion.

I sped to the playroom, where my shipboard mate, Cecil, had earlier taught me the basics of tossing darts and was now coaching a thickset boy. "You hold it this way." Cecil's instructions were squeezed through clenched teeth. Nigel squinted dumbly at him through thick glasses. "You have to hit the target somewhere, old fellow, and the bull's-eye gives you the most points." Cecil twitched his nose as Nigel's blindly hurled darts peppered the wall or ricocheted wildly.

"You are an idiot!" Cecil exploded. Nigel's magnified eyes brimmed with tears. "Can't you see he can't see?" I gestured the meaning to Cecil by arching a hand over my eyes and motioning toward the boy's eyeglasses.

Shouting words I couldn't make out, Cecil stalked off to practice cartwheels at the far end of the room, and I curled an arm around Nigel to console him in the same way I had comforted Petit-Jean. I staggered backward at his sharp blow to my chest, but refrained from striking back. Maybe news of such violence would be reported to the Mister Bs, who might return me to the Sisters as an incorrigible.

"Leave me alone." His face pink with rage, Nigel ran off to sulk, leaving Cecil to torment someone else. I collected and replaced the darts, consoling myself with memories of Petit-Jean, who would fondly kiss my eyelashes and cheeks.

Every year the tall, stooped doctor came to measure our heights and weights. Petit-Jean defied change. At age eight he resembled a four-year-old; a handsome boy with a thick shrub of springy brown curls and moist, dark eyes. Anne and I adopted him as our pet, a random amusement shared with Chantal and Marie.

We would lift him in our arms like a stuffed toy, squeeze him and heave him into the air, pinch his nose, tweak his ears, and run our fingers through his ringlets. He might momentarily protest with a yelp, a kick, or a show of tears. But, quickly pacified, he would soon revive his good-natured smile.

Petit-Jean had slept opposite me until I turned seven. Eight beds were ranked on each side of the wall; ours were farthest from the hallway door and nearest the steps leading to the Sisters' sleeping quarters. Crossing the cold floor on bare feet, I tiptoed to his bed when he cried out; nightmares woke him. I brushed back his damp hair, stroked his hot forehead, kissed his eyes. He would often follow me back to my bed, clasp my arms and plead to join me. Only fear of discovery by the Sisters and the inevitable punishment restrained us both.

Erratic Petit-Jean. Adept at coquettish remarks and nimble wit, he was shaken by terrors at night. Slow and inclined to give wrong answers in school, he could instantly commit the multiplication table to memory and rattle off the names of saints and historical dates. But a curtain was drawn on his parentage, on those questions that sometimes obsessed the other children. Did parents exist for him as well as for me, I wondered?

We docked in Southampton and changed ships on a foggy morning that Branigan assured me was *typiquement Anglaise*. Over the mournful hoots of fog horns, he sounded out each French syllable, animating the red hairs of his moustache. "The fog has only to lift," he raised upturned palms to demonstrate ascent, "and we'll be sailing for America."

In what was now a ritual, I squeezed my arm to confirm this nebulous realm of ringing bells, gongs and clamoring horns, that it was real. "We'll depart on the dot of three," Bale confidently added, pointing to his watch for emphasis. I was convinced that self-assured and dignified people were reliable about facts.

Such was the case with Mother Superior, whose marshal bearing and firm directives gave her a stamp of certainty beyond question or protest. Cold eyes surveyed our failings behind spectacles that rested on the bridge of a red and bulbous nose, her only feature betraying weakness. She patted it constantly with a handkerchief, as if grieving for the institute's intractable inmates. Where would she be now? Surely frowning into the ledger of infractions and offenses.

Are you dozing?" Bale tapped my shoulder from an adjoining deck chair. "Here, let me arrange your blanket." It had turned cold in the lingering fog of morning. He pulled the fringed, plaid lap robe up to my chin, lit a cigarette, and returned to his book. A mystery, he replied to my question. And to another, "We'll arrive in New York in five days."

The Mister Bs seemed much alike in their whims and behaviors: drawing on their cigarettes, sipping straw-colored liquids, playing cards, writing letters and sharing newspaper headlines. While Bale deflected my stream of questions with unfailing tact, I sometimes caught Branigan clenching his teeth or narrowing his eyes when I persisted. He lacked Bale's patience and gift of concealing displeasure.

Our stateroom was fitted with a single mirror hung high above a dresser. To catch sight of myself in the glass, I half-opened its drawers, clambering up them like a ladder, descending and shutting them with a bang. "It is not a toy," Branigan reproved, freezing me with a glacial stare. But I stole back to the empty stateroom; the joy of sliding and slamming drawers proved irresistible.

The cabin's furniture reminded me of the polished, ornate desk drawers in Mother Superior's quarters that seemed like symbols of her high office. The dresser drawers in Berthe Hermann's private room declared her privilege, the modest affluence of her parents. For the rest of us, our few possessions were folded on shelves in a large communal closet. Spring and winter coats were hung on open racks. Our uniformly dark shoes lined up on the floor: two pairs, heavy and light, as well as a set of brown plaid felt slippers.

Our ocean liner dwarfed the vessel that had ferried us from Antwerp; its topmost deck rail was beyond my reach, and the yawning corridors opened to state rooms and lounges whose luxury left me gasping. I regained composure after escaping to the children's play area, where I pulled a jump rope from its peg and made up a reassuring skipsong. "A" I'm called Anne, "B" your name's Brigitte, "C" is for Claire who jumps on muddy feet."

Jumping rope was one of our few approved amusements at the institute. The nuns might have reasoned that the cooperative nature of the pastime protected jumpers and spinners from any offense. Since no one lost, no one won, how could our heads be turned by envy or conceit? Boasting was wicked. The braggart's soul would float in Purgatory, that country somewhere below the door of Heaven, but above the gateposts of Hell.

The ship's foghorn sounded three blasts: notes of departure, I guessed, returning the skip rope to its peg and rejoining the Mister

Bs on the promenade deck. Three o'clock, *exactement,* Bale smiled at me and motioned to his watch. Passengers, collected two deep behind the railings, waved at onlookers on the receding dock. The sky cleared, a good sign.

The cold spring days at sea passed quickly. I woke at dawn and knelt to pray "*Notre Père* . . . Our Father . . ." then dressed in the dark. Bundled in my new blue coat, I escaped the snores of my sleeping guardians for the gentler deck sounds of wind and sea. I greeted the early risers: the nun I caught sight of on the first ship and her cluster of English children, a bearded old man with a wooden leg and his small dog that yapped at passersby.

Good morning! I cried in English. *Bonjour,* I called out to man or beast, whichever I passed. I gaped through the railings at high waves dashing against the ship's hull, their spray dampening my face, hair, socks, and shoes. The rocking of the ship, which distressed many passengers who took refuge below deck, elated me. *"Mal de mer,"* Branigan moaned, pushing aside an untouched lunch brought by Bale who, like me, seemed immune.

Cecil was equally unscathed when I found him in the play area urging an ashen-faced Dutch boy to ride the swing to cure his queasiness. The trusting boy looping higher and higher until he braked to a stop with his feet, covered his mouth and dashed from the room, heaving up his breakfast.

I may have been Cecil's only non-victim, a confederate who, in his offhand, arrogant way, he sought out and liked. Stretching the skin around his eyes, pulling the corners of his mouth downward like a clown, he acknowledged me with grotesque faces in an odd show of fondness. My feelings toward him were mixed: admiration for a gangly ten-year-old gamely setting out alone to a new country, uneasiness at being audience to his taunting of others.

Sometimes we met in the ship's chapel, where he seemed tempered by prayer, head down and eyes clamped shut in a fervent solemnity I could not begin to rival. From Cecil I had expected a hasty bob instead of a deep genuflection, a nonchalant signing of the cross instead of the fixed and pensive stare he aimed at the altar. He had studied with the Jesuits in an English Catholic school for boys, Bale remarked.

Cecil and I shared the dawn light, played shuffleboard before being evicted by adults, and at breakfast mashed runny eggs or drowned clumped oatmeal and raisins in sugar and cream. I practiced English to his high-pitched, horsy guffaws—which erupted at "I am a gull," my monkey imitations, my dog yaps, and even at my parodies of his braying laugh.

In fumbling French, Cecil told me of his adoption by American relatives after the recent loss of his parents, aping death by sprawling on the deck with hands crossed over his chest. "*Ma mère,* my mother," he announced, pointing skyward. "*Mon père,* my father," he made devil's horns with crooked index fingers and gestured toward the floor.

Cloudless skies and calm seas gave us hours on deck. Branigan recovered, and only then did I dare ask him about my mysterious aunt, describing her as a *triste,* pious lady with a gold tooth and prayer book.

"Was she a professor like you?" He blinked, and after a moment's hesitation, shook his head, saying with a note of finality, "I don't know what you are talking about." The subject was closed.

Cecil was first to announce it. "New York, we've arrived old girl!" He winked at me, fell to his knees and mewled, "Pray marry me, fair lady." Sticking a finger down his throat, he made a heaving sound. Typical Cecil.

The midmorning fog was so thick, the famous *gratteciels,* as Bale called skyscrapers in his labored French, had vanished. Gone, too, was the Lady of the Harbor, France's gift to America. "A gift like you," Bale gallantly added as I stared with dismay into the swirling mists.

Even though it was past my bedtime, I was allowed to attend the departure party held the night before we arrived. Festooned with fluttering twists of red, white, and blue paper garlands and small replicas of English and American flags, the salon was transformed for a night of celebration. Our table overlooked a staircase down which women descended in jewels and evening gowns.

Arm-in-arm with escorts in dinner jackets, these dreamlike figures took seats in the section reserved for cabin and first-class passengers. We sat apart in our Sunday best: I, in my red dress embroidered with flowers, astounded by this mixture of elegance and commonplace.

A cataract of tri-colored balloons bubbled from the ceiling, drifting lazily among the guests who sang "The Star-Spangled Banner" and "God Save the King." I could barely detect Cecil's high, cracked voice and mock angelic expression with eyes tilted upward, singing as he fished in his pockets for a jackknife to stab the balloons.

"Cheers," Branigan toasted with champagne, a salute that echoed around our table of American couples and the Mister Bs' card partners. "Cheese," I ventured, lifting a glass of ginger ale. Baffling laughter.

"Cheese is what you say to smile for the camera." Bale's handsome face twisted into a demonstrating grin.

3

While customs officers stamped our passports, I glimpsed Cecil among the group of other English children squired by the nuns. He was stooped and irritable. I pitied him and, at that moment, even missed his eccentric companionship. I found it hard not to be beguiled by his hot-tempered, devout, bullying, and antic moods, which shifted and swirled like the winds at sea. He answered my wave by wrinkling his forehead and hiking up his shoulders in an exaggerated shrug.

Relatives were soon to meet him, but not before he broke away and handed me his American address penciled on a slip of paper I folded into a pocket. When he asked for mine, without thinking I answered "rue Chant d'Oiseaux in Brussels," forgetting for the moment it was a place of the past that would forward no mail.

"He may write to you in care of me." Bale dashed some lines on a page torn from a pad and handed it to Cecil. Even so, I assumed, like Cecil, my relatives were just beyond the customs office door. I tugged at Branigan's sleeve for reassurance. Would we be met? He nodded and spoke in short bursts between puffs on a pipe.

"Of course, there's no need to worry, all will be well." Both he and Bale were given to that expression: all will be well. Standing on my toes, I craned my neck toward the exit while we inched forward for luggage inspection.

Hours passed before we moved into a vast reception hall congested with people rushing toward and embracing returnees and newcomers like me. I heard thunderclaps and the heavy spatter of rain above the clamor of greetings. It was an affront to be welcomed by mournful grey and not a shimmering day more fitting for our arrival. The Mister Bs swept the crowd with their eyes; Branigan peered about through horn-rimmed glasses, squinting and frowning.

At a distance, Cecil was energetically hugged by his English aunt and her American husband, a sturdy, jovial couple. A last look and final wave, but in vain as Cecil disappeared in a commotion of bodies and arms. Would we meet again?

A slim, blond woman approached us and called out, "Bob . . . Paul!" She wore a dark, blue suit and plain, white blouse. Balanced on her shiny hair was a saucer-like hat trimmed with a scrap of veil resembling my first communion cap. A small crucifix on a fine, gold chain swung from her neck.

Bale introduced me to Inez Londeborg, who lightly pressed my hand. Her blue eyes settled on my face, probed it, read it, and then scanned the length of my body. This woman was not my mother, but who then? Branigan's lady friend, a bachelor's acquaintance? She seemed to know both equally well. Bewilderment clouded her face when I asked if she knew my family. She spoke to Bale in rapid English while vigorously shaking her head.

Branigan leaned down and gently touched my shoulder. "Mrs. Londeborg is a friend who lives in California." I knew the state bordered the Pacific Ocean. It was extravagant, I suspected, for her to cross the continent just to meet two old companions. So she must be a messenger, a news bearer who at God's discretion came with word about my parents.

"Where is my mother, where?"

"There has been a delay. We will have to wait. *En retard.*" Branigan relit his pipe and spoke in clipped phrases. I yearned to know more, but held back at his gesture for silence, a finger held against closed lips.

Jammed between boxes and valises, we wove by taxi through the soaked streets of a sprawling city. New York. Pressing my nose against the window, I saw rows of trees coming into green. Surely it was no less than an admiral or general who carried our suitcases through the hotel's revolving door, a white-haired dignitary in a blue tunic with epaulets and gold buttons. Incredible, I thought, as Bale handed him a small, silver coin. America was a remarkable country.

We glided up to Mrs. Londeborg's floor in a mirrored elevator. Tiptoeing across her suite's lush carpeting, I decided *this* would be the place to invite Anne for tea and pastries; my letter on engraved hotel stationery would soon follow.

My hosts seemed oddly formal for schoolmates. When Mrs. Londeborg withdrew a cigarette from a silver case, the Mister Bs leapt toward her with flaming lighters. She removed her jacket and in a skirt and blouse looked as youthful as a novitiate in our Sisters' order, despite the forked lines between her eyebrows and at the corners of her mouth.

Bale called his wife to announce our arrival; the telephone was passed to Branigan and then to Mrs. Londeborg who spoke to Sue in turn. How had the women met? At school, at Bale's wedding? The receiver was handed to me. "Ello . . . ello?"

"Pronounce it with a haitch," Branigan corrected. Sue's greeting instantly won me over. "*Bienvenue,* welcome." The still unexplained Mrs. Londeborg urged me to nap while she and the Mister Bs shared afternoon cocktails in the hotel lounge. I hesitated, afraid to crease the taffeta spread.

To curl up on a lavish double bed also seemed an insult to the memory of Saint Rose of Lima, who had slept on a pallet of handhewn stones with a band of steel spikes circling her shaven skull.

But, fully clothed and exhausted, I drifted into sleep. That night I would stay in a Manhattan hotel in a bed of my own, my male escorts asleep at the other end of the room. Fitful dreams of important documents unfolded and vanished.

"This is a railroad timetable," Bale explained as I rubbed sleep from my eyes. "Tomorrow we're going by train to Rockville Centre. You'll meet Sue and stay with us." Forever? I dared not ask.

At Pennsylvania Station, Branigan pecked me lightly on the forehead and promised to write from his college in Massachusetts. "Soon, please?" I gripped his rough tweed sleeve and inhaled its clinging aroma of tobacco. "Certainly," he nodded. "And practice your English." He glanced back once before disappearing into the depths of the terminal.

Mrs. Londeborg exhorted me to pray to God for patience and strength, words distressingly like the incantations of the Sisters. "He has shown you his mercy and love. One day you will understand his will." I knew these assurances were often given before despairing news about mortal illness or crippling accidents. My parents?

"I must return to California. Let's not kiss, I have a terrible cold." She blotted her eyes and nose as Bale translated. Waving a handkerchief and blowing a kiss, she raced off before Bale and I boarded our Long Island–bound train.

"Don't worry, all will be well," he mumbled automatically from behind a spread newspaper. "All will be well."

We sped past towns glistening in the soft green blur of an early-morning rain. "Lynnbrook . . . Baldwin," the conductor intoned down the aisle. "Rockville Centre." I spied a large church through the train window. A cathedral, I thought, admiring its spires, and asked to attend Sunday services. "Of course," Bale nodded without looking at me.

Small-boned, dark and more fetching than her snapshot, Sue welcomed us at the door. Her stomach bulged noticeably under a loose fitting smock. Bale was even less talkative than usual during the weeks I settled into the cozy quarters of their one-bedroom apartment. Nothing more revealing was said about my parents. Again, "All will be well." Nightly, Sue draped sheets and plumped a pillow on the sofa on which I slept until dawn flickered through the gauzy drapes of their living room windows.

On weekdays at seven-thirty, Bale surfaced from behind his paper and washed down a few remaining fragments of toast and eggs with slowly sipped coffee. After the meal, Sue and I shared his eggy, hasty kiss before he drove to the station for his city commute.

Make yourself invisible, I told my hungry self, tiptoeing at daybreak to the refrigerator to gnaw a slice of packaged bread or peel a breakfast orange. Its pocked skin and spicy, biting juice, so innocent of purpose, were indulgences allowed only to the ill at the institute.

A hot spring day. We celebrated Sunday Mass at the Rockville Centre cathedral, kneeling on prayer cushions, the pews emptying row by row as congregants filed to the altar to receive the Host. I sat between Bale and Sue, who could have been my parents if God had willed it. If *they* would will it.

At night I heard raised but muffled voices through the bedroom wall, and breathy, distressed whispers on the telephone they tirelessly used during the day. Bale conferring with his colleagues? Sue calling her sister or mother in Virginia? She sometimes lowered her voice and turned away when I entered the room.

After church services, they changed into leisure clothes for our drive to the seashore: Jones Beach, an undulating stretch of sand dunes and fences interspaced by low stone buildings with shops and outdoor cafes.

"Say cheese," Bale ordered while aiming his box camera at us as I squinted in the sun and stood pigeon-toed on the boardwalk, whose railings simulated those of a ship. "No, not in my delicate condition," Sue protested, but drew her arm around my shoulders and smiled. Click, click, in the late April light. Then Bale and, click, only Colette. Then Sue, click, with her back to the sea. Then the Bales and Colette by an obliging passerby. "Stand closer to your daughter," he said, then click, click.

During fine spring days Sue and I hung the weekly laundry on a clothesline, relishing the snapping sound of wet sheets in the wind and the scent of freshly washed pillowcases cool against my cheek. I watched Sue sprinkle and iron the wash, bewitched by the bulge that would become a baby.

"Le petit bébé." I formed my hands and arms into a rocking cradle to acknowledge I understood. She laughed, cupped my face in her hands and brought me cocoa and cookies.

One Saturday, we drove to the Shelter Pines Country Club. Bale had briefly described the game of golf, which seemed to me a queer amusement. But for him, frowning under a small straw hat, glowering down at the fairway before each swing, golf was a passion. Sue and I trailed him in the hot sun. She declined playing, blaming fatigue I couldn't quite connect with this almost inert game.

"Nice going, Bob," she would say when he sunk holes he often accused of scooting from place to place before his very eyes. The bright sun spilled heat on the spongy turf underfoot. The course's hilly acres unraveled and danced like a mirage.

"Dizzy, I am dizzy," I murmured to Sue who grasped the meaning of the circles I drew in the air over my head. Yes, she would help, offering me an arm as we slowly walked to the clubhouse.

Sue sat at my side in the dark bar, dabbing my forehead with a cool, damp cloth, pressing my wrist with a delicate thumb, holding my hand and kissing it. It seemed unnatural, their excessive indulgence and refusal to find fault with a sometimes exasperating and over-inquisitive child. Something was amiss.

Accusations of blundering were part of the old order I accepted. I should have told Sue about my sensitivity to sunlight. Had she been Sister Henri, I would be informed of my stupidity with the sting of a ruler on my palm and a rebuke: "You act without thinking. Why do you test me?" To be rewarded with so much sympathy was simply bizarre. But over club soda in a chilled glass, turning my sunburned face toward her, I believed Sue, with her sympathetic ways, to be the ideal mother.

"Do you feel better?" I was just fine; she signed the check.

At the apartment, Sue fussed over me with cool, wet tea bags applied to my face, arms and legs. Poultices and packs, as well as a dispensary of healing herbs, were the antidotes of my childhood. Mustard plasters were strapped to my chest by Sister Paul in her prescription for the flu. Anne contended that slices of raw onion would soak up the poisons of bee stings and colds. Licorice was doled out for coughs or other lung ailments. Camphor or onions boiled in molasses and stuffed into flannel bags were strung around our necks to medicate sore throats. From her grandmother, Marie learned about holy oils and the saints to invoke for healing each complaint: Saint Appollonia for broken teeth and Saint Theresa of Avila for headaches. But few remedies were more comforting than the solace of Sue's cool fingers stroking my forehead.

As an ambitious young lawyer, Bale was preoccupied with professional concerns. House-hunting was also mentioned, their need for larger quarters. "We'll be crowded when the baby comes," he repeated to Sue a number of times. My skin had begun to crack and peel when a few days later Bale abruptly folded his morning paper.

"War's going to break out in Europe." *La Guerre,* he translated, but I only dimly knew the word's significance. Sitting on my hands to keep from picking at thin shreds of dead, itching skin, I watched him lift and drain his coffee cup.

"It's time," he asserted to Sue, wiping his lips with a napkin, "it's time to tell her."

"This evening after dinner, after the meat loaf?" Her festive dish afloat in a sea of tomato sauce was among my more savory American discoveries. I looked forward to it, understood her question to Bale, although not its meaning. "No, now, she'll need time to get used to the idea."

With a start, I realized that something important was about to be said. We left for the living room; I sat on the sofa that doubled as my bed. Bale and Sue pulled up matching club chairs into an intimate circle. Were the Bales going to give their new baby a sister? Would they keep me? Bale harrumphed and lit a cigarette. While he slowly gathered his thoughts, I watched a wispy trail of smoke curve toward the ceiling and dissolve. In halting French: "Your family is here and wants to meet you." Turning his face aside, he stubbed out the cigarette.

Looking out the train window, following the blur of trees budding into leaf, I recited my rosary in tempo with the speeding towns and beseeched the Blessed Virgin for a mother as affectionate as Sue, for a father with Bale's regal bearing.

They were waiting in his office when we arrived. *Ma mère,* mother in a Persian lamb cape and matching hat pierced with a jeweled sword, black hair coiffed into three ringlets pressed flat across her forehead. Beneath the row of curls, large, glistening eyes fixed on mine. Blue eyelids, thick eyelashes; *chère mama* in leather gloves, a gold bangle bracelet, high-heeled pumps, and leather purse with a thin strap. She stood there, elegant.

I flung my arms around her, could not keep myself from touching her, but her body tightened and I pulled away, startled and hurt for the moment by her cool response. I would soon be happy, I comforted myself, once safely inside the grand house I fancied they lived in. It would be my house, too, for I was their daughter, their child. Beyond new English words, I must practice patience, remembering the Sisters calling attention to my willful nature.

It seemed that Bale's ringing telephone and scurrying clerks with papers for his signature distracted everyone, dismissing me from the center of concern. While he conferred, I wondered if my mother had asked him to relay her regrets at our long separation, how much she missed me. I hoped this strangely mute couple would tell me how and why we were apart these many years.

Puzzled, I was more guarded with the man, who was not the father of my daydreams. Short, with thick strands of slicked-back, graying hair, nattily dressed in a derby and Prince Albert coat, he stared at me vacantly through glassy blue eyes set close above a large pinkish nose. Hair-thin red veins branched along his cheeks and disappeared in the shadow of pale gray jowls. When he drew closer, his breath held an unpleasant scent of tobacco and something stronger than communion wine.

Raymond and Ruth, my family? Ray tossed off his first words of greeting: English words sprinkled with a few bungled French phrases.

"Au revoir, Colette." Bale's kiss rested on my forehead as lightly as the smudge of ash daubed on my brow on the first day of Lent. The forty days of Lent were over, but I had made no pledges or recited extra prayers for souls adrift in Purgatory. I had found a family, but still felt deprived and wondered if losing the Bales was punishment for committing the venial sin of gluttony aboard ship.

"We'll see each other again," Bale assured me and turned to Ray, "and let's set up a golf date for next Saturday." His only revelation about my new parents was that both families met while members of the Shelter Pines Country Club.

4

The spiffily dressed couple escorted me back to a Pennsylvania Station commuter train for our trip to Merrick, Long Island. I later learned what French Ray spoke was picked up while serving with the U.S. horse cavalry in France and on furloughs in Paris during World War I.

Like Bale, he retreated behind the daily paper. I decided that this was a ritual of American men. The scattering of women on the train passed their time with books or fashion magazines or knitted wool garments from balls of yarn concealed in bags with wooden handles. Others crocheted.

But not *mama,* who sat composed, seemingly unruffled by the excitement I could barely suppress. I was left to admire the doll-like features of someone who spoke no French and wanly smiled at me as the train clattered through the towns. When it rattled past the Rockville Centre cathedral, I recalled High Mass with the Bales, branches of gold light flooding the aisles, haloed saints profiled in stained glass windows, candle sticks glowing on the altar.

Ruthie, as *mama* was called, clicked open a compact extracted from her purse, studied herself in its mirror, powdered her cheeks with a pink puff, then dabbed the pale violet circles under her eyes. A few pats subdued the shinier skin of a perfect nose. Blinking, then widening her eyes in the glass, she darkened her lashes with a tiny black brush. Lips were burnished with crimson lipstick, first the upper lip, which she pressed against the lower. After blotting her mouth on a scrap of paper which she crumpled into the ashtray, she looked up at me.

"Jolie," I exclaimed, entranced with my first spectacle of cosmetic sorcery. My adoration was repaid with a brightly rouged smile. "Freeport," called the conductor as we shrugged into our coats. Then Merrick. *"Merique . . . Amérique!"* I shouted, struck by their similar sounds, the coincidence of it. Ray and Ruth seemed embarrassed and annoyed by my outburst.

"No parle," commanded Ray. No speak? Primitive French, but I knew enough to cup a hand over my mouth in a gesture learned when told to curb my chatter.

We arrived at Bayview Avenue, and the buff-colored, two-story stucco house, a replica of others along a street lined with anemic trees, struck me as small and drab, hardly the mansion I assumed this debonair couple would own. Certainly, it was less spacious than Uncle Luc's Baltimore home, my image of the ideal American house. I anticipated more, much more, when Ray eased us into the car parked at the station, a luxurious new vehicle gleaming in high polish and suitable for the Pope.

Ray told me to expect a crowded household. *"Deux grandmères, un grandpère."* He held up three fingers.

Assembled in the dimly lit, overheated living room, they were posed and waiting like figures in a jury box. Nana: upswept white hair and tight lips blotched with dark cherry lipstick. Ray's gaunt, widowed mother sat imperiously in a straight-back chair. Maude Burt: Ruthie's mother overflowed her armchair and frowned behind rimless glasses when I offered my hand.

I was drawn to Ruthie's father, Mr. Burt, a tall, sullen figure with ashen skin and a bald head. Intrigued and wanting to alert him to my presence, I cocked my head to a side and curtsied.

"Ello, bonjour," I chirped. To my surprise, moments after being introduced, a yawning Ray and Ruthie left for their upstairs bedroom.

"Fatigue," Ray complained. Exhausted by late afternoon? So unlike our Sisters. Watchful as blackbirds, they were first to rise and last to retire, bearing witness to our days from dawn to dusk. My astonishment at Ruthie and Ray's abrupt departure was not shared by the elders, who remained gathered in the sitting room, ogling me as if I were an oddity, a curiosity brought into the house for their unwelcomed diversion. I broke the stillness with the universal language of gestures.

"Souper," I asked for supper, a finger crooked toward my gaping mouth, a hand circling my belly. Family life in my new home began with a bowl of Campbell's tomato soup, Ritz crackers, and a glass of cold milk. The grandmothers later escorted me to my small upstairs room, a cheerful space with white furniture: a bed, a chair, a dresser, and a round mirror. My own mirror! In my eagerness to pose and prance before it, a throw rug bunched under my feet and spilled me to the floor.

Frowning at the face in the mirror, I worried about my new parents in the adjoining room. I yearned for them to dream of me jumping on their laps as they laughed and blew smoke rings like Bale while reclining in his chair, for them to stroke my feverish forehead as did Sister Paul. I prayed to Blessed Isabel of France, who mended the clothing of the poor; to Blessed Michelina, who had kissed the sores of lepers and by a miracle restored them to health; and to Mary Mother, entreating her to enter the hearts of my new family.

Spring days, 1938. "Mama fatigay," Ruthie announced, draping a hand over her eyes. She had taken a leave of absence from her secretarial job at the Kraft Cheese Company and was drained by my exuberance. But, doing what she thought properly maternal, one afternoon

The house on Bayview Avenue

she decided to bathe me, run the tub, and swish a hand in the water to test its temperature. As she kneeled there, I noticed her face, bare of cosmetics, was defenseless and sad. Her puffy eyes followed me as I played with a bar of floating soap, and when *mama* bent toward me, I caught a whiff of her mingled scents, cologne barely masking the bitter odor from her mouth.

During the first few weeks, I had been too exhilarated to wonder about her despondency. *Mea culpa,* I thought, believing if all was not well in one way or another, I was at fault.

To blend in with the family, I began to master some of the house rules: to tiptoe in silence past Raymond and Ruthie's door on mornings and weekends when they slept late, to avoid speech or noise when sharing breakfast with two generations of gruff and brooding people.

Bathing me was a tenuous affair, with Ruthie hesitantly soaping my shoulders and back. Once excited by her touch, the unexpected attention, I reached out and caressed her face with sopping fingers.

"Mama!" Soapy water streaked down her cheek.

She recoiled, covered her eyes and stomped out, slamming the door. I had offended the hard to please *jolie mama. Finis.* I would be shipped back to Belgium. I would never be the child that Nana later told me had been prescribed by a doctor to relieve Ruthie's depression, her pinched nerves and headaches, the frayed marriage of thirteen years.

Late one night, I stumbled on Ruthie's nude body sprawled across the bathroom floor, the first I saw of such episodic collapses. My heart squeezed like a fist as I raced down the hallway and hammered on the grandmothers' doors. *"Elle est morte!"* She is dead, I cried.

"She is nothing of the sort," Nana remarked, covering Ruthie with a towel while Grandma Burt held smelling salts to her daughter's nose. She is sick, they explained. She would be fine. Ruthie's heavy eyelids twitched; she mumbled as the women lifted and steered her to the bedroom in what appeared a common ritual.

Not a word was said next morning about the night's mishap. Ruthie drank a second cup of coffee brewed by her mother who urged,

"Eat something, please honey." A hulking shape in a lavender robe tailored from material similar to Nana's bedspread, Grandma Burt pleaded, "Do it for me." Ruthie leafed through the pages of *Screen Romances,* ignoring everyone.

Was it a bad dream? *Mama* was flawlessly composed in a smart dress with white cuffs. She smiled at me complaisantly as I sat with head in hands observing her every move. Did she know I had trespassed on some private indiscretion, and was I forgiven?

Some days later, Ruthie took another fling at mothering. "You need summer clothes." Suddenly animated, she suggested a shopping trip by drawing a hand along the long rank of skirts, blouses, and dresses spanning the length her closet. She surveyed me with the eye of a consultant facing a trying challenge. At that moment I was a child with a ribbon slumped in a tangle of curls, socks drooping at the ankles, shoes scuffed from running, not sensibly walking the reaches of her new world, but racing down streets that branched outward from Bayview Avenue bordered by Merrick Avenue to the north and stumbling through weed-congested lots that intercepted the shoreline of the bay.

But despite a *tsk tsk* click of the tongue and upward-rolled eyes, Ruthie's manner implied that correction was possible. I was delivered into the hands of someone described by a neighbor as the best dressed woman on the morning train to Pennsylvania Station.

"Try this one," she commanded, handing me a swimsuit covered with flowers and stitched with tiers of elastic that pinched my skin. It was a style that emphasized my child's potbelly, and I disliked it.

"*Jolie,* we'll take it." Ruthie flashed her red smile and had me model it with another twirl. "You'll want summer dresses, blouses, skirts, and a bathrobe."

Yes, a bathrobe would do very well. Alien to institute wards who shuffled from bed at dawn in grey-white muslin gowns, such a garment would blend me nicely into the ways of the household. I could now be at one with a family frequently eating breakfast in robes and slippers and join their reluctant excursions into morning.

But at the same time I began to wonder if I were equally at one with the America I had imagined. The household seemed disturbingly different from those in family pictures of tranquil domesticity I found in *Life* and the *Saturday Evening Post,* magazines that along with *Modern Screen* and *True Confessions* were stacked on the nightstand on which Ruthie parked a bedtime cocktail. I had learned the word cocktail from Ray, who had begun to appraise me with a speculative, moony look I could not then fathom.

Petite Colette was her mannequin, her plaything to ornament with white shoes and a white clutch bag lined in satin. Things must match, insisted Ruthie, whose dresser lamps were identically flounced. On our return, she sighed deeply while shielding her eyes from the light blaring through the windows.

"Malade?" I asked when she dropped onto her bedroom lounge chair.

"Une tasse de thé?" I offered her tea, remembering the restorative teas Sisters infused for headaches and fatigue and returned with a cup whose design matched the paper napkin I carefully folded down the middle.

I knocked on her door and called *"mama . . . mama,"* while wiggling the doorknob. No answer.

I quickly roused Grandma Burt from her kitchen vigil, beckoning her to follow. She heaved her bulk on dainty feet with impressive speed up the staircase to Ruthie's door. Silence met her furious pounding. "Woofie, are you all right? Come to the door."

It slowly swung open. Mama stood framed in the doorway, her wobbly breasts tipping from a loose robe. I was faintly repelled by her mouth wiped clean of lipstick, her lips the color of cooked liver. "Goddamn it, why can't you all leave me alone?" Her voice sounded fuzzy and far off.

Grandma Burt scooted me away with a wave of her plump hand, *"Faché, faché!"* The French word for *angry* was a frequent utterance the family learned from a neighbor, Mrs. Morse, a grizzled widow who took pride in the French she learned at convent school. After Ruthie's relapse and recovery, maternal gestures ceased. She left the next week with Ray for her early commute to the Kraft Cheese Company, never again wholly playing the role of mother to an increasingly perplexed child.

Bayview Avenue was a second home for this family, which had emigrated from Chicago. "Chicago, Bang, Bang" was the name the institute children had coined, linking it to gangland murders learned of through adult talk about movies we were not allowed to see.

The family brought with them a weapon almost as lethal as the guns of the Windy City: silence, both aggressive and defensive, often lasting a week or longer. Silence could come as the aftermath of a squabble over Grandpa Burt's public binges, when he unbuttoned his fly and watered our front stoop. I heard Grandma Burt claim he had sprayed his son-in-law's name into the dusty top step of the house. The use of the wee wee as a pen, and piss as ink, had not occurred to me, although I was impressed with the notion.

I never fully understood why Grandpa Burt broke his pledges to refrain from drink, but his pendulum swing from sobriety to drunkenness resembled that of the Church of the Redeemer bell calling parishioners to pray for remission of their sins.

Silence sometimes followed an affront to Ruthie by Nana, who expressed her disdain for her daughter-in-law's extravagance. Ruthie hated the bargain-basement atmospheres in which Nana thrived and despised the frenzy of women elbowing one another aside for cut-rate garments at Namm's in Brooklyn or Gimbel's basement in Manhattan.

After shopping sprees, Ruthie would spread out white boxes with black lettering from Best and Company, Peck and Peck, or Saks Fifth Avenue and ceremoniously open them before her awed mother, a frowning Nana, and an inquisitive child.

"You should have waited for the January sale on those pillowcases." Nana put great stock in post-holiday discounts. "What business is it of yours how I choose to spend my money?" Ruthie bristled. "You are not to speak to me in that tone of voice." Nana wheeled around and headed for her room. Whatever matter prompted a quarrel, it flashed through the family like a contagion inoculated by silence.

The otherwise chatty and acid-tongued Nana lapsed into stillness behind her locked door. The few words Ray and Ruthie exchanged at home or at the country club ebbed to zero as they sulked upstairs. Grandpa Burt rode the hours in his usual torpor, his speech muzzled and locked in a cage to which no one held the key.

I was exempted, told to hush up or tiptoe up the stairs. "Ruthie is sleeping . . . Don't touch the telephone . . . Shush, don't disturb Raymond at his desk." The grandmothers momentarily broke the silence to divide up duties: who would cook what for each meal; whose turn to shop, clean, dust, polish the silver, set and clear the table; whose to wash the clothes and the linens, hang them on the line, starch and iron them, mend them.

I hungrily turned to English with hopes that I might bridge these silences or mediate between the warring factions, picking up words like bright stones held to the light, gathering them from the grandmothers and from labels on medicine bottles. Aspirin, cough syrup, iodine. I harvested words from newspaper headlines and from grocery lists penned in Grandma Burt's neat hand or in Nana's scratchy scrawl. And there were the words of neighborhood children.

"You're a stupid frog," jeered the boy whose bicycle I wheeled away without asking, never doubting for once that items left unattended in front yards were collective property. Thanks to Mrs. Burt and Nana, "stupid" was already in my English lexicon, sounding much like its French equivalent, but "frog"? I was building a sprightly personal dictionary while discovering some words meant for me were quite bizarre.

"Frenchie Babu lived in a shoe, always slept to half-past two," chanted Donna and Dorothy, twin redheads down the block who crossed their eyes and thumbed their noses during a mocking, jittery dance. I wondered, too, at the poorly informed boy who waggled his hips while crooning, "They don't wear pants in the southern part of France."

I was bewildered, but also pleased by these welcomes to Bayview

Avenue. Being French made me an authority with some standing in local circles. I was the eye in their storm of questions. Do the French put French dressing on their French toast and French fries? Give me a French kiss.

Since I had arrived in late April, it was decided I would not attend classes until fall, when I was registered by Nana in the town's elementary school, a pleasant red brick building on Merrick Avenue. A week after Ruthie abandoned me for her desk job, Mrs. Morse, our French-speaking neighbor, shed some light on Ruth and Raymond's history. Counting on Nana as an intermittent ally, I had earlier pressed her for details.

"If Ruthie and Ray had a nice car and a house in America, why didn't they send for me sooner? Why did they leave me with the Sisters in Belgium?"

Secure in her belief that speaking any language other than English was a weakness to overcome, Nana never stooped to making exaggerated gestures or parroting French words, badly pronounced, as did Ray and Grandma Burt. She turned to Mrs. Morse whose serviceable French helped unravel the knot by one loop.

Ray, a salesman, and Ruthie, his stenographer, were employed at the Chicago headquarters of a large fabric firm. After their 1925 marriage—she had just turned seventeen and he was a boyish-looking thirty-five—they relocated with his Iowa-born mother to a Jackson Heights apartment in the borough of Queens.

Ray prospered as a sales representative for the Cortiselli Silk Company, and in the early nineteen-thirties bought the Bayview Avenue house for more space and the fresh air of the suburbs. Soon after, Ruthie's parents joined them, Mrs. Morse elaborated.

"Is he my real father?" I asked. My feelings toward Ray were muddled. He was the rooster around which the hens of our household clucked. Only Nana was permitted to peck at him or complain of his crowing. His strutting and boastfulness repelled me even as I liked, even envied his physical grace, his surefooted lightness when holding Ruthie in a dance.

If I had a true, living father, he would surely be someone less the peacock, less the windbag. Ray, my real father? The question was dodged by the women, implying he was *not* my blood relation. Do I have brothers and sisters? "Heavens no, one of you is more than enough." Nana changed the subject.

Returning one Saturday to our mid-block brown-shuttered house, I spied Ray's Cadillac in the driveway. He and Ruthie were mixing midday cocktails while tuned to sportscasts wafting from the basement radio.

More answers would come that night from a taciturn Ruthie whose speech was liberated by drinks. I learned that no, she did not attend church, and no, she was not a Roman Catholic. I had earlier mentioned to Nana my fear that Ruthie could not enter Heaven, and was once again hustled off to Mrs. Morse.

"We are Episcopalians," Nana explained, "and we practice baptism and holy communion, but, thank the Lord, we don't recognize the Pope." Because of him, Catholics breed like rabbits, she added, without regard for a pained Mrs. Morse, our faithful translator.

Sundays with Nana brought me the comforting and heartening sight of the Episcopal church's priest, even though the aged reverend's craggy face and arched eyebrows looked satanic. Likenesses of Christ and his apostles peered at me benignly from stained glass windows.

But gone were the bells of Mass and incense curling from the swinging brass censor. Gone, too, were the holy saints and the vault for the statue of Mary Mother, and not one confessional booth was to be seen. I missed them, longed for the familiar consolation in the presence of such holy artifacts. Here, worshippers neither genuflected nor buried their faces in their hands in fervent prayer. Episcopalians seemed like watered-down Catholics, even though they practiced communion.

For my first holy communion I had been measured with the other girls for a white dress. "Little brides," the dressmaker mumbled through a mouthful of pins while snaking a long yellow tape around our bodies. "You will always remember this day." We had learned our catechism: *Who made us? God made us. God is the Supreme Being, infinitely perfect, who made all things . . . ,* and committed it to memory. On that day Anne, Marie, Chantal, and I trooped to our communal closet; slipped on our garments; and, under Sister Jerome's stern guidance, pinned circlets of shirred, white veil to our hair.

How weary the priest seemed. I shared his fatigue, a lassitude that deepened with each lulling cadence of the chant. Bunches of lilies drooped behind the altar, expelling a fragrance that mingled with the dense perfume of incense cycling from the censor.

The priest placed a wafer on my tongue, and it lay there, fragile as a moth. Behind the rail, ghostly sprays of white flowers seemed to sway. My teeth must not graze or chew the Host, the immutable body of Christ given to join mine. They must not touch the Host.

Was it perversity or vileness? A back tooth fractured the wafer. A puny figure with a crown of thorns and bloody lacerations floated before me. I had wounded Jesus. My body, flaccid as a cloth doll, collapsed over the railing. As a Sister later pointed out, I had completely misinterpreted the symbolic nature of the Host.

Ruthie and Ray waltzed into the living with freshly topped highballs and settled into the sofa, she in a soft blouse and pleated skirt, he in one of his many three-piece tailored suits accented with a monogrammed pocket handkerchief.

Ray's tongue was loosened by several scotches when I probed for the answers Nana withheld. Are you my father? Is *mama* my real mother? In his light, nasal voice: "You are someone special we chose in a marriage *sans enfants.*" Do you know anything about my real parents? No. Does Bale or Branigan? No. He exaggerated a shrug while Ruth smiled wanly, playing with her drink's maraschino cherry.

"We chose you from all the others," Ruthie insisted. What *others* I wondered, had she been shopping for a child? One that blinked its eyes and mewed "mama" when you tipped it on the side? I imagined children propped up like dolls on a department store counter. Ruthie points one out to a salesgirl. "I want this one if she doesn't cry, wet her bed, suck her thumb, pick her nose, eat her snot. I'll take that one if she doesn't sass back, throw up, scream in her sleep. I want her gift-wrapped if she does what I tell her to do, combs her hair, rinses her mouth, curtsies, says thank you and please."

I bit my lower lip, choking back the confusion and anger I knew would provoke them. If they were annoyed too often, I could be returned to the institute. I felt tricked and betrayed by them and the Sisters and by Bale and Branigan, who had led me to assume I would join my authentic family.

Ray and Ruth invited me to the Whoopee Room, a wood-paneled basement with a full-service bar, stools, and glass shelving for ranks of liquor bottles sparkling under recessed lighting. Ray had also installed a linoleum dance floor, a concession to his passion for the samba, rumba, mambo, and tango, all danced with a compliant Ruthie during evenings of drinking.

Both were *cum laude* graduates of the Arthur Murray Dance School. Ray was in glassy-eyed rapture when spinning across the floor to the songs of Carmen Miranda, to the beat of Xavier Cugat's orchestra.

Ruthie fetched me a ginger ale and kicked off her sling-back shoes. Dialing the radio to swing band music, Ray snapped his fingers, at which Ruthie stood, gliding toward him, yielding as he spun her in spirals around the room. Her head tilted back, she smiled dreamily, eyes shut. In this dance, they were film stars of equal billing in a Hollywood romance.

Transfixed, I followed the turns and dips of these now familiar strangers to whom, as Ray and his mother were later to remind me, I was not related by blood. I was swept by contradictory emotions: mortified at being deserted by my true parents, relief that these people *were* outsiders after all.

Nana later argued that taking me was Ruthie's idea, that she had been urged by her doctor to take in a child. An agreement was struck soon after I arrived. Bale told Ruthie of my predicament, displaying my photo during cocktails at the country club.

"Mr. Bale wanted his own child, and, of course, he was stuck because no one else wanted you." Nana seldom minced words. "Ruth said 'cuddly as a puppy,' or something like that, when she saw your picture." Nana's dry, rattly voice drifted off.

I missed the Bales, especially Sue, and was told they believed visits would interfere with my adjustment to a new life. No one spoke of them, but one afternoon at the country club, while playing ping-pong with other golf orphans in the community room behind the bar, I overheard an older child say the Bales had moved to Virginia.

Hot weather steamed in. Was it with reluctant hands that the grandmothers filled my glass with lemonade? I sensed more than ever that I was an irritant, an unwelcome rival for their grown children's affection, an unasked-for addition to their workload.

Lean, dry-eyed Nana scorned stout, whiny Grandma Burt, who, in turn, loathed Nana's condescension and bossiness.

"Raymond wants his roast medium rare, and this is clearly overcooked, Mrs. Burt." Cool in a V-necked summer dress, Nana jabbed contemptuously at the meat.

"It's all I can do to keep up with chores around here without your incessant complaints." Grandma Burt fished a hanky from the deep furrow between her breasts and mopped her forehead. Accord was reached only in their mutual disgust toward Grandpa Burt, who was routinely dragged by the women from a Merrick Road tavern, each tugging at one of his arms. "A sorry excuse for a man," Nana retorted, shaking her head.

"He's off on one of his binges, Mrs. Burt." A "toot," it was also called, which sounded to my French ear like a dental term, which I dutifully added to my growing stockpile of American slang.

"You go for toot?" I asked him on his way out the door. With a knifing glare, hands clapped over his ears, he stumbled down the steps. I waited curiously, secretly hoping to see him unbutton his fly and pee on the top stoop, marking our house front with his scent, like a dog anointing a hydrant. I was eager to see if his thing spelled out Ray's name in full: Raymond. But not this time or ever; such exhibitions were staged only for the elders.

Yet, in this household there were instances of generosity as rare as they were baffling. Nana would invite me into her bedroom to rummage through a box of Louis Sherry chocolates sent by her Chicago niece, Elizabeth. I preferred those wrapped in gold foil and marveled how, stripped of their paper, the candies' sweet, chocolaty bursts of cherry syrup squirted into my mouth. The lavender candy box with its entwined violets blended with Nana's chenille bedspread and scatter rugs.

I was allowed to watch her preen at her dressing table. Brushing her white hair upward in long strokes, she swept it into a topknot briskly secured with wavy hairpins and silver combs. Nana was proud of her mirrored image, the dignified face that nodded back at her.

"Raymond and I are blessed with a lion's mane," she said, preening her hair. I touched my short curls, more poodle-like than jungle cat, I thought.

"May I comb your hair, Nana?" To my surprise she assented.

"Softly, I'm not a horse." Grateful kisses were discouraged. "Don't maul me, child, get your paws off me."

And there were private pleasures: a small basement library of dusty books, which tested my beginner's English while nourishing an early devotion to the look and sounds of words, their tiny insect shapes parading across the page, their tones and shadings when spoken aloud. In the collection were Zane Grey's western potboilers, a frayed *Anthony Adverse* and the *Holy Bible*. From the *Collected Works of Rudyard Kipling* I later memorized "Gunga Din," not understanding it, but basking in the sounds, the muscular swagger of "you limping lump of brick dust," wrapping my tongue around pure rhymes and Burmese words, the steamy glamour of "Mandalay."

Summer arrived. A peculiar ritual called "getting a tan" was practiced in the backyard. Through kitchen windows on clear, hot days, I caught sight of Ray and Ruthie in tight swimsuits, supine on a blanket, their greased bodies like pale lumps of biscuit dough baking in the sun.

And, there were skip-rope games with the twin girls whose taunts had vanished with the breezes of early summer. "Strawberry shortcake, cream on top, what's the name of my sweetheart? . . . A, my name is Anna, I eat a ripe banana." "My mother sent me to the store, and this is what she sent me for . . . salt, pepper, cider, vinegar." We lashed the rope faster and faster while reciting the last four words, aiming to trip the jumper.

"All together, girls, how is the weather, girls? January, February, March . . . " Following the rules, I leapt in at June, my birthday month, and out again when it was called a second time. The rope spun to the same pounding rhythms as in Belgium, a country whose memories were forsaking my thoughts like islands absorbed in the larger sea of life in America.

5

I had disappointed Ray and Ruthie, though differently than the unaccountable aunt who visited me in Brussels. I was not the cure for their childless marriage. They were *not* comforted by my nearness. Increasingly, they fled from the household's tensions and constraints to the distractions of the country club.

Prepared for a party, Ruthie would pose at the doorstep, glamorous in fluttery clothes and wait for Ray, her courtier and chauffeur. I would hold back my desire to kiss her dusty blue eyelids, to caress the flawless oval of her face. I believed her beauty had the power to stop passersby and render me invisible.

"You don't look like your mother," I was informed during casual introductions at the country club, and understood it to mean I was far less exquisite than she. I recalled Sister Bernard's adages: "She who studies the mirror, neglects the spirit," and "Beauty is empty," an emptiness I occasionally hungered for.

"Isn't she stunning?" Ray beamed, chucking her under the chin, holding Ruthie as I might not. I had learned to comply with *ne touchez pas,* one of her few French phrases, when my hand heedlessly approached her rouged and powdered face. "Am I nice looking?" I would ask Nana, eager for her praise. "Well," she would pause, "you'll do in a pinch."

When I was not simply dismissed, Ruthie would greet me with a frown or a hand draped across her forehead. Or more ominously, I was summoned to the master bedroom. Something was missing from her dressing table, a green comb. Had I taken it? No. Are you sure? In fact, blameless, I nodded yes.

Ray set aside his highball. "What you need is a good spanking." Recalling the protocols of the institute, I draped myself across his knees and winced as he smacked me with an open hand. The punishment's only surprise was Ruthie's reaction to it; her eyes welled up with tears, smearing the painstakingly applied mascara. She pointed to my flyaway curls. "Your hair, go comb your hair." My often intractable hair was a target of her disfavor.

Another punishment was to be locked in my room without supper, which, to my relief meant I was then spared from Ray's eager hands on my *derrière,* a word he enjoyed using. His in-laws, the Burts, he defined as: "Goddamned leeches sitting on their *derrières*." And he would say of F.D.R.: "He and his Commie pals in Washington give me a pain in the *derrière*.

Ray was at odds with the grandmothers, who listened to the President's Fireside Chats. I, too, stared expectantly at the half-moon of Nana's radio speaker and bent toward it as the announcer intoned, "Ladies and gentleman, the President of the United States of America." It shocked me to hear insults hurled at the leader of a nation. At the dinner table, Ray once proudly admitted taping Roosevelt's picture to the office toilet seat.

"You go too far," challenged Nana, stalking out of the room.

In September I brought my increasingly flexible English to the Merrick Grade School. A coronet of dark hair framed the impish, olive-complected face of Miss Piscotta, my third grade teacher. I shared not only her French, but her warm indulgence of an outsider, a newcomer. I accepted her as a mentor who favored me with attentions, sometimes interrupting lessons to translate words she thought were beyond me.

"Water," she pronounced, lifting a rose from the vase she jiggled until droplets scattered from its lip. "Water." Eager to please her, I repeated a word learned as a shipboard passenger, reading it as a teardrop, saliva, pee pee, blood, water by the glassful, by the tubful and in an oceanful of high waves at Jones Beach driven by the huge hurricane that struck the northeast coast that very September.

A procession of alphabet posters circled the walls of the classroom: the *a* shaped a baby carriage, the *t* a crucifix and the *z* a mute swan or lightning bolt.

Sepia photographs of Lincoln, Washington, and Roosevelt lent benign authority to the wall behind Miss Piscotta's desk. Chalk dust sometimes whorled like snow flurries reluctant to fall. As she monitored our work, gliding through aisles of nailed-down desks, her slender hips were at our shoulders when leaning over us, cajoling, correcting. And we, her loving subjects, hunched over blue-lined notebooks and penciled words in high, gray loops.

I labored for Miss Piscotta's round and tidy A's and earned them in spelling, geography, and reading skills. An A for conduct and its particulars: attitude, cooperation, effort, neatness, self-reliance and self-control. And an A for music from agitated, lip-biting, Miss Dowling for whom, along with my twin girl friends, I was an on-key *Robin,* not a discordant *Sparrow.* I was selected to nest with the class's most tuneful warblers.

Sturdy letter *A* was a ladder with a single rung, pronounced to rhyme with "stay," not spoken broadly as "ah" as in "father," but sounded as in "grace," which no one I ever knew said. I delighted in the vertical row of my inked-in A's, but never received one for arithmetic. Or for penmanship, which was then taught in the Palmer Method, perversely created for right-handed writers. While my left-handedness was seen by the Sisters as an adversity ordained by God and not to be tampered with, the pedagogues here were more intolerant.

Colette, the name, began to gain a forward slant, the looping double *ts* and *es* resembling keyholes. I was pleased to omit Raymond's ugly-sounding family name from papers that did not require it.

We worked to please our teacher, our monarch in that airy first floor room whose odors, foremost her cologne—*Evening in Paris,* she told us—mingled with the sharp smells of ink, waxy crayons, brown soap, paste, and paints that greeted us each day. We obediently copied "We may . . . We can . . . We will" into our notebooks, with other rallying cries Miss Piscotta scratched on the blackboard.

I dreaded arithmetic, how fractions hobbled on the page in a cavalcade of mutilated numbers, digits on a chopping block. I panicked when fractions were subtracted from other fractions; things dissected in half and less than whole unnerved me.

Crisp, blue skies lapsed into wintry gray. The school day over, I would sometimes find Nana at the kitchen table, presiding over a tray of tollhouse cookies, pouring cold milk into emptied Kraft cheese jars imprinted with cornflowers or tulips. In the Catholic spirit of sharing food, I offered a cookie to Grandma Burt, who had come for a cup of tea.

"Mrs. Burt is fat enough without sweets," Nana lashed out, slapping my extended hand. I felt an unexpected rush of pity for the woman whose misfortune, like left-handedness, might also be ordained by God. Her small and slowly eaten, picked-at meals made no visible difference in her weight.

Stealth was out of the question in that crowded household whose larder was scrupulously watched; no missing cherry pies wolfed at midnight could explain Grandma Burt's heft. Nor could I quite accept Nana's gibes at a woman who bore the indignity of corpulence without the offsetting pleasures of eating well.

"Witch, witch, witch!" Grandma Burt stammered between tears, a pudgy finger aimed at Nana, who replied, "Don't you dare point your finger at me." It seemed odd to be offended by finger-pointing, but even with her vagaries and whims, I was grateful to Nana who, despite her declared antipathy for children, became my fitful and sometimes bad-tempered custodian. "You were a mistake, but they can't send you back," she claimed.

Mistake, a misunderstanding, a wrong action. A different child could have better soothed the household's discords. Would a docile Episcopalian girl have pleased them more? Ruthie and Ray were hardly religious. Unlike Nana, who had snatched away my rosary and declared it Catholic hocus-pocus, they remained unconcerned that I attended Sunday services.

"Listen, there's only one God up there," Ray gestured toward the ceiling, "but a lot of different people are sitting in different pews."

While Nana agreed with her son's homespun theory of the church and the almighty, in those early years I yearned for fish on Fridays, even the once-dreaded confessional booth, and chafed at losing the religious freedom espoused by the turkey-eating pilgrims we studied in school just before the Thanksgiving holiday.

I soon learned that no one cared about my studies or grades, and was shooed away when asking Ruthie or Ray to sign my first report card with its row of A's and two C's.

"Mal a la tête," she moaned, with fingers pressed to her forehead. "I'm busy, tomorrow," he contended, consulting his watch. A second attempt was also deferred, so I turned to Nana, who also declined.

"Only Raymond or Ruth may sign, they are your guardians."

The Palmer Method to the rescue. Modeling Ray's name from a cancelled check left on his desk, I applied the method to copying the outsized flourishes of the *y* and *g* in his bold, extraverted signature. With pride in craft, and with a trembling hand, I presented the first in an unbroken series of report card forgeries to Miss Piscotta.

Nana, whose deductive powers were impressive, oddly said nothing about my report card frauds through the years I lived with them. I was never caught nor questioned. Fiercely loyal to her son, she believed his imperfections traced to demon rum and Ruthie's bad influence. "Drink runs in her family" was Nana's explanation for Ruthie's collapses and morning-after blahs. No doubt, she assumed Raymond had signed the cards, doing what was required and right.

"Right," was one of her freely used words. "It's not *right* they lock the door to that child," she would confide to Grandma Burt when they were on speaking terms. "It's not *right* that Ruthie's gone back to work, leaving us to raise her."

"As if we didn't have enough to do," sighed Grandma Burt, vigorously rubbing a stain on the dining tablecloth. Nodding in rare agreement, the women would speak about me as if I were a phantom in their midst.

The care and management of George Burt were other ordeals both women continued to endure. Weekly, they would escort him home from his boozy escapades, as much out of concern for his well-being as for the need of his labors: minor household repairs, mowing and watering the lawn, washing the car, and what they called "puttering in the garden."

I once tagged along as they trooped down Bayview Avenue and up Merrick Road into a dark roadside bar with its bunch of local drunks. Mostly wrecked and rumpled, they howled at the sight of two old women, one lean, one stout, yanking an ashen-faced carcass from his bar stool. How easily Grandpa Burt surrendered, childlike, head hanging as if in shame, lurching between us as we trooped home at dusk.

"And tomorrow is our wedding anniversary," Grandma Burt recalled to Nana, who clicked her tongue and shrugged.

Nana had told me George and Maude Burt had met and married in Chicago. "She worked as a salesgirl at the tobacconist where George bought his cigars. Maude said she was won over by his educated speech and he was taken by her peaches-and-cream complexion." Nana claimed, seeing early photographs of the youthful Maude, "A very handsome woman going to fat even when young."

"Did Grandpa Burt have a family?" She looked at me wide-eyed. "Everyone has, and George was born into a good family in Ogdensburg, New York. But he struggled with the bottle even when working for his father's bank.

"Maude said he wasn't cut out for doing accounts and he frequented local bars, suffered blackouts and so on. A black sheep, no question about it. I suppose his family was relieved when he took off to Chicago with a drinking pal." While there, George was supported by Maude's income as a salesgirl and seamstress. Later, daughters Ruth and her sister, Gwendolyn, left grade school to help pay family expenses.

"Why haven't I met Ruthie's sister?" I had seen a photograph of a blond, full-lipped Gwendolyn on Grandma Burt's dressing table, but nobody seemed willing to talk about her.

"Not that it's any of your affair, but Gwendolyn inherited her father's liking for liquor. She's a beautician now on her second or third husband. Of the girls, Ruth was the more ambitious, studied shorthand and typing, and landed a job at the company in Chicago, where Raymond became her boss."

When the armistice was broken and the Grandmother Wars resumed, I feared Mrs. Burt's wrath. Why had I forgotten her orders to scrape my shoes before trekking mud across the freshly mopped kitchen floor? Why?

Trying to reach Ruth at her office, I slipped the phone off its cradle. *"Mama, mama,"* I shouted into the mouthpiece. "No, no, *stupide,*" Grandma Burt shook me by the shoulders, wagging a pink finger in my face, tempting me to bite it. "The child's not stupid, and she's certainly not deaf." Each word Nana pelted at Grandma Burt was edged in ice.

In a feeble gesture of rage, Grandma Burt stamped her foot, a small, swollen foot squeezed into a cross-strapped, square shoe. That night, through my bedroom wall, I overheard her ranting at her voiceless husband, followed by high-pitched sobbing. My anger and sympathy toward her alternated like the names of the days on Miss Piscotta's wall chart: Monday, fury; Tuesday, pity; Wednesday, tantrum; Thursday, remorse; Friday, futility. Christmas arrived and another truce was declared. A sober Grandpa Burt played endless hours of solitaire, slapping down cards on the dining room table. Working overtime, Ray took the early train. Once again, Ruthie's exuberance foretold a spell of shopping. Only six days before Christmas, and her thoughts leapt to gifts; wrapping paper; greeting cards; the blue spruce Grandpa Burt would select and erect on Christmas Eve; and gallons of brandy, eggs, and heavy cream for the eggnog.

"Santa Claus is coming and will leave presents under the tree." Her eyes glowed. "To Bayview Avenue?" I asked incredulously. I had heard the saga of Santa Claus in class but had trouble reconciling this burly, red-suited grandfather with the institute's Saint Nicholas, a chaste European who must have abhorred chimneys. The twins maintained Santa Claus was a hoax, one of the falsehoods parents bestowed on children with gifts in his name.

But for me, the truth of Christmas was found in singing with the Junior Choir led by Mr. Carn, whose silver moustache trembled above the open circle of his lips energetically mouthing the words to each carol and hymn.

I found myself recalling Brussels and the somber Advent in which candles were lit on each of the four Sundays before Noel. In reedy voices, we sang "Un Flambeau" . . . "Il Est Né, le Petit Enfant" . . . "Minuit Chrétian," "Sainte Nuit," and "O Holy Night"; we recited our prayers, knees ridged from the cold chapel floor.

These were now fading images of L'Institut de Puériculture, exempt from the ring of doorbells and telephones, vacuum cleaners and electric fans, a hushed world I had inhabited, but was not entirely lost to mind. I could still pluck French words out of the air and sing them without effort, and could still recall the statue of our Blessed Mother, her folded hands and downcast eyes.

At breakfast, Ruthie offered to treat her parents to the Radio City Music Hall Christmas show. "Christmas comes only once a year," she observed, patting her mother's hand, "and Dad needs a change of scenery."

"Getting your father to go anywhere is a major undertaking. We'll see."

"We'll see" was a remark that often meant "no" after an extended and fruitless period of hopefulness. "We'll see," said Nana when I prodded her to ask Ray for roller skates like those owned by children in the neighborhood.

"We'll see," she repeated at her vanity table, applying a gash of dark red to her lips, a slap of rouge to her cheeks. I also asked if Santa would advance my education with a jigsaw puzzle of an American map like that gifted to the children next door. "Hey, Frenchie Babu, what's the capital of Mississippi?" they teased. "Frenchie Babu, what's the capital of Ohio?" The answer to which I assumed from Nana's talk of her sisters' house was in Cleveland.

"The weather's warm for December," Ruthie said, explaining the yellow wool cape she substituted for her mouton coat. I hardly noticed the weather; for me the air was charged with surprises—among them a Christmas greeting and photograph from the Bales in Virginia who were posed on the lawn fronting their new home. Bale's arm circled Sue who cradled a bundled baby held to her chest. The message: Love to all, Bob & Sue & Robert Jr. Another personally addressed card for reforwarding to me was tucked into Bale's envelope:

> Dear Colette: I hope you get this. I am fine and go to Catholic school here in Buffalo near Niagara Falls. I don't have to study as hard as in England, so there is time for sports and chess, etc. Do you remember the ship? What jolly fun. How do you like the States? I eat hamburgers and hot dogs and ice cream. I guess you found your family. Write, if you're not too busy. Happy Christmas. Cecil

Got you, tootsie." A sudden kiss wet my mouth as I passed through the archway leading to the kitchen. "Mistletoe," Ray named the cluster of berries and leaves dangling overhead.

It was Ruthie's turn next. I watched her under the green branch twist in Ray's grasp and wrench her face away before following him to their room; a fuddle of voices on the stairs, sliding steps and the bang of a door. I could not understand why standing under bits of shrubbery oddly prompted holiday kissing in America, as Nana forewarned earlier that week. My first Christmas Eve in America was puzzling to me. I almost missed the familiarity of our chapel services in Belgium.

"Oh, my poor head." An ice pack at her temple, Ruthie cautiously clopped down the staircase and began opening the gifts strewn under the tree. *"Joyeux Nöel,"* I shouted.

"Shush," warned Grandma Burt, her hair set for the holidays into a cap of tightly-ridged waves. "Too much office partying," groaned Ray. Like a waiter aboard the ship, he entered the room balancing a tray with two tomato-red drinks for himself and Ruthie. "Hair of the dog." How unkind, I thought, to shear off the pelts of innocent animals for this purpose. "A cure for what ails us," Ray added.

Grandpa Burt sat deeply entombed in his accustomed club chair and glowered, clapping both hands to his ears at my gaily twittered "Merry Christmas," a futile effort to rouse him from the silence in which he lived, a traffic of sentences roadblocked in his throat, gagged paragraphs, a clamor of stories suppressed and untold. "Why doesn't Grandpa Burt speak?" had been answered by Nana with a hunch of bony shoulders.

It was my first American Christmas, and I was dismayed at how quickly its excitement had fizzled—like that of ginger ale bubbles in the Shirley Temples Ray served me in the Whoopee Room. Dazed, I felt like a boat marooned in a sea of floating paper, cast-off ends and snippets of ribbons, tinsel and twine.

Would Anne envy me now that I was engulfed with presents in America? I supposed she had adjusted to empty-handed holiday visits from her aunt and uncle, her gaggle of farm cousins with scarcely more to give than bored looks and stiff words of greeting.

The gift from Grandma Burt, a jigsaw puzzle of a sky and flowery meadow was likely designed to keep me out from underfoot. But the gleaming roller skates! "For me?" I gushed, about to throw my arms around a sleepy-eyed Ruthie, but held off, fearful of disturbing her carefully achieved powder and rouge.

I was embraced by *mama* only when posed before the camera, whose snapshots repeatedly captured us with her arm around my shoulders as we sat side by side on the porch glider or stood by the shiny Cadillac, Ruthie's lips parted in a wispy smile, mine in a gap-toothed grin. We squatted on the boardwalk of Jones Beach; her arms enfolding me as I scowled into the lens, my eyes squeezed shut in the blazing sunlight.

At the edge of the kiddy pool in the West Bath House, I stood pigeon-toed in the shirred bathing suit she had selected for me. On our front stoop, I peered up at *mama,* who held my hand languidly in her white gloved fingers.

"Don't move." It was Ruthie's turn behind the camera. I leaned coyly against a tanned and jaunty Ray, slimly erect in a lightweight summer suit; he wore a Panama hat with authority, its brim smartly snapped down.

"Okay, let's have a big smile." Ray abandoned his eggnog to flash pictures of Ruthie and me kneeling beside the tree, holding up our gifts. "We'll see" sometimes *does* mean yes, I speculated while buckling on the roller skates. I chanted new words, *tinsel, mistletoe, tootsie,* while skating past doors with wreathes, trying to recall the capitals of Nebraska and Wyoming, savoring the air which was warm for December. Suddenly, my back wheels struck a sidewalk crack, spilling me to the ground; blood trickled down my white knee socks.

A whiny Grandma Burt would lecture me about my clumsiness. "You're doing this to spite me," she would moan, wiping her glasses with a little pink cloth.

Nana had already latched her door and slipped off to Cleveland without so much as a good-bye. "How I come and go is nobody's business but mine," she would sniff if questioned why. I imagined her also saying of my mishap, "You never look where you're going. I'm not going to play doctor to your cuts and bruises."

Scraps of their reproofs collected in my head, rolling into a heavy ball of discordant sentences that pressed against my skull. I hobbled to Mrs. Morse's door.

"Pauvre chère," she cooed, dabbing on iodine that stung my bleeding knees, which she then bandaged. "Poor dear, have a glass of milk with grenadine." Pomegranate syrup lingered on my tongue.

She tapped a spot on her cheek for my kiss. "*Joyeux Nöel,* Madame Morse," I chirped, surveying the crèche under her tree. A porcelain audience of cows, donkeys, and three kings on camelback seemed transfixed by the trumpeting of glass angels inside a doll house. Mrs. Morse nodded at the nativity scene, at our secret homage, our shared Catholic lineage.

"*Courage, mon enfant,* and this is for you." The laminated prayer card she slipped into my hand read, "I believe in these and all the truths, which the Holy Catholic Church teaches because Thou hast revealed them . . . Act of Contrition." I hid the card in the bottom of my dresser drawer to safeguard it from Nana's prying.

Nana returned early in January after Grandpa Burt had dismantled the Christmas tree. We met on the stairway. "Nana, you're back from the capital of Ohio!" In her absence I had stared repeatedly at her locked door, pretending my eyes shed beams of light that would magically open it to the scent of lavender sachets tucked among her handkerchiefs, to the aroma of oil of cloves and wintergreen she inhaled when colds threatened.

I missed the taste of her honeyed cough drops, the feel of her oily-smooth amber beads rolling between my fingertips. I yearned to caress the limp dresses she allowed me to remove from their hangers and spread across the bed. I longed to don the feathered hats with pins and satin bows she stored in boxes.

But at the moment, Nana acknowledged me with tensed lips and a curt nod. I knew the look; she was in a black mood. I suspected a difficult visit with her relatives. Or was it something I had done?

I felt captive to the household's fast-shifting outbreaks of gloom and anger and prayed for deliverance, recollecting the old dominion, the supreme authority of the nuns. Their rule of law was at least predictable. I looked back in wonder at the clear-cut routines of a place I had no wish to see again and remained both absorbed and mystified by this family at loggerheads.

I basked in a nearness to Miss Piscotta's perfumed scent, her crisply tailored dresses, starched lace collars, the tiny gold icons clipped to her ears. "Happy New Year, 1939. Today's Lesson" was neatly chalked on the blackboard. "The Assignment is the Writing of Thank You Notes. Form: Date (upper right-hand corner), Salutation, Content, Complimentary Close, Signature."

The words of her dusty white instructions swirled and speckled like flurries of snow outside the window. I asked for permission to compose a thank-you note for a letter just received. A look of concern furrowed Miss Piscotta's forehead. "Such notes are normally written to express gratitude for a gift or a visit. But if you follow the proper form, I don't see why not."

> Dear Cecil: Thank you for your letter. What a surprise. I found a family, not my real one. This family will adopt me. I have two grandmothers and a grandfather, but no brothers or sisters. I attend school and we are writing thank-you notes. My teacher is pretty. I hope you liked the holidays. I had lots of cadeaux, gifts. Do you remember French? The English ship was fun. I saw the ocean at Jones Beach. I am glad you live near the water. God bless you. Write soon. Sincerely, Colette

6

As cold weather settled in, Nana's good humor revived, as if her sullen behavior of the other day had been no more than a mirage, a hallucination. Her activities at the Church of the Redeemer recommenced, and she baked cookies and pies to raise funds for the Ladies Auxiliary.

On a basement worktable, Grandpa Burt repaired our neighbors' broken toasters, lamps, fans and electric irons for small change. "There's no free lunch, my friend." Ray thumped his father-in-law's back. And in her rare spells of leisure Grandma Burt crocheted squares for an afghan Ruthie requested for the basement sofa.

Her daughter and son-in-law evaded avoided dinner at home except on Sundays, when the grandmothers competed to impress "the children" (as they called Ray and Ruthie) with baked chicken and gravy, roast pork and applesauce, roast beef and horse radish, mashed potatoes, buttermilk biscuits, fruit Jell-O, devil's food, and mocha cakes.

Our silent meals were punctuated by Grandma Burt's "Have another biscuit. I baked them for you especially, you're looking so peaked, Woofie." It was true. Her daughter had grown pale and thin, deepening the bluish circles under her eyes. She seemed to slip even further into despondency, and I felt the weight of her sadness pushing me farther out of her concerns.

During a Sunday dinner, the family was electrified by Ray, who slapped down his *Daily News* and tapped his highball glass with a knife. An announcement. He and Ruthie were embarking with another country-club couple on a Caribbean cruise to Tobago, Trinidad, and Barbados. Impressed, I chanted the exotic place names before being muffled by Nana's hush followed by a swift kick under the table.

"We've got to put some color back into that face." Raymond leaned over and pinched his wife's cheek, "And you've got to get your strength back, honey. There's a whole goddamned new wardrobe to shop for." Ruthie brightened. Shopping. Cruise clothes. I pictured her gliding in a low-cut evening gown, in ankle-strap shoes, flinging high kicks in a conga line that wove along the promenade deck of a moonlit liner vibrant with Latin music pulsing over Caribbean waters.

"Some new duds, just the thing for what ails you." Ray opened his newspaper to accounts of Poland's surrender to Hitler's invading army.

During the following week our house was pacified by their absence. I was entranced by snow silhouetting our lawn, by shrubs limned in whiteness that brought back memories of the children skating on the pond near the trolley line on rue Chant d'Oiseaux. I shared the after-school hours with Donna and Dorothy, belly-flopping on their sled down a nearby slope, and brought my giant jigsaw puzzle to their home for help in patching together a sky from its many defiant pieces.

In turn, I was the patient diagnosed as suffering from an advanced case of Frog's Disease (an affliction of the French, they insisted), and could be healed only by eating green vegetables. Spinach will do it, predicted Donna. I called her a featherbrain. She scrambled the puzzle, leaving a broken meadow bereft of its disordered sky of concentrated blue.

It was later that I became the girlfriend of outgoing, redhaired Roone Arledge who I met during a 1942 grade school air raid drill. That summer, with his brother, we lashed together a raft we paddled around Merrick Bay. At times I joined him in his backyard tent that held photographs of actress Brenda Marshall, who he said I resembled, and his baseball idol, Mel Ott of the New York Giants.

I was again Nana's companionable child, privileged to share her Sunday radio favorites while seated before the Emerson; I had grown accustomed to these bits of American furniture that actually spoke with often curious messages. Charlie McCarthy, I charged, was not deferential to his master, Edgar Bergen. And how could penny-pinching Jack Benny afford to pay his gravelly-voiced valet, Rochester? Nana refused to comment on such idiocies, the blather of a know-nothing child.

Weekdays were tuned to *One Man's Family; The Lux Radio Theater;* and *The Goldbergs,* whose star chatted in a curious accent that even my beginner's English divined. "Hexcuse me, I heff to go, mine leg's in de oven." Nana would toss her head back in uproarious laughter that brought tears she would blot with the hanky I fetched from her bureau drawer.

Now there's a beauty," Nana insisted one evening as she propped a photograph on the bureau. "She's my late brother Jimmy's only daughter and is married to a Chicago muck-a-muck in politics." I would meet them the year after next. Nana received letters from Elizabeth Corley addressed in twining curlicues; her classically modeled face was framed by abundant hair gathered at the neck with a large bow. As hard as I tried, I could not push aside my jealousy of her looks and the praise Nana heaped on them. Whenever Nana was out of the room, I would turn Miss Perfection and her Crowning Glory to the wall.

Shortly before Ruthie and Ray returned from their cruise, a

warm spell thawed away the snow. As with the words *thief, thin, thick, thimble,* and *thorn,* I struggled before our bathroom mirror to enunciate "thaw" with my tongue drawn across the ridges of my top teeth.

The car pulled up our driveway. Ray and Ruthie climbed out, bronzed and blithe, a happier couple than we knew the week before. "Look at our nut-brown maiden and her Indian chief," exclaimed Nana with a flourish of her hand. Ray's eyes lit up when greeting his mother with a pat on the back. Nana was pleased at her prodigal son's homecoming and later assured him they both needed their reprieve from family warfare.

After Ray's late returns from work Nana would sometimes loosen his tie and shirt for a body massage. Stretched full-length across the sofa, he would groan with delight as she kneaded the muscles of his legs, back and neck. "More there," he would plead, "a little lower, yes, higher. Yes, that's it." The rite usually ended with Ruthie's call from the open door of their bedroom. "Raymond, is that you, Raymond?" Bolting upright, he would straighten his tie and wordlessly race to her up the staircase.

But these were brief intermissions in the family's symphony of discord. Nana resumed her attacks on her daughter-in-law's extravagance, but Ray stood his ground. Ruthie was not to be criticized. I relished such moments: Ray in command, Nana subdued and both stalemated in an eerily similar exchange of pale-eyed glares. Even in their intonations and the rhythms of their speech, they echoed each other. Ruthie had Grandpa Burt's large, down-curved brown eyes, his pointed lips and her mother's luxurious hair. When combed back, their hairlines dipped across their foreheads in the same smooth way.

This sameness of looks and manner led me to speculate on whom *I* resembled, whose gestures might duplicate mine, whose voice would speak out with the same timbre and pitch. I mused on having a twin somewhere on earth, a faithful copy I would one day meet. I knew no one I looked like.

The couple unpacked their booty from luggage spattered with tropical island travel stickers. Gifts for everyone. Mine was a grass skirt Ruthie wrested from my hands, brushing past me as I melted into the concealing shadows of the furniture. She clutched the skirt to her body and swayed while chanting "Hula, Hula, look at me doing the Hula," her hips wildly oscillating.

"She thinks she's been to Hawaii," Nana sneered. "Why must you always be so sarcastic?" Grandma Burt asked, eyes brimmed with tears. Nana turned away with a snort and recited, "I yam what I yam: I yam Popeye the sailor man."

A new siege followed, during which neither spoke. As weeks of the newly declared Grandmother Wars dragged on, I was the appointed courier. "Tell Mrs. B, we've run out of starch for Raymond's shirts. . . . Ask Mrs. Burt to turn down those screeching hyenas on her radio." At the end of another hostile day, I would ask the Blessed Mother to enter the hearts of the adversaries that they might receive charitable thoughts of mercy and calm.

In this blight of silence, Ruthie's festive post-cruise mood soon evaporated. On my way to the bathroom, I saw her weaving toward me, a spectral figure half-dancing down the hallway, holding a tall glass at arm's length, or worse, unconscious on the floor.

I could never pair with anyone, as did Ruthie and her mother stumbling down the corridor—Grandma Burt's heroic figure wrapped in yards of pink chenille, shielding her daughter.

"Did Raymond say anything to you about my parents?" I asked Nana as she mended her son's black silk sock stretched over a wooden darning egg. "You've asked me that before and I've always given you the same answer. No, and no means no."

If I could learn nothing about my real family, I decided to pump Nana for stories about *her* parents. "When was I born? Good lord, five years after the close of the Civil War, if that means anything to you. In Clinton, Iowa, December 10, 1870. I was the fifth and last daughter in a family of twelve. My father, James, settled in Colorado, where he worked in the silver mines. He liked to tell us that his aunt and uncle from Scotland were scalped by a Cheyenne war party." Nana stopped for a moment to let that grisly fact sink in. "And as for my mother, she was a Baxter."

"What's a Baxter?" I asked

"For heaven's sakes, it's a family name. What is the matter with you?"

"Where did James Miller meet your mother?" I persisted.

"He bought a piece of farmland in Clinton, where my mother's people were homesteading. The Baxters, who were also from Scotland, claimed Ulysses S. Grant as a cousin. The Grants had known drunkards among them, and Ulysses had the love of liquor in his blood, our mother told us. As children we were not allowed to mention his name at the table. Whether to rile me or not, for some reason Raymond got it into his head to use Grant as his middle name."

I recalled the care I had used in forging the loops of his large *G* when signing my report cards, and it crossed my mind that Nana's handwriting, with its sharp angles and large curves resembled her son's. "Did you look like your mother when you were a girl?" It was difficult to call up the image of a youthful Nana.

"Here I am." The tintype she extracted pictured a face with clenched lips and a firm chin, suggesting a willfulness that contrasted with the wide, soft eyes gazing flirtatiously beneath a frizz of forehead curls. "I was a pretty young thing, if I say so myself, with a flock of beaux, but Raymond's father won out over the others." Without my asking, Nana handed me a picture of Arthur, a shy-looking, bespectacled man gripping a violin.

"Arthur punched tickets on the trolley line in Clinton and played at church socials, but it was clear to me and others who knew him that he would go on to better himself."

"How did he propose?"

"On his knees in our parlor, and I warned Arthur that if I ever smelled even a whiff of alcohol on his breath, I would never speak to him again. I asked if he understood that I meant what I said. He said yes, and I believed him."

A dreamy expression softened her face. "Once when Raymond was a schoolboy, Arthur floated home from a Masonic Lodge meeting, and I sniffed his breath. There was no mistaking it. Liquor.

"It's a harmless glass of wine to celebrate a friend's promotion, he lied to me. For weeks I did not utter a word to him, not once, not a whisper until one day a weeping, pleading Arthur crawled the length of the floor to my shoe tops and begged for pardon, implored me for a word, a reprieve from an unhappiness so great, he said, it would force him to leave me."

"What did you say?" I felt sorry for Arthur and hoped he would be forgiven. "I told him, for God sakes, stand up, Arthur, and he did, and that was that."

No, no, make it into a heart, not a tomato. No blobs, please, I want big, red hearts." In art class, we were each constructing a Valentine's Day card from red construction paper and lace cutouts in a project orchestrated by our teacher, Miss Hartman, a squarish woman in a bright blue, rumpled smock. She waved her hands when she spoke, accentuating the sparkle of her gold rings.

"Children, make no mistake, it's Love Day. Hot love is soon cold. He who falls in love with himself will have no rival, et cetera. Children, what is love? Let's have some definitions." "Love is mush," groaned a boy in the back row.

"Who disagrees? Let's see some hands."

Miss Hartman ran manicured fingers through her shock of orange hair and chalked words we might print on our cards: *sweetheart, darling, honey, patootie, sweetie pie*. The blackboard blossomed with enormous letters. When we laughed at her jokes, she would clap her hands or blow us a kiss, stretching her heavy, red lips upward like the clown during special attractions between feature films at Freeport's Grove Theater.

The Saint Valentine I once learned about was an unlikely champion of love. A martyr beheaded by a Roman emperor for restoring a blind girl's sight and converting her family to Christianity, he seemed wholly unrelated to *this* Saint Valentine. But my models for sanctification were themselves transformed by living in America; I accepted it as a given of my new existence.

I withheld sending my Valentine's Day card to Cecil, who had not yet answered my letter. I was also restrained by Nana's counsels which began to build walls of suspicion and fear around my fantasies of honeybunches and darlings doing *it* behind closed doors.

"Never run after a boy. Never go into a cellar alone with a boy. Never let a boy touch you *down there*." I tried in vain *not* to touch myself in that secret place where curly hairs would soon sprout. But at night, my hands were small animals that sought out warm crevices and lairs, lingering there as I dozed in soft-colored half-dreams.

I gave the card to Ruthie, hoping that the invocation of Saint Valentine might relieve her fainting spells. She received the card without comment, smiling wanly, slipping it into a mound of bills and papers on the end table.

Ray decided they needed to entertain more often. During weekends that followed, Ruthie's disposition improved when guests gathered in the Whoopee Room. She invited me to join the party for a friendly inspection, for guests to meet *petite* Colette, a "genuine import."

I was trotted out to "sing something for us in French." "Sur le Pont D'Avignon" and "Frère Jacques" were favorites. I reveled in the spotlight during one such soirée with Ernie and Esther Luce, a tall, weather-beaten couple who were Ruth and Ray's golf and Caribbean-cruise companions.

"Bonjour, sweetie pie," Ernie bellowed in the voice I recalled booming out golf scores at the country club.

"You should be in bed, kiddo." Esther smiled through prodigious teeth like those of the wolf I encountered in Little Red Riding Hood. A swizzle stick tapping against a glass was Ray's cue to begin my tune. How cute, how sweet, such a little puppet, such an actress, they enthused in a huddle of clumsy embraces, and offered me sips of their drinks, which I politely refused.

"Your kid is about her age, right, Ernie?" Ray wondered, jiggling a cocktail shaker to the beat of "The Peanut Vendor," a popular Latin tune of the day. "Did you hear the one about . . . stop me if you heard the one about . . ." I would be sent off to bed before Ray fed his visitors obscene jokes, deftly narrated in various accents.

One April morning, after returning with Nana from Palm Sunday services, Ruthie called me to the master bedroom.

Tout de suite, she summoned, draining her meager horde of French commands. The giggle behind her call and Ray's passive expression were reassuring. I was not about to be accused of insolence or theft or reprimanded for talking back to Grandma Burt.

The Sunday funnies were littered about the room, upturned to "Casper Milquetoast," "Jiggs and Maggie," and "The Katzenjammer Kids," Ray's prized comic strips. An empty coffee pot and scattered pastry crumbs crowded a tray waiting for removal. The night table on Ruthie's side of the bed held a stack of travel folders and brochures. Lounging in a silk robe and white scarf, Ray examined maps.

"Next week we're going to Niagara Falls," Ruthie announced, toying with a kiss curl. "Do you remember Mr. and Mrs. Luce?" I nodded. "They're coming, too, and are bringing their son, Skippy. You're both off from school for Easter. Do you remember we mentioned Skippy? Won't that be nice?"

Niagara Falls. I recalled Sister Jerome's class calendar with its tinted photograph of what she described as one of America's great natural wonders. I longed to see it, but not with Ruth and Ray nor with the tipsy and boisterous Luces. But it was wrong to feel that way about my guardians. Nana insisted often enough that I should be grateful to them for giving me room and board.

"You're our French Orphan Annie, even if Raymond is no Daddy Warbucks," she would say, clear out of the blue. I resented comparisons with the saucer-eyed, floor-scrubbing child.

"May I also see my friend Cecil, who lives nearby?"

Ruthie vaguely recalled Bale's account of my shipmate, the English orphan who tossed a mean game of darts. "I don't see why not," Ruthie agreed, "What do you think, hon?" Ray glanced up from the sports pages. "As long as I don't have to pay for the honeymoon, it's okay with me."

I had been told many newlyweds spent their wedding nights at Niagara Falls. Doing *it* under a spray of mist? I wondered. "Have you ever been there?" I asked Ruthie. "Listen, I take her on a honeymoon every year," boasted Ray who resumed reading the funnies.

Early Friday, we met the Luces at the information booth of Grand Central Station. It was dislike at first sight of elephant-eared Skippy Luce, a tall, stringy boy who stood sullenly beside his parents, clutching a pack of battered baseball cards. He was ten, he insisted, a year or so older than I, who would reach nine in June.

"Now you be nice to Colette, do you hear," his mother urged as she nudged him toward me. The couples fled to the bar car on the ride north. While I studied the passing scenery, Skippy squandered his allowance on Milky Way and Hershey bars bought from a vendor and withdrew to absorb the statistics on the backs of his baseball cards. He handed me a stick of Spearmint gum, which I obligingly chewed and, to his disgust, promptly gulped down. Except for the Host at communion, it seemed natural to swallow anything placed in the mouth.

"I'll bet you never heard of Mickey Owen."

"No, but I've seen Mickey Rooney," recalling an inexplicable Andy Hardy film I had seen at the Gables Theater. Freckled, pug-nosed adolescents wearing porkpie hats with upturned brims and aged and discerning fathers were not native to my Bayview Avenue life. "You're hopeless," he declared, shaking his head and withdrawing from his mouth a gray rubbery wad, which he glued under the seat.

After a guided tour of Niagara's cataracts and islands, we boarded the *Maid of the Mist,* and in yellow raingear cruised across a deep pool, dwarfed by towering walls of plunging water. Here my body might be thrashed against boulders that rose from cold and swarming waters. My spirit would join the souls of the drowned who I guessed ascended to heaven in a thick mist. I had known such fear when Ray flung me from a high diving board into the big pool at Jones Beach: a beginner's swimming lesson. The memory of flailing my arms and gulping water in near-suffocation now returned.

"Don't move; hold that pose." Ray's camera caught the instant on the deck, snapped the Luces, Ruthie, and a glowering Skippy, his arm draped like a limp snake over my shoulders. I could hardly wait to share my impressions with Cecil, who by prearrangement would be delivered by his aunt to our hotel.

He was recognizably the same, gangly and stooped, but less windblown than I remembered, with a crop of wetted-down blond hair parted at the side. "Who's the boyfriend?" He motioned toward Skippy left behind by his parents during their daylong Canadian excursion with Ruth and Ray. The Luces would return by late evening, satisfied that I was safely minded by their intrepid son.

"You probably can't tell me who Whitlow Wyatt is, or the Brooklyn Dodgers," Skippy challenged when we gathered in the lobby. "What is he talking about, can't we get rid of him?" *"Je deteste cet idiot,"* I remarked in an easy test of Cecil's French. Indignant and confused, my erstwhile escort wheeled around and tramped off. "What's the matter with you foreigners, don't you like baseball? It's un-American not to."

Alone in the hotel, we made prank phone calls. To a tobacconist: "Do you have Prince Albert in a can? Well, let him out." To a hardware store: "Do you have long nails? Yes? then scratch my back." To the hotel clerk: "Do you have a horse in the lobby? No, well why not?" We spoke of his aunt and uncle, who he liked well enough, and of America, which was "smashing, *formidable,*" the French word articulated with drawn-out vowels in a mock falsetto. He screwed up his face and crossed his eyes. Authentic Cecil.

"Put the tip on the bill," he instructed the waiter who brought sandwiches ordered from room service. We folded hotel stationery into paper airplanes and sailed them out the window, watching them lift in the wind and drift in slow, lazy spirals down to the street. "Let's wrestle." He seemed at a loss for something else to do. "But that's for boys," I protested. "The Amazons were wrestlers," he insisted. I agreed to sham combat, convinced by his assurance that women warriors invented the hammerlock.

The bout began. Pinned gently against the floor, I could have struggled and twisted loose, but did not. I lingered under the weight of his light, sharp-boned body, inhaling the sweet, clean odor of his skin, lulled by the sound of his heart drumming under a rib cage I likened to a bridge spanning his floating organs, the body structures I had seen illustrated in a butcher shop poster while buying meats with Nana. Heart, liver, kidney, spleen. Clutched by Cecil's unaccustomed hold, I pushed away hard to dislodge his hands on my shoulders.

"You're quite strong for a girl, and your English has certainly improved," observed Cecil.

I considered the word *improve,* that it meant to advance, to make headway, to go forward, to gain ground. In America, one could change for the better; it was expected. And Cecil *had* changed. Even his escapades were less impulsive. "Let's find old flappy ears."

"Skippy? But you said he was an *imbécile*."

"But he's the imbecile we need. Don't you want the parents to find us all as happy as ducks in a pond?"

Skippy was settled in the lobby, undressing another candy bar. With a stab at civility, Cecil suggested playing a game of chess borrowed at the hotel's courtesy desk. "It's a stupid game and boring," Skippy objected, licking chocolate from his upper lip.

"You must be a cretin, what's the matter with you?" Cecil replied in a flash of his shipboard self. But he mellowed as the afternoon waned and reluctantly agreed to hear Skippy discourse on baseball heroes and their records, although nothing he said won us over to the great American pastime.

As the hours slipped by, Cecil's English accent seemed less assertive, and I sensed we were shedding our origins. Our speech and mannerisms were transforming—the ways in which we gripped our knives and forks, cut food—the transforming language of numbers and words that we pronounced and dreamed. Orphans at sea, we had emigrated in the spirit of castaways to accept the fullness of a seductive new world.

As our rendezvous in Niagara Falls ended, we parted with the hope of meeting again to share that world, even if briefly. "In New

York City, then?" I suspected a second trip here, to the honeymoon capital, would not happen. "New York? We've already been there. Last year, remember? Let's meet in Hollywood, *dahlin',* okay?" Cecil slobbered little kisses up and down my hand. "Okay, okay." We exchanged our final farewells.

7

GERMAN INVASION OF THE LOWLANDS. DEFEAT OF THE NETHERLANDS. OCCUPATION OF BELGIUM. May 1940. A year had passed since the trip to Niagara Falls, and two years since I had left Belgium. I could now decipher all the words in headlines bannered across the front pages of Ray's morning papers. "It's lucky you're not still in that orphanage," Nana advised me. "You'd be eating slops with the Huns looking on."

German soldiers in jackboots goose-stepping through our refectory, Nazis occupying the apple orchard, tanks planted on rue Chant d'Oiseaux, barring Sunday visitors from their trolley rides. Reverend Mother would never allow it, would order the invaders to heed the No Trespassing sign and leave Belgium at once. But what if she were forced to submit? Even she would be helpless to bend a whole army to her will.

The papers reported that King Leopold had capitulated, that the nation's poorly armed defenders had surrendered in droves to advancing German troops.

How might the war touch the life of Anne? Was she crouching under a dormitory bed, alert for the thud of bombs after the whine of the sirens? Did little Jean-Pierre still wriggle and squirm at evening devotions? Was he huddled in a basement shelter, picking at his nose, fingering his rosaries, intoning "Our Father" in a high, agitated voice? Were they victims of machine-gun fire or crushed under fallen bricks loosened by fiery explosions? I pictured a small troop of nuns, with Sisters Jerome and Paul among them, loading rifles aboard a street car whose conductor wore the uniform of a German officer.

I wanted to write to Anne, having neglected my promise to do so from an elegant hotel, but the letter could be lost on a falling plane or torpedoed ship, the envelope singed by flames plummeting from the sky or nibbled by fish at the bottom of the sea. No, I would send her my prayers, confident that they alone would safely scale the violent seas and skies of the far-off war.

Watching Nana primp before the mirror, I suspected preparations for a singular event. While daubing her fingernails with maroon lacquer, she hummed a radio jingle that glorified Rinso's "Happy little washday song." She abstractly dusted violet powder over her eyelids and splashed puddles of rouge on her cheeks. Halloween, I thought, but dared not say. Out of vanity, Nana refused to correct her myopia with eyeglasses, and the effect of her makeup was sometimes startling.

"There's nothing wrong with my vision. I see all that I need to see and that's more than enough." Nana pressed her pudding-like hairdo with agile fingers.

"Why won't you tell me where you're going?"

"I'm entitled to my secrets, but if you must know, I'm about to be taken out."

"By a man?" I was astounded.

"Could be, although there's hardly one worth the effort. There's no bigger fool in the world than a man." She pressed her mouth on a tissue, leaving a purplish imprint of her narrow lips. Nana stood up, glanced sideways into the mirror and patted her hips. "I hope you're fortunate enough to have my figure when you're my age." Although her energy belied the years that filigreed her face with wrinkles, Nana would not admit to having turned seventy last December, and was proudly tagged by Ray as "my mother, the septuagenarian," a substantial word I could neither spell nor pronounce.

At breakfast the next day Nana poked listlessly at her corn flakes. "What are you staring at?" She scowled at her son.

"No conniptions, please, we're waiting to hear about last night." Ray gave her his sly, wet-lipped smile.

His paper remained folded beside his plate; Ruthie's *Silver Screen* was untouched. "Let me guess," Ray said to Ruthie, who was gingerly wiping the corners of her mouth. "You remember my cousin, Bill Culiman, the skinny chiropractor with the funny mustache?" Ruthie giggled. Ignored by everyone, my elbows on the table, I listened with rapt attention. "He called me yesterday at the office to say he's in town with the new wife, Mary Joan. She has a big practice in Cleveland and he's supposed to have married her for her clients." Ray spoke in an exuberant way, although I detected no liquor on his breath during a glancing kiss in the hallway.

"Maybe he loves her." Ruthie sighed, looking up from her plate. "Love? She's fat and fifty if she's a day. The upshot is that Mary Joan planned to fix up a couple of septuagenarians—her widower father from Westchester and the duchess, here. The whole thing's a howl."

All eyes turned toward a grim Nana tipping prune juice into her glass.

"I'll bet you ate him up and spat him out in pieces, right mother?" Ray took another swig of his hangover brew.

"If I did, and I'm not saying one way or the other, the old coot gave me a bad case of indigestion."

"What's the story?" Ray persisted.

"There is no story. Unlike your father, who knew enough not to speak when he was uninformed, this old codger yammered the whole evening long. I don't know what Mary Joan was thinking."

Later that day I found Nana preparing one of her notable pies.

The rolling pin wheeled smoothly in expert strokes across a thin sheet of dough she deftly fitted into a baking tin. A stew of apples fragrant with cinnamon and sprinkled with sugar was loosely sandwiched under a crust brushed with unbeaten egg white. "To make it nice and glossy," she explained before forking steam holes into the pie, which then vanished into the maw of the oven.

"Did he ask you to marry him?" I wondered while she rinsed her hands under the faucet. I found it hard to believe anyone would willingly marry Nana, but anything seemed possible in the topsy-turvy unions I witnessed in America.

"Marry me? Where on earth did you get that notion? Me marry that antique chatterbox? What a joke." She tilted back her head and loosed a high, staccato laugh. "For heaven's sake, don't you have any homework to do?" Nana untied her apron, but before returning to her room for the day's episodes of *Ma Perkins* and *Young Widow Brown,* she added as if in afterthought, "By the way, next week you're coming with me to Cleveland. And we'll be staying with my sisters and with Kate's husband, Ed."

I was elated by the news, a chance to see more of America and even visit the Great Lakes, whose shapes on the map resembled the petals of a flower. When asked by our teacher about our vacation plans, I could impress classmates with descriptions of my trip to Ohio.

It was time to bid Ruthie good-bye, but she had taken to her bed, the fringe of her peach-colored bed jacket peeking from behind the sheet. I carried up a rum and coke on a red lacquered tray with parasols stenciled in gold. "Just what the doctor ordered," Ray claimed, warning me not to spill a drop. I placed down the tray and plumped up her pillows. Ruthie's skin tone was not so much a waxy pallor as a faint yellowish tinge glistening with perspiration.

I leaned against the bed, shifting from one foot to the other. She broke the silence. "My ankles are swollen, and I can't play golf with Ray and the Luces today, not that I'm any great shakes as a golfer." Unexpectedly, she was confiding in me, her large, mascara-fringed eyes searching mine. Was she about to say she would miss me? I checked the impulse to reach for her hand, to lift it to my face, trapping its scent of tobacco and hand lotion. And I was overwhelmed with the desire to do something for her, to make some gesture before the good-byes, to leave my fingerprint on something she would use, a candy bar, a slice of toast, a movie magazine.

"Can I go to the store for you? Do you want a paper, a pack of cigarettes, Alka-Seltzer, aspirins?"

"No, I have all I need."

"Isn't there something I can do? An errand, anything, please?"

"Yes," she paused for a few seconds. "Go comb your hair."

It could have been a Belgian farmer—even Anne's Uncle Charles—who met us at the Cleveland bus depot. We had traveled the better part of a day, sustained by Nana's brown-bag lunch of hard boiled eggs and ripe bananas.

Shadowed by a battered hat, Uncle Ed was a hunched six-footer whose thread-worn blue pants bunched at the top of scuffed brown shoes. Bowing from the waist, he peered at me benignly and said, "Welcome to Cleveland, mamselle." My era of Ohio summers was under way.

The houses planted along the length of Columbia Avenue slumped under the heat of July, as if the weight of weariness and time bore down on them, sagging the roofs and rusting the hinges of doors. In a rite of daily waiting, I rocked on the front porch swing, listening for the crunch of tires on gravel. Uncle Ed's dilapidated Ford coupe would soon belch to a halt in the driveway.

In the kitchen, Aunt Kate husked corn, the definitive vegetable that nourished our days: corn soup; fritters; bread; muffins; succotash; and a concoction called corn oysters blended from cornmeal, eggs, flour, baking powder, and cracker crumbs stirred in a hot skillet.

Tall, gaunt, as if her body had been sewn together by a stingy seamstress, Aunt Kate was an unsettling presence in a soiled bandana. The fold of skin under one eye, pulled and twisted from its lower lid, gave her the look of a cat clawed in a back alley fight. Nana related the impairment was caused by a blazing potato hurled at her by their drunken father for some girlish impertinence.

It did not take long to discover from her scowls and peevishness that she disliked me, an interloper and rival for her husband's affection, which, in any case, she received in scant amounts. When brushing past each other in the hallway or on the stairs she would say, "Get out from under my feet." By unspoken agreement, we kept our distance. While cranky toward me, Kate cocked a patient ear to Nana's advice. How more might she scrimp to survive on Ed's meager and irregular income as an itinerant piano tuner for the theater trade? Nana, the confident youngest sister, basked in her role of counselor and respected summer guest.

Another sister hovered about, communing with the walls and ceilings of the kitchen and parlor. Stout and humpbacked Agnes gazed blankly from a face in whose planes and structures lingered the residue of a dimmed radiance, a glow I had seen in the illustrated faces of saints. Passive and dreamy, she seemed attached to another reality far from the shabby boundaries of our street. But at times, Agnes would spring suddenly to life, aim a gnarled finger at me and ask, "Who are you, what do you want?" Or she would sidle up to Nana and mutter, "You killed our father." Because he drank, Nana had ceased speaking to her father, toward whom she remained unforgiving these many years after his death.

Still licking off telltale bits of crust and meringue from her lips, Agnes accused me of theft on the day she alone bolted down an entire lemon pie Nana had left cooling on the steps. I was vindicated by Nana with a caution, "Agnes is not right in the head, and you are not to challenge or bother her in any way, even if provoked. Especially if provoked. Do you understand?"

I learned that Nana's tolerance of Agnes traced to her middle sister's superior education; among the surviving Miller daughters, only Agnes had earned a high school diploma, followed by informal studies in human anatomy. But her hopes for a career in chiropractic medicine were dashed by the profession's general exclusion of women. A discouraged Agnes toyed with thoughts of marriage.

"She couldn't find a man good enough, and by the time she was in her thirties, all the men were taken," Nana recounted. "Then she took up with some Hindu guru with peculiar ideas about standing on your head and mumbling the same word over and over, and god knows what. Little by little, over the years, she became demented, although she does have clear moments. Ed wants her out of the house, and Kate rightly refuses to put her away."

Can I cut some tiger lilies for Uncle Ed?" His garden in the cramped backyard was thronged with flowers: beds of marigolds, lilies, petunias, hollyhocks, and gladioli separated by narrow strips of grass on which I imagined myself a female Gulliver circled by a swarming population of Lilliputian visitors, transient butterflies, grasshoppers, houseflies, crickets, and praying mantises.

"A few flowers, what of it, Kate?" Aunt Agnes asked, nodding toward the sunlight that flooded through the kitchen windows. Her momentary radiance was spoiled by the sight of food stains on her bib.

I longed for Uncle Ed to return home and escort me to a vaudeville theater assignment at The Alhambra or The Palace. I had accompanied him before and listened while he tuned a grand piano, his fingers reflected in the sheen of its polished face board. Onstage he was my maestro, flinging bright arpeggios into the theater's shadowy emptiness, and I was his gifted protégé. I peeked into the piano's interior, at the trembling ribs wired like a harp. His freckled bald pate was canted forward as if in prayer, and he probed the notes along the scale, occasionally lingering, plink-plink on the treble, a throb on the keyboard's bass. When testing the action of the pedal, he whispered in a hushed, reverential voice, "It's where the soul of the piano resides."

Poised before the red velvet curtain that opened every night like the Red Sea for Moses, I invented a dance to his "Tiptoe through the Tulips." One, two, side, close, back and one, two, back and forth, side, close, turn, turn, blowing kisses to the dark loge and balcony, and then a deep curtsy to fancied applause blooming from vacant orchestra seats.

"Look," I called to him in the midst of a pirouette.

"Dance away, my princess." Gruff to his wife, snappish even with friends, not on speaking terms with his son, he had singled me out for unwavering affection during this and following summers.

"I think Uncle Ed really likes me," I pronounced to Nana's scrawny back in the double bed we shared. "Don't let it go to your head. He pities you because you're an orphan."

That first month I met Bill and Mary Joan Culiman at their chiropractic offices in the Euclid Avenue Arcade. A small, neatly made man with a square black moustache, Bill resembled neither parent, although his stature and manner were similar to Ray's. Had Bill been deposited on the Culimans' doorstep by Gypsies, who failed to find a nearby church? His dark eyes gleamed when he pressed my hand.

"Comentallay voo mamselle," he attempted, bowing from the waist.

"She speaks English better than you speak French," Nana huffed, backing away from his arms outstretched in greeting.

"Please, for heaven's sake, no kisses." The corners of her mouth turned down in distaste.

"Bill likes to get his hands on women," remarked Mary Joan as she entered the reception room in her white medical coat.

Sturdy and buxom with a pink and white complexion, Mary Joan seemed younger than her reputed fifty-some years. I was impressed by the self-assurance her big body exuded. As expected, the couple had perfect posture. Did they nightly massage and manipulate each other's spines and bones? That's what chiropractors did. I caught Bill appraising me as I stiffened to a ramrod, head held high.

"We'll have to watch Frenchie, here. She'll be a cute little number one of these years," he said.

"She's cute right now," Mary Joan added, perhaps to amend an unintended slight. A dimpled smile brightened her face.

"Orry Vor," Bill mispronounced after our brief meeting, his rendering of *au revoir* sent my imagination spinning in a windmill of words starting with letter *o* followed by *r:* orry vor origins, orry vor orangeade . . . orry vor oration . . . orry vor ordinary . . . orry vor

Oregon . . . orry vor orchestra . . . orry vor ordained minister. And as the women debated whether to lunch at Halle's, Higbee's Department Store, or in the Arcade, I was handed a lollipop.

"No, thank you, Uncle Bill." I was convinced that lollipops bulging in the cheeks of children made them look moronic; except for Shirley Temple who every movie-goer knew was hopelessly adorable. Along with runny eggs, waxy toast, fat on meat, bubble gum, and tiny fish bones, lollipops were high on my index of irks.

"Let's get a move on," urged Nana. From the corner of her eye, she had again caught me daydreaming.

Uncle Ed's car rattled and wheezed into the driveway. He had picked up Nana at the Euclid Avenue Arcade after another visit with Bill and Mary Joan. She wore the usual clenched-lip, pinched-nose look she assumed when something was amiss. I hoped it did not signal a tiff that would cancel next week's invitation to Bill and Mary Joan's Parma Heights house tended by a Mexican couple who gardened and cooked.

Maybe Nana had tried softening Ed's disapproval of Bill's marriage, the "May-December medicos," as she called them. Or had she quarreled with Ed in a flareup of buried resentments? During our bus trip west, Nana confided that Ed had been among her more ardent girlhood suitors.

"He was handsome with wavy, red hair and considered a catch, but not for me. Of course, Ed married Kate on the rebound."

I prodded her for details, eager to learn more about their meeting and courtship, why he was spurned and if Kate ever learned she was a spitefully selected second choice, and why Arthur's violin was more tuneful to Nana's ear than were Ed's beloved pianos.

"That's enough. Not one word more. I was not put here on earth for your entertainment." Weeks would pass before I learned her reasons for repulsing Ed.

"When I found out he frequented cathouses (an expression she tactfully explained to me), I washed my hands of him." In another version of the story, Nana hinted Kate was in the family way before they married and she miscarried, but Ed chose to responsibly endure a union in which he felt trapped. A frail and sickly child, Bill was born to the couple in their early forties.

"Bill looks so different from his parents," I observed during the trolley ride back to the Culimans' house.

"Children don't always take after their parents." Nana's clamped mouth signaled the futility of more questions. But as the days of summer steamed ahead like ships on the calm waters of nearby Lake Erie, I persisted and pried loose bits and pieces of the tale.

Ed suspected the baby was not his and withdrew from Kate, who clung even more needfully to her only child. A gulf opened between father and son. While Nana remained vague about Bill's legitimacy, I supposed Ed might have been astonished, as was I, that any man would choose Kate; her sulky disposition and disfigured face seemed poor incentives for a sensual spree.

In the kitchen, I filled a basin with vinegar and water and washed Uncle Ed's knobby feet. "You are my revered foot doctor," he offered with a crisp military salute.

"Am I like Mary Magdalene?" I asked. He knew his New Testament. "No more than I am like Jesus." His laughter came in loud, short bursts.

Uncle Ed was nowhere to be seen at the local church to which Nana squired me on Sundays. Yet, rising to full height, in a booming voice he would quote the Sermon on the Mount or passages memorized from the Apostles, sometimes vocalized to the rhythm of a tap dance or soft shoe shuffle. I was anxious about his mockery of religion, fearing it might deny him salvation.

To resurrect the young Uncle Ed, I erased his wrinkles and liver spots, planted waves of carrot-colored hair on his bald crown, and tacked above his lip the moustache of a man-about-town. But his high-bridged nose and light blue eyes above deep pouches gave proof of bygone charms.

Like his orations of Bible verses, Uncle Ed's readings of poems published daily in the *Cleveland Plain Dealer* were full of sweeping flourishes with outflung arms and eyes rolled heavenward. I applauded and begged for more. When we retired to the parlor, he cranked up the Victrola.

"Music sounds better when you're horizontal." Uncle Ed stretched out on the bare floor. I joined him, the two of us side by side on our backs, but not touching. I pretended we were fish drifting on the surface of a pond, sea creatures washed and lulled by the music of "The Lost Chord," "Song of India," and Caruso's arias from *Pagliacci*.

"Did you hear the one about the moron who killed his mother and father?" He rolled over to face me.

"No," I exclaimed with a jolt.

"He wanted to attend the orphan's picnic."

"You two laughing fools will catch your death of a cold on that floor," Aunt Kate cautioned with hands on hips, her dull, uncombed hair resembling the feather duster she flicked and jiggled late at night over heaps of stacked newspapers no one threw out.

"Who in the world could that be at this hour?" she wondered when the telephone rang. "Go answer it," Ed snapped.

I heard radio voices from upstairs droning like insects circling the gummed fly paper dangling from our light fixtures.

An unexpected call from Ray brought Nana to the parlor. To allow her privacy, Ed and I climbed into the porch swing, whose rusty hinges Ed vowed to repair. Without speaking, we absorbed the twanging notes of a mandolin plucked somewhere down the street, then the distant sound of shattering glass, likely a liquor bottle hurled to the curb. Nearby, the clamor of cicada music high in the trees blended with the silky drawl of southern voices nearby.

Columbia Avenue, which today spears the city's Hough district, was home for migrating blacks, some lured from the rural south by better paying jobs in Cleveland's industrial plants and foundries. Two years after war was declared (I returned five more summers), ours and that of an orthodox Jewish family were the only resident Caucasian households on the block; a lonely predicament, since playing with black children was forbidden by Nana and Kate. When

I once ventured into conversation with a pretty black girl skipping rope, her mother came to their screen door and called her away.

"They want to be with their own. Don't go where you're not wanted," Nana instructed. Uncle Ed seemed to agree. I had overheard his slurs, a litany of ugly names for nationalities other than his own mix of German and English. I remembered my discomfort and confusion at being labeled a "frog," a "Frenchie Babu." Our Jewish neighbors also prohibited their children, including twin girls my age, to play with me.

Nana announced that Ruthie had been rushed to the hospital.

"Pack up your things. We're taking the train," she commanded. Not the bus. The costlier choice of faster travel implied a crisis. Uncle Ed's parting gift glowed in my pocket, a green, velvet-lined, gold-painted ring box fashioned from a walnut. Its attached card read: *For my Beloved Foot Doktor for her foot service to me in this summer of 1940.*

Ruth was laid out in a beige lace dress cinched with a lavender sash and adorned, as she would have chosen, with a single strand of pearls. Visitors whispered how peaceful she looked, shook their heads and muttered condolences in counterpoint to Grandma Burt's whimpered refrain, "Woofie, my baby, gone."

Studying the face under its cosmetic mask, the beauty spot on her left cheek, the mouth thickened with blood-red lipstick, I half believed she could magically revive. I had not been told earlier that she died, but I sensed it from Nana's unaccustomed silence aboard the train. Grandma Burt, veiled in black, collapsed in a heap. Nana counted telegrams of condolence and computed the cost of every floral wreath. To her disgust, a sobbing Ray had earlier flung himself across the casket. He had ordered the Burts out of the house that very morning saying, "I'm done supporting those leeches. They'll have to find another goddamned Santa Claus."

Days later, they packed and left for the one-bedroom Jackson Heights apartment of their surviving daughter, Gwen, who attended the funeral in an elaborate hairdo, her face tense with resentment at her new predicament. Throughout the services she competed with Ray for the loudest wails. Grandpa Burt absented himself from the affair, probably to scavenge among unguarded liquor bottles in the Whoopee Room.

At the age of thirty-two, Ruth had succumbed to cirrhosis of the liver and pneumonia. I could hardly pronounce her killers or make much sense of the doctor's claim that she had lost the will to live.

"You're a cool little number," Grandma Burt had accused the night before as I hummed in the kitchen. I was hardly bereft. It was difficult to pretend grief when I no longer felt fear at being forced to tiptoe up the stairs, or lower my voice, or comb my hair properly for inspection.

I would be free from finding her sprawled on the bathroom floor, free from feeling like a pigeon to her peacock as she adorned herself with stylish clothes. For the moment, I was hostage to such mean and selfish thoughts, the hard-heartedness I so despised in others, and shuddered at what God was conjuring up in his future plans for me.

Her body had suddenly failed, like a clock or toaster beyond repair laying dismembered on Grandpa Burt's worktable. Why had God failed to mend her? And why, as I now supposed, had He earlier summoned my real mother and father to his heavenly realm? Unfamiliar women at the funeral cooed and pinched my cheek. "Ruthie loved you so much." Why had she not shown it or told me?

Nana had previously urged a horrified Ray to instruct the undertaker to remove Ruthie's wedding band. "She would want it used again." Hating to see anything go to waste, Nana had pointedly advised, "The dead don't care, the dead eat dirt."

She handed me a nosegay to place in Ruthie's hands. I had just begun grieving for *myself* in a reverie she interrupted by pushing me toward the casket. Repelled by the thought of prying open those rigid fingers, each flecked with blood-red nail polish, I flung the flowers across her chest and bolted into the crowd.

I later entered Ruthie's bedroom and puffed a haze of breath on her three-way mirror, met my flushed and flawed self in triplicate, pinched my arm and squeezed my wrist to test reality. The dent in my palm dug by my fingernails also proclaimed I was alive. I discovered Ruthie could indeed be ordered to come and go at the snap of my fingers and to lift her tweezers to pluck out the scattered hairs between her brows. At my bidding she stretched out on the chaise lounge and flipped through the pages of *Photoplay*. She vanished when I blinked my eyes twice, only to again return at my command; I relished my newfound control over her entrances and exits.

I circled my cheeks with her rouge, darkened my brows with her Maybelline pencil and rolled her shiny lipstick over my mouth. Rummaging through the closet, I extracted her paisley dress with fringed epaulets and pressed it against me, draping its length along my body. Wobbling in her spike-heeled shoes, I danced a clumsy rumba with the empty sleeves, startled back into awareness at the approaching sounds of stumbling and gasping from the stairs. Ray stood in the doorway. In disbelief, he eyed my garishly made up face and Ruthie's dress in my hands, dragging its train of crumpled silk.

He laughed and drew me to him, planting a noisy kiss on my ear. His words were barely audible over the roar in my eardrum. "From now on, you're going to be my very special girl."

After the funeral, calm settled on the house, and with it, dust gathered in the master bedroom where Ray snatched a few hours of sleep, dimpling his side of the double bed. Now that his door was unlocked, we entered as we pleased. Nana sometimes sat primping before Ruthie's vanity table, from which nothing had been removed, not a flacon of perfume, mascara brush, jar of vanishing cream, nor the apple-green comb I had been accused of stealing. I stretched out on the chaise lounge and pretended I was a fine lady sipping a cocktail through a straw, buffing fingernails to a high polish, eyes downcast and lips puckered like Ruthie.

One day toward summer's end, Nana opened the basement cedar closets in which Ruthie's garments still hung. Out came her dresses from their zippered skins, slithering like snakes over her head, and I caught a glimmer of Ruthie's apparition inhabiting her mother-in-law's body.

"How dare you wear her things!" Ray shouted. He had returned earlier than expected.

"Why should they go to waste?" Nana threw back her shoulders and grimaced with her throwing-down-the-gauntlet look, and Ray took up the challenge.

"I don't ever want to *see* you wearing her clothes. Do you understand?" He articulated every word. But icy glances and slammed doors were not routinely followed by the marathon silences that had once held the household in suppressed rancor. Mother and son were more forgiving after such tiffs.

As Nana began to further neglect her role as my caretaker, I explored the paths of a town still surrounded by meadows and open fields, its fly-ridden beaches spread haphazardly along the bay. After Labor Day, I eased into the comforting routines of school. Assignment: Draft a composition on How I Spent My Summer Vacation. I wrote of Uncle Ed's arpeggios in an empty vaudeville theater, trolley trips that clattered miles up Cleveland's Euclid Avenue, of lofting box kites in Wade Park and along the shores of Lake Erie.

I did not report Ruthie's death to my schoolmates, nor her entering heaven in a ravishing outfit, out of concern the news would elicit moans of sympathy I did not deserve. I had not wept for her; during whole hours, even for days, I did not think of her once.

The Burts had begun to fade from memory, until I stumbled on a cigar box while rummaging through the basement. It opened to folded sheets of stationery on which rhymed verses were penned and signed in a fine blue script. I was surprised, even moved by their sentiments, so unexpected from the dour man and his mystifying silences, and was riveted by a poem that begged for forgiveness.

FOR MY GIRLS, RUTH AND GWEN

Deep in my soul I am proud. I have not lost
the sight of your bright curls tossed
hither and yon in the wind. I have sinned
against you, and my life, my heart, grows dumb,
hoping for the day your pardon will come.

I suggested that we mail the box to the Burts in care of their daughter, Gwen.

"Don't go poking into things that are none of your business,"

Nana cautioned. When I searched for it weeks later the box was gone.

"Did you ever return Grandpa Burt's things?" I asked.

"Maybe yes and maybe no."

Nana economized on stamps by having me bicycle her letters and cards to local addresses; she would hardly bother wrapping and posting off my discovery. I suspected she had incinerated the poems in the back lot, where garbage was burned in an open pit. Good riddance to bad rubbish, she would say, symbolically wiping her hands.

I had begun to practice on the piano at the Church of the Redeemer parish house, whose doors were always open. Sometimes after choir practice, Mr. Carn, our choirmaster, provided informal instruction to a group of us eager to learn the keyboard. I had a good ear, he assured me, and I quickly learned to sight read music.

After classes, I rode my new blue bicycle around the block to a favorite tree, a towering maple overlooking the backyards of Bayview and Hewlett Avenues. In a crook of its boughs, high above the backyards of neighboring homes, I voraciously read books borrowed from the Merrick Free Library.

"You'll ruin your eyes, and then who'll take care of you? Mark my words, books are a waste of time." Nana never went so far as to forbid my reading and, in fact, proved a remarkably undemanding custodian, who ignored muddy tracks on the kitchen floor, dirty dishes in the sink, and gatherings of dust bunnies under the beds.

The kitchen radio entertained our catch-as-catch-can dinners of grilled cheese sandwiches and ginger ale, hot dogs, canned brown beans, French toast, soup and crackers, minute steaks awash in ketchup or Worcestershire sauce from the basement bar where Raymond concocted his Bloody Marys.

I was appointed to shop at the local Bohack store and was mesmerized by the clerk who learned to decode Nana's garbled grocery lists and gracefully plucked goods with pickup tongs from high shelves. But washing laundry with a scrub board in the cellar was less entertaining. When I brought Nana my soiled clothes, she pressed a cake of brown soap into my hand. Chore by chore, Ma Burt's duties were being reassigned.

In high spirits, Nana rolled out a thin sheet of pie dough with accustomed skill and speed. Licking flour from her lips, her eyes glinting, she handed me a shard of pie crust.

"What's better than a good home-baked pie?"

"A good book," I maintained, feeling safe to sass back.

"You may think twice about sticking your head in a book tomorrow. Raymond is taking us to the World's Fair." As a concession to my birthplace, we toured the Belgian pavilion and its exhibits of lace articles, which I imagined Anne with the older girls, despite the war, still dutifully embroidered for sale to support the African missions. Under photo murals of a bemedaled King Leopold and his Queen Astrid, we feasted on Belgian waffles, which I'd never been served at the institute.

Would the streets and shadowy cathedrals of Brussels ever transform into palaces of glass and chrome modeled by Democrocity, a diorama of tomorrow's urban centers within the soaring cupola of the Perisphere? I clutched a leaking orange sherbet cone, fancying the scoop a miniature Perisphere cradled in a Trylon sugar cone, the symbols of the fair. An earlier school outing to the event had been guided by our spellbound art teacher who announced as we descended a large ramp called the Helicline. "Never mind the war clouds, this is the World of Tomorrow."

That evening at the Aquacade, I was seated between Nana and Ray, who was in a blue blazer with a carnation boutonniere. Squinting without glasses—she had been lulled by the water's haze and saw it hypnotically daubed with indistinct white splashes—Nana nodded off and began to snore. Engulfed by Ray's odorous hair oil, cologne, and peppermint and alcohol breath, I gradually relaxed against my hard backed seat. He draped an arm around my shoulders.

"Some mermaids, huh? Maybe when you grow up you'll be a Billy Rose aqua-gal." I was flattered that Ray saw such possibilities. "Practice your butterfly stroke, kiddo," he whispered in my ear, kissing it noisily while he pinched my waist.

"Tomorrow, I'll take you to Jones Beach. It's a promise."

"It's a promise," was a phrase he often tossed into the air with the casual ease of an Aquacade clown juggling balls above the water.

"We'll be going to the zoo, to the Empire State Building, on the Staten Island Ferry. We'll be off to Coney Island, to Radio City Music Hall, to the Aquarium next month, next week, tomorrow. It's a promise."

"Don't think the world revolves around you and what you want," Nana snapped when I reported his vows.

"But he made a *promise,*" I insisted, believing the words themselves constituted oaths as solemn as Lenten pledges.

On Bayview Avenue, the acrid smell of burning mounds of raked leaves filled the air and darkness arrived in the late afternoon. The Thanksgiving dinner plates were cleared. Ray puffed on an after dinner cigar, tipped back his chair, and announced he had met "a helluva gal" in a Flushing bar and grill near the World's Fair.

"She's lace-curtain Irish and a knockout. Wait until you see her." His watery blue eyes glistened.

Was she one of the bathing beauties, I asked Nana, "a long-stemmed rose" as the girls were called in Aquacade? "God only knows." She was clearly perturbed with the news that Raymond had made claim on another woman so soon after Ruthie's death.

"We'll see," she said, fitting leftovers into the refrigerator.

The following week the furniture had been rubbed with lemon wax, the carpets pummeled clean with a broom stick. Nana had taught me the fine art of ironing doilies between sheets of wax paper to keep the lace crisp. And I learned that crumpled and dampened newspapers polished windows to a high gloss.

"Our house is as good as anybody else's," Nana huffed when Ray reported his lady friend had been reared in a fine home unlike ours, which began to resemble a pigsty.

Escorted by Ray sporting a tailored three-piece glen-plaid suit, Dee appeared at the door in a white ski outfit whose hood framed a shiny fall of dark red hair. She inspected us through mascara-caked eyes and chain smoked red tipped filter cigarettes.

"Do you care for winter sports?" asked Nana, who believed in dark clothes for winter, riveting her eyes on Dee's meringue ski suit. It was a mild December day without a hint of snow.

"I don't much care much one way or the other," Dee allowed, twirling the stem of her martini glass and playing with a strand of heavy hair.

"But she's going to make a great golfer, aren't you?" Ray flashed an idolizing smile.

"I don't know if I want to knock little white balls around in the grass." Her laughter was as husky as her voice.

Not exactly the film star I first assumed, she was nonetheless, Ray had told us, an ex-model, who high kicked in a chorus line, although he couldn't recall for whom or where. And she had spent a year at college, a fact that awed Ray, a sophomore-year high school dropout. The daughter of a justice of the peace, she had lived in Flushing and attended Catholic schools. Ray rattled off these credentials to an impassive Nana who fixed him with eyes dusted with reddish purple eye shadow I had convinced her to tone down.

Dee asked about my hobbies.

"Books. I like to read and ride my bicycle."

She studied her lacquered fingernails, removed another cigarette from a silver case engraved with her initials. D.C., as in Washington.

"Ray tells me you're Catholic." She eyed me with a spark of interest.

"No, an Episcopalian, as are we," Nana replied.

"That's too bad. I heard she has an interesting Catholic background." There was an edge to her voice, and when she smiled her teeth resembled Chiclets. Were they real? Nana and Ray wore dentures that soaked in tumblers overnight.

What she must have meant by "interesting Catholic background" was my life with the Sisters in Belgium. Yes, that was it.

Dazzled by her cover-girl looks, I complimented her clothing and hair while feeling vaguely anxious. What if she were to live with us? Her self-absorption and cockiness would likely collide with Nana's bossiness and signal a return to warfare in the house. I stared uneasily at her penciled eyebrows, the evenly applied pancake makeup.

The three martini interview was over as she amputated an olive with one bite of her flawless teeth.

An adoring Ray tapped his watch: "We're running late." Through the living room window, I watched him guide the Cadillac down the driveway and speed off to the city.

"Very full of herself and a barfly in the bargain," Nana proclaimed, dismissing Dee as a widower's passing fancy, a flirtation to mollify grief. But something in Ray's jaunty step, the Irish ballads he sang in the shower, his whistling, told me otherwise.

I was anxious about the prospect of another foster mother, an intruder in these peaceful days. At twenty-nine, she could have been Ray's daughter. What he saw in her was obvious; what she saw in him, less so. But his colleagues at work, who admired his professional pitch, allowed that Ray was a salesman to his fingertips.

They married three months later, in January 1941, a small wedding to which Nana and I were not invited. I asked why they were not wed by her father, the justice, and learned that Dee was not on speaking terms with her family and was not to be pestered with personal questions. We later learned that Dee's previous marriage had been annulled through a dispensation by the church.

"Why all this Catholic business? She certainly doesn't seem religious to me." Nana wore her high and mighty look, nose tipped in the air.

"Don't you sneer at my wife. She's to be treated with respect in this house," snapped Ray.

"Respect ought to be earned," Nana shot back. Again the clash of loud voices. Feet pounding up the stairs. Slammed doors.

I plugged my ears, trying to finish a homework composition, "My Favorite Exhibit at the New York World's Fair." I wrote of moving through the General Motors' Futurama in an upholstered seat past a toylike scale model of the world of 1960, past eight-lane highways and cloverleafs, mini-dams and tiny bridges, a checkerboard of houses generations in advance of those on rue Chant d'Oiseaux or Bayview Avenue.

She looks potted," Nana observed, sizing up the wedding photos of Dee in spiked heels, her low-cut beaded gown split up to the knee, exposing show-girl legs. More than half a head shorter than his bride, Ray hiked a champagne bottle into the air as if it were a trophy.

Dee called him Shortie, he called her Legs. Fans of the Li'l Abner comic strip, they shouted "Pappy" and "Mammy" to one another with drinks in hand. They were afflicted in love; not for them the conventional endearments. He was her Spike and she his Butch. She was his Mick, he her Shrimp. When she snapped her fingers, he ran.

"Pappy, you skinny S.O.B., freshen my cocktail. Shortie, get a move on, is this any way to treat your little wifey?"

Wedged in a room between theirs and Nana's, I would hear late night moans and hoots through the wall, and Dee's cuss words sailing out. Was it drunkenness? Trying to interpret the yelps and shrieks, I grew intrigued. The rhythms climbed and peaked like the course of Ray's dirty jokes. Were they doing what dogs did? Whatever it was, I no longer believed that children grew from garden seeds.

Leaving bed at noon or midday, Dee sometimes strutted around the house in the nude, flaunting a straight-hipped, long-waisted body. Though I would be eleven that summer, my pointy breasts were larger than her flat circles, and I was embarrassed by what Ray called my milkmaid figure, fully developed at ten. I was shocked by Dee's immodesty and stared wide-eyed at a space above her head, squeamish in the presence of her bare body.

"Jesus Christ, haven't you seen a naked woman before?" she groaned.

I said no, and tried to blot from memory Ruthie's figure curled on the bathroom floor, not daring to mention her by name to her successor.

"Hasn't anyone told you that the human body is natural? Those old biddy nuns must have really worked on you."

In fleeting confrontations, the brand of Catholicism she stirred seemed like a strange potion combining indifference, contempt, and sentiment. Once after challenging Nana's allegiance to the Church of England, Dee yanked a crucifix from a jewelry box laden with gold chains and bangles.

"It's a tough religion to follow. That's why it's great. Although, God knows, I'm no saint." She lit a cigarette and blew smoke through her nostrils like a dragon.

During those early days Dee kept her distance from her mother-in-law, biding her time for an attack. A couple of belts of rum and coke fortified her groggy hours after waking; she would not be spoken to until dressed, and even then only by invitation. There was to be no noise to aggravate her migraines or disrupt her beauty sleep.

"She doesn't get up until past lunchtime, and then she prances around as naked as a jaybird," Nana grumbled.

"The hours she keeps are nobody's business. And if she wants to dance without clothes before the Pope himself, that's her affair. You are not to disturb her. You are not to criticize anything she chooses to do. You are not to touch her food in the fridge, do you understand?" Reinforced with bourbon, Ray laid down the rules.

Returning home after school, I gingerly closed the door and pretended to be invisible as she leaned, bare bottomed, into the fridge, her square, freckled, be-ringed hands probing for slices of cold cuts. I slipped out the back door on seeing her in the living room flipping through fashion magazines, or skimming through books rented from the local drug store library. She favored lurid historical novels of high romance, such as *Forever Amber*.

She waited daily for Ray's homecoming, a restless presence in skintight pedal pushers, silk shirt, long strands of gold chains, chunky bracelets, and occasional hats with turned-down brims. Dee chose to wear pants as if she were the man of the house. During our seven year relationship, she donned a dress but once, when appearing at my 1944 grade school graduation, as soused as Ray.

Once I overheard him on the telephone. "She's a minx, leads me around by the nose, drinks me under the table, and cusses like a sailor. And I love her to death." He shrugged off her boredom with golf, baseball, football, basketball, and tennis.

Ray was captivated by Dee's indifference to the opinions of others, which rankled fellow members of the Shelter Pines Country Club. He was drifting away from his golfing partners, from Sundays pinned to radio sportscasts, from evenings awhirl with Latin dances. Dee's contempt for such pastimes encouraged him to abdicate to her apathy almost everything but the bottle. It was enough that she was his drinking buddy and pinup girl extraordinaire, enough that she laughed at his jokes and acquiesced after hours in a suburban alliance of fantasies.

"It's the talk of the club," confided Mrs. Luce, who Nana and I ran into while shopping in Freeport. "We all grieved at Ruth's death, and although I wasn't one to turn my back on Ray's new wife, others just shunned her. Some people said right to her face that Ruth was not yet cold in her grave, to which she replied with dirty names and throwing drinks in their faces. And then Ray got into a slugfest. When the two were asked to leave, they said they didn't have to be asked. They quit on the spot and said they were never coming back.

"I'll give your best to Skippy. He's shooting up so fast. And you, too," Mrs. Luce continued, leaning down like a long-necked bird, pecking me on the cheek while eying my bodice. "Tell your Granny to buy you a brassiere."

Once home, I rubbed off Mrs. Luce's greasy lip prints, surveying the pink-cheeked face nodding toward me in the mirror, tilting my head this way and that. A pair of Dee's garnet earrings, the color of Ruthie's favorite lipstick had been left on the bath sink; I held one up to the light and slowly turned the stone.

Last spring I'd found a sticky blotch in my underpants. How could I have cut myself where I pee? I felt weak, dizzy. Would I be found dead, like a saint with a stigmata smeared on my palms? I scrubbed out my panties, but the dark stain returned like a malevolent spirit. It trickled down my thighs again the day after and I prayed to the Holy Mother for comprehension. How could I tell Nana, whose various expressions of alarm and disgust beckoned to me at night?

At school I found the courage to ask an older, eighth grade, schoolmate the meaning of blood between the legs.

"You're going to have a baby," she wagged her finger.

"Only people who are married have babies." I smugly refused to be bullied by her ignorance.

Later that day I visited our school nurse, Miss Cruikshank, who plunked a box of Kotex in my lap, and declared I could expect a discharge every month for the next forty years.

It became a monthly routine. With eyes averted, I scrubbed out thick cotton rags Nana had cut from old flannel night gowns. "No point wasting household money on sanitary napkins," she ruled, waving away my look of disgust.

"Could I please have some money?" I asked Dee hesitantly.

"What for?" Flush from winning in Poker or Bingo, and stretched across the chaise lounge, she seemed accessible.

"For Ko-ko-kotex." I fumbled with the word out of embarrassment. It was no secret to her that I menstruated. She had breezily told me now I was a full-fledged woman and better keep my legs closed.

"Why don't you ask the Duchess?"

"She refuses."

"Why should I give you anything? I'm not a bank." The gleaming whites of her eyeballs resembled hard boiled eggs. I made a motion to leave.

"Just a minute." Dee lifted herself and walked to the other side of the room. Was she fishing change from a purse? I had rightly guessed her approachability, after all.

"Here," she retorted, dumping a pillow case packed with dirty laundry in my lap, "earn your keep."

In the spring, I received a letter from Uncle Ed, with its recognizable imprint of a grand piano and a motto, *A Piano Is a Musical Instrument Only When It Is in Tune.* But I had forgotten his weakness in spelling, a frailty shared with Nana, whose grocery lists mangled words now appearing in our class spelling bees: carrots, celery, asparagus, rutabagas, rhubarb. Written on tan paper in brown ink:

> My Dear Foot Doktor,
> I am overjoyed with news that you are to grace us with a visit this sumer and await eagerly the treat of your health giving treatmints.
>
> Ever thine,
> Enkle Ed

You didn't say anything to me about going to Cleveland again." Brandishing Ed's letter, I confronted Nana on her way out the door. "There is no rule that says you have to know everything."

Out of sorts because of Dee's presence, which had become a large stone heaved into the placid waters of our lives, Nana had begun to reflect on the time when our housework was shared and even found a good word for her former foe, Grandma Burt.

"Say what you will, that woman was a hard worker. And so was Ruth, not like this hussy, who is too lazy to wash a dish or make her own bed.

One afternoon I found Nana inspecting recent pictures of her niece, Elizabeth, slipping them under a magnifying glass. "She made heads turn. You know, I took take care of Elizabeth after she was orphaned. Her mother had passed on, and her father, my brother, James, was killed in a train wreck. She received an insurance settlement, and since Raymond dropped out of high school to play in amateur golf tournaments, it seemed right for us to have her."

I enjoyed Nana when she reached into the past for stories as if she were digging into her knitting bag for hanks of yarn to wind around my extended hands. But I bristled with jealousy at compliments reserved for Elizabeth. I knew I could never approach her good looks, and it was best to change the subject by coaxing Nana to speak of herself.

"What were you like when you were a child?" As I had done with Uncle Ed to imagine him as young, I ironed away her wrinkles and brushed the white hair to a brownish gold.

"Well, I knew enough to behave myself."

"Was your mother nice to you?"

"My mother was a proud, thrifty, God-fearing woman and tough as a general. Even after losing her youngest, twins, to fever, and she favored those boys, she did not weep. 'Tears don't bring back the dead,' she would say."

"Did you run errands for her like I do for you?"

"I haven't thought of it for ages, but once when she was feeling poorly, I offered to bring her a glass of water. I was just a little thing then, and I wanted to help. No, she said, go to bed and leave me alone, but I brought the water for her anyway, poured it in a glass and carried it to her bedside, where she knocked it out of my hand. That will teach you to do as you're told, she said. Don't do people favors they don't want. I have never forgotten that lesson and neither should you."

May 1941. Dee had been in bed all day with a "monster migraine" when I brought her a sandwich and ice for her Cuba Libres. From the store I delivered a carton of cigarettes and box of Tampax, which she insisted I was too young to use. "They could spoil your virginity," she fancied. I had no idea what she meant.

Unlike Ruthie, Dee ordered me to shop for her, accepting such services without a *please* or *thank you.*

Her given name was Margaret, and her middle name, Dee, was contracted from Deirdre, an Irish goddess. The first daughter of four offspring born to the judge and his wife, she was a self-described tomboy and hellion, who fought with her fists like a boy, pummeling her two older brothers, who admired her spunkiness, but beat her up all the same.

Dee loathed her younger sister. "A regular crybaby always tattling on me," she chided, exposing lips and teeth of Hedy Lamarr perfection when laughing. During a rare confession, she admitted not having seen her sister in years. "She's a brood mare with seven kids who goes to Mass daily like our mother after she dried out at some sanitarium where pop sent her."

I met Dee's father only once, after he was paralyzed by a stroke and wheelchair bound. An Irishman from the old sod, he hoisted himself up from Hell's Kitchen by cracking legal tracts into the early hours. Night school helped earn him a law degree, which he transformed into a sinecure among ward heelers running the city when an army of immigrants poured through its boroughs.

He prospered sufficiently to ask for the hand of the convent bred daughter of a Queens property owner and counselor-at-law. An early photo of Dee's mother at seventeen showed her shrouded in lace, as slim as a ballerina. She would step lightly down the aisle on the arm of her father in a cutaway, and into the mysteries of the marriage bed without a murmur of dissent. So she told us at a later date.

9

"Try your luck! Three throws for a dime! Win the pink dog! C'mon up, ladies and gents! It's easy as one, two, three! Pretty lady, let me guess your weight! Win the little girl a baby panda to take home!"

As a gift for my eleventh birthday, and before my trip to Cleveland, Dee treated me to a Coney Island outing. She had purchased mother-and-daughter slack suits with sailor collars. Hers fit flawlessly, mine was tight and too high in the seat. She scowled when asked might I please wear something else.

"You need some lessons in gratitude," she threatened. I saw no reason to be thankful for ill-fitting clothes, but knew enough to hold my tongue. She had never asked that I call her "mother," and seemed repelled by the idea. It was my first time alone with her outside of the house, and I felt wary. "I don't care to talk while driving," she said without explanation.

As Dee drove the Caddie with the top down, her hair lifted in the wind like the mane of a race horse. From the corner of my eye I glanced at her bare arms flecked with silky, gold hair, the familiar square, freckled hands resting lightly on the steering wheel. *Black Beauty,* I thought, although her hair was russet.

"It comes out of a bottle along with her war paint, which she takes all day to put on," Nana exclaimed, calling her daughter-in-law a lounge lizard, hard looking, not naturally attractive like Ruthie, when I sighed over Dee's drop-dead good looks.

In the House of Mirrors, Dee was rendered stubby in the convex glass, rippled and skinny in the concave glass. Her face swelled to the size of a goldfish bowl, as did mine, in an enlarging glass. Magnified, her eyelashes resembled spider legs, her teeth, huge dice. The mirrors tricked her. It was thrilling to see she had no power to control her reflections in all their grotesque spectra.

On the Loop-the-Loop, my half-digested hot dog, washed down with Cracker Jacks and cotton candy, bunched in my chest. I clenched my lips and held my breath. The moment before the roller coaster swooped giddily down, I glimpsed Dee at my side in the hot glaze of the sun and marveled at her cool nonchalance, as if lunging down a steep incline was a commonplace amusement. I was also irritated at that poise, which distanced her from me as she stared fixedly ahead, her eyes eclipsed behind film-star sunglasses.

Willpower, I told myself as I tried to contain the lunch we had consumed at a concession counter. "Eating on the hoof like a horse," was how Ray described vertical dining, and it always surprised me to discover him standing in the kitchen with a messy fried-egg sandwich running yellow at the edges, how it contrasted with his tailoring. I was equally surprised when he would prop his hands under my arms, lift me to his lips for a full eggy, saliva-filled kiss I would later wipe away with a damp kitchen cloth. Other times he would pinch or whack my bottom for a laugh I did not share.

"You look like death warmed over. Don't toss your cookies over me," Dee warned. Her laughter was hollow. I didn't tell her that a drop of blood like gummy syrup had dribbled between my legs. The Curse. The red flag up a week earlier than expected. I did not want to show her my weakness, and besides, one must not protest noisily over minor discomforts.

Bypassers, especially teenage boys, hooted long wolf whistles as she strode, straight-hipped and long-legged as if she were a Radio City Music Hall Rockette.

Fortunately, Dee's stamina had begun to flag. "I've had enough; I'm pooped." But as we headed toward the car, a concessionaire beckoned and she handed me a dime for three parting tosses in the stuffed animal target range. I missed every throw, but not Dee, who then flung three balls and leveled a moving wooden duck with each. Good. Right on the mark.

"Here's a pink dog for you . . . how about that? I'm a pretty good shot." Gaping at the prize, I dimly recalled the auntie who, ignorant of the rules, handed Sister Paul or Sister Bernard a stuffed animal as a gift for me. A dog, a bear? The memory clouded over. There was no question about accepting Dee's prize, which I didn't want and felt I had outgrown. With the pink creature under an arm, I followed her in the middle of the afternoon into a dark, half empty bar in which she perched on a stool.

"One Cuba Libre, a double shot of rum for me and a ginger ale for my daughter, here."

Astonished, I jerked my head around toward her.

"You're kidding," the bartender lifted his eyebrows. "You're too young to have a daughter." He looked at her speculatively, then at me, pinched into an identical outfit, and shook his head.

"Naw," he guessed, peering harder at Dee, "You must be a model? Right?"

"Say, d'you reahhly buhlieve so?" After one stiff drink, Dee acquired a tinge of an English accent I found as affected as Nana's dropped *r*s when speaking over the telephone to women designated as socially prominent among the church's Ladies Auxiliary. "O my deah," Nana would say, her head thrown back like that of a singer reaching for a high note, "perhaps we should have had more dahlias on the altah."

Dee ordered another round. I wanted her to fuss over my birthday, which she obviously forgot, but Nana remembered. Back home, on the dining table, a misspelled note, "Happy Brithday from

Nana," was attached to a tin of homemade fudge wrapped in recycled Christmas paper. I raced upstairs but found her door locked.

"Nana, Nana!" I jiggled the knob, pounded on the door and kicked it. I shouted her name, tears leaking down my face.

"What the hell is going on?" Dee's eyes tightened with anger. I smelled rum on her breath, mingled with her favorite scent of Tabu cologne.

"Where is Nana?"

"Nana has gone to Chicago. Now shut up and go to bed."

"But she didn't say good-bye. When is she coming back? I want Nana." A whining sob crept into my voice.

"Did you hear me? Are you hard of hearing?" With the speed of the balls with which she downed the Coney Island ducks, I was slammed against the door of my room and struck across the face. Another slap to the side of my head, and I cried out in shock and pain. But only Dee was at home, stepping unsteadily down the stairs for another refill of her nightcap.

I remembered standing in a nun's office and touching my mouth to the lips of Jesus, his image on a crucifix. My rush of ardent kisses had brushed the figure's knees and thighs, profaning our savior. Drawn to Christ's tortured body, wanting to show my adoration, I had anointed the martyr with my tongue.

"Blasphemy!" The accusation burst from Sister Henri's lips. My ecstasy was shattered by a slap across my face that knocked me to the floor. Dazed, but swept by a fit of rage, I climbed to my feet and shouted I forget what at the imperious Sister who backed away in surprise.

Fury was allowed to nuns, but never to children. We had to beg for forgiveness, but expect no apology. It was no different in the world outside, Anne had rightly observed.

In America I had stopped reciting the "Our Father" except in church, but I recited it that night, covering my face with my hands, pleading for Nana's return. I implored God to sober up Dee with black coffee and asked Him to let her slide behind the wheel of the

Caddie, start the engine and drive off permanently to the Flushing bar and grill where she first met Ray. I pressed my hands hard against my cheeks, dug my knees hard into the floor to prove my sincerity.

The next day I woke to the song of birds in the maple whose branches leaned against the shady side of the house where my window drew in the morning light. I wriggled into the red swimsuit Nana had picked up "for a song" at a church fair. Only *I* knew that it was under the dress I wore for Sunday services, to be followed by an afternoon at Jones Beach with my new friend Nancy and her family.

In the way they smoothed over the normal run of frictions, the clashes of wants among their children, the Cantwells served as my model for the perfect family. With them, for hours at a time, I could find refuge from Ray and Dee and from Nana at her crankiest.

It was a breezy day at Field Nine as Nancy's father lit the barbecue, cupping the flame with his hands, and once ignited nursed a blaze from crumpled newspaper with his breath. His sharp features reminded me of those of Dick Tracy, whose adventures Ray still followed in the *Daily News*.

Nancy's mother was ten years older than her husband and had been his nurse when he was hospitalized for tuberculosis contracted on an Indian reservation out West.

"She saved his life," Nancy confided. I was moved at her open admiration for her parents, a pride rarely expressed among school friends, who often regarded mothers and fathers as well-meaning tyrants.

Nancy's father relished telling stories about noble Cheyenne warriors battling with Comanches, Kiowa, and Sioux, Indians of the plains who hunted bison and lived in skin tepees. "The name Cheyenne meant to speak a strange language in an Algonquin dialect," he informed our circle of listeners with legs folded before us.

Sometimes at church socials or in the Cantwells' backyard, Nancy's dad opened a story, perhaps of an old Mississippi River potter who fell in love with a chieftain's daughter, with: "Once upon a time, there was an old man who was widely known for the beauty of his pots." Or a tale about a boy who discovered an ear of magic corn: "One day a Shoshone boy who had gone out into the field to hunt for quail saw something shining on the ground."

His face glowing, he asked: "And what do you think happened next? Does the old potter marry the woman he loves? Or, what would you do if you found an ear of magic corn? My hand flailing with eagerness, I would answer: "If I had that ear of corn, I would ask it three wishes. A corn violin that would play Christmas music when you drew a bow across it. A corn door that would open to a room where you would always feel safe. And I would have the old potter meet a weaver and give them a magic fish to make them love each other until they die."

"That's good, yes, indeed. You've got plenty of imagination. You'll be a writer some day."

"Now who's ready for a swim? Girls, one to get ready and two to go." We dashed to the water's edge, waded out, plunged inside the first ascending wave and dove through another, which we rode until reaching a sand bar. From a distance, beach blankets and umbrellas, canvas chairs and sling-back lounges resembled diminutive furnishings in the doll house Mr. Cantwell was building for his daughters in the basement. Nancy invited me to see it the following winter.

"We live with my Grandmother, Julia, who wanted my father to be a banker like Granddad. Mother says our father hated money, which was fine because he didn't make any as a missionary." When Nancy laughed her teeth were smooth and even as the cultured pearls she wore to church under her choir robes.

Grandmother Julia was standing before the fire, which flushed her long, pointed face. As I greeted her, she peered through a lorgnette and lifted a glass filled with ginger ale, or was it champagne? *"Bonne Sante, Claudette,"* she eyed me appreciatively. "Yes, I think you look absolutely French. French complexion, pink and white. Nancy, pour out some ginger ale for your little friend, *votre petite amie.*"

"Do you understand what I am saying, child?" I nodded. Everything in the room gleamed: the fire, the glasses holding our beverage, Grandmother Julia's earrings and the necklace looped around her neck in multiple ropes. Nancy poked the fire while her mother, sensibly dressed in loose-fitting slacks, leaned over the phonograph and put on a record.

"Grandmother J. admires anything French except French beans, isn't that right, mother?" There was a hint of mockery in her tone, and I wondered how the women got along. Better, apparently, than Nana and Dee who weren't on speaking terms these days. I put them out of mind and bit into my sponge cake, hoping Nancy would forget about the doll house. Nothing must intrude on these pleasures.

It was in this big cedar-shingled house that I first heard *The Nutcracker Suite* and, spellbound, knew this was a far cry from Grandma Burt's Saturday opera streaming from the radio or Uncle Ed's sprightly tunes on the piano.

That same evening on Bayview Avenue, Latin dance music pounded from the basement; Ray had not entirely abandoned his rhumbas, sambas, and congas, even for the love of Dee.

"Do you like Tchaikovsky?" I once asked Nana. She was foraging for pins in her hair and dropped them one by one into a Louis Sherry candy box.

"We have too many foreigners in this country as it is."

"The composer."

"For real music, give me John Philip Sousa every time." Nana had the usual last word.

We marched smartly to Sousa into assembly and out again; looking forward to waving good-bye to alphabet posters circling the walls, to the Palmer Method, nailed-down desks, rolled-down maps, pens with scratchy nibs, yellow pencils, inkwells, song books, graph paper, twelve-inch rulers, and compasses, the paraphernalia of school.

The calendar page for the month of June was ripped out and flung into a wastepaper basket. Summer rolled into town. My late June birthday had come and gone with memories of the trip to

Coney Island with Dee. Ray was swapping jokes with business cronies in North Carolina textile mills. Having patched things up with her mother, Dee was visiting in Queens. Nana remained in Chicago from where she would pack for her annual visit to her sisters in Cleveland later that summer.

I traveled alone by Greyhound bus, and once again Uncle Ed awaited my arrival at the Cleveland depot. Like a suitor, he pressed into my hands a homemade bouquet of floppy petunias mixed with sweet peas from his garden. Parked outside the station, the old Ford seemed even more battered than its owner, who, doffing his crumpled hat, revealed a ruddy face scattered with freckles and large brown spots.

Little had changed in the house on Columbia Avenue. The skimpy furnishings, bare floors and stained window shades spoke of neglect and a shabby poverty its residents were too proud to admit. I circled the rooms. The big Victrola in the living room would entertain us with music. Uncle Ed's pipe rack, redolent with tobacco, sat in its accustomed place on the mantle, and next to the empty magazine rack slept his barely used shoe shine kit draped in a chamois cloth. The browning stacks of *Cleveland Plain Dealer*s, some wrapped in fraying rope, had grown taller by a year, pressed flush against the walls in remote corners, and the vestibule mirror, marred with streaks, was reminiscent of a Coney Island funhouse prop.

Pinch-faced with the one eye still contorted, and hands tucked in the pockets of her faded duster, Aunt Kate ordered me to set the table after unpacking. I had already smelled cornbread and boiled chicken on entering the house. "We're having a Sunday dinner on Monday, "she wearily explained.

Aunt Agnes looked up from her astrology book, caught sight of me and cackled, "Who are you, and what are you doing in my sister's house?"

"She's the orphan Alice's son took in. You know, Raymond. Now, I told you she was coming again."

"What? What? When was she born?" She waggled a gnarled finger in my face. I told her my birth date and year, and her head shook.

"What time of day?"

"I don't know." How could I?

Agnes cupped a hand to her ear and aimed a question at Kate.

"Why doesn't the child know a simple thing like that? Who is she, who?"

Nothing had changed. I was to remain an unexplained visitor to her for all the summers to come, an alien presence she met with indifference and hostility.

The summer days blossomed and waned like Uncle Ed's roses and petunias. After finishing chores for Kate, I asked if there was anything else to be done. Staring listlessly, she would say, "You are dismissed," as if this were school and she the headmistress.

I had finished the breakfast dishes, tidied the rooms, made the beds. I had pinned up the laundry on a line strung across the narrow garden: sheets, towels, rags, Ed's union suits, short-sleeved white shirts, ribbed black socks, Kate's and Agnes's saggy pink underpants, full slips, aprons, flannel nightgowns worn even in summer—almost everything old and soft with wear, sprouting small holes, threadbare and in danger of tearing into shreds. I swept the sagging front steps and bought what was needed: Silvercup bread, Crisco shortening, a half pound of butter. And root beer and lemons and onions, a penny apiece at Merrick prices. Nana had instructed me to be alert to such things.

Ed had routinely shopped for the family ever since Kate had decided not to leave the house; it was never made clear to me why. The mangling of her face had occurred more than fifty years ago, and afterward she had married, given birth and raised a child. No, it was something else that kept her housebound. Perhaps it was her covenant of misery with Ed or a decision to repudiate their son, Bill. I would never receive a satisfactory explanation.

I inspected my face in the cloudy vestibule mirror, reluctantly drawn into the dark corridor to look at whatever the glass decided to flash back. The image that valiantly grinned back from the glass was inescapably me, frizzy-haired, gap-toothed, a child trapped in a young woman's body, high round breasts, wide hips unsuccessfully confined under dresses gathered at the waist and fastened with a bow at the back. Who was I, and at what hour had I been born? How do ghosts differ from souls? Kate told us that Agnes had once spoken to their dead mother at a séance, that her ghost hovered about the room and spoke through the voice of the medium.

"Fake as a three dollar bill," Uncle Ed exclaimed. "You have to be dead from the neck up to believe it." I favored the notion that after death the departed were merely souls, soft as old underwear or moths circling light bulbs.

My boredom was relieved with library books, some that Uncle Ed admired and teasingly professed he read centuries ago. I catered to him, eager to nourish his affection, frightened of losing it, knowing that Kate and his son had at one time basked in his approval, but were now banished from it.

I read Kipling's *Jungle Stories, The Collected Poems of Longfellow,* the poems of James Greenleaf Whittier, Stevenson's *Kidnapped* and *Treasure Island,* Dumas's *The Three Musketeers,* Halliburton's *Book of Marvels,* happily grappling with a vocabulary beyond my means as I sat in the reading room of the library or on the front porch swing, momentarily distracted by the few cars that drove up the tree-lined street, while waiting for Uncle Ed's Ford to snort up the driveway.

He left the house daily, even if no assignments were pending, and met with other members of the piano tuners' guild to discuss pay, temperamental pianists and working conditions over cups of coffee or mugs of beer. He was not opposed to a glass of brew, Ed declared, although liquor was not kept at home. Whatever he sipped with his cronies, I never saw him unsteady or "acting the fool," as Nana called it.

"A postcard from Alice," Kate announced as she handed it to me. I was barely acquainted with Nana's proper first name, but recognized it from the tall, angular handwriting. She would soon arrive by bus and stay through August. The card was signed, "Regards to one and all," followed by the initial *A*. A . . . I began playing with my mental word list: *A* for Able, Achieve, Admire, Affable, Aghast, Aha,

Ajar, All right, Annotate, Amend, Applause, Apple pie, Arise, Atoll, Avowal . . .

Nana would energize the house. But since we were to share the same bed, I would have to contend with her snoring, her moodiness and temper, the sight of her horny feet, whose toenails I would be obliged to clip and file. Escorted by Nana, I could once more meet Bill and Mary Jane at their Euclid Arcade chiropractic offices; Ed and Kate had not patched up their differences with the son and his wife over the passing year.

Now I could also join her at church and sing Sunday hymns, having felt uneasy about appearing at services alone. The piety I clung to in my first year in America was drifting away. All thoughts of God and Jesus fled during solitary moments when I caressed my breasts, tweaked my nipples into hardness, or nervously twirled the crisp dark hairs between my thighs. And I sometimes felt pleasure—not compassion—in finding Nana frustrated in her efforts to change the priorities of this unsettling household.

"I did not kill our father, and I want you to stop saying that," Nana commanded.

"You broke his heart, you witch, you broke it in two," Agnes replied, glaring at her sister.

"I will not be spoken to in that tone of voice." Nana was losing patience.

"Let her be. Don't provoke her," Kate whimpered as she wiped dribbles of food from Agnes's bib. Nana for the moment had forgotten her sister's craziness. Her head was filled with country club lunches, teas, drives in the country, the purebred Dalmatians or scotties Elizabeth was raising for shows. As Nana began to supply the details, Kate's injured face took on an expression I had never before noticed; it flickered with warmth and amiability. For the rest of the summer, the companionship of Nana, her favorite sister, helped ease her loneliness.

During the weeks that followed, Nana and I visited Bill and Mary Joan at their offices, and once, at a newly opened Chinese restaurant, shared a lunch of exotic chop suey, the bulk of which Nana abandoned on her plate with a pained look.

We met for tea and pastries at Higbee's and shopped with Mary Joan for gloves that she fitted over her small, plump hands. I was fascinated by the confident way she slid her fingers one by one into the slack fabric.

We were later invited by Bill and Mary Joan to Sunday dinner in their Parma Heights house, a spacious single-level dwelling decorated with gaily colored, striped Mexican rugs spread on the floors and hung as tapestries.

"We honeymooned south of the border and bought everything in sight." Bill greeted me, noisily kissing both my hands. "It's the way they do in France, mamselle." He licked his lips, caught my eye and winked. "Here's our humble abode. What do you think?"

I had never seen its equal. In corners of the room and inside the fireplace, huge clay pots held flamboyant paper flowers and cactus plants needled with thorns. Cabinets with shelves of costumed dolls and a bright menagerie of small glass animals stood against white walls. The furniture included carved oak chairs, end tables, and a leather sofa strewn with pillows of all sizes and shapes.

Mary Joan acknowledged us with red-rimmed eyes—an infection, she explained—dabbing her face as we toured the house and its landscaped acre. From the modest appearance of their office, I had not expected such affluence, like that of homes pictured in women's magazines. Mary Joan had private means, Nana confided to Kate. "Why do you think his nibs married her?" I wondered at Kate's failure to rush to her son's defense, as did Nana when excusing Ray's blunders.

With his shoe-button eyes and black moustache, Bill reminded me of Charlie Chaplin, but as if the loveable little tramp had suddenly prospered. While he stirred fruit drinks for Nana and me, I caught the gleam of diamond rings.

He seemed elated in the role of host and bowed theatrically when he presented us to the Mexican cook, Luisa, who was as pretty as any of the dolls on display. Outfitted in a short black uniform, she ladled chicken parts from an immense casserole onto our earthenware plates. Outside the windows, her solidly built handyman husband slowly watered colorful arrangements of marigolds and zinnias as profuse as those in Uncle Ed's backyard.

The next evening, Nana claimed she was positive, having noticed his ogling, that Bill was fooling around with the Mexican cook—which would explain Mary Joan's weeping. "Make no mistake," said Nana, who didn't like the look of the cook's husband. "That's what they say he is, and Bill had better watch his step. People like that are known to use knives, and this one carries around those hedge clippers." Nana paused to let the import of her comments sink in. Kate's hair was swathed in a brown net secured over curlers Nana had just fastened; she leaned in so as not to miss a word.

"Fooling around," seemed to me as innocent as frolicking on the floor after dinner with Uncle Ed when the women had gone upstairs. As innocent as swapping moron jokes, or listening to new records by Rudy Vallee and Frank Munn (I had asked him for *The Nutcracker Suite*), or listening to poems emoted aloud, or reading passages from books, or dipping into bowls of homemade popcorn as we built playing card towers and blew them down. Our amusements would come to a stop when Kate entered the room armed with feather duster, dustpan, and broom.

"Have you looked at the time, woman? It's almost eleven o'clock. Who asked you to come in here . . . what in hell are you doing?" His voice coarsened when he shouted at his wife.

"Dust doesn't care what time it is. Besides, this is the coolest part of the day." Kate, hands on her hips, stood her ground. Ed glowered and stomped up to their shared bed, which Kate had just left. Nana's hoarse breathing, sounding like a swarm of bees, could be heard at the top of the stairs.

"Well, what do you think?" Nana asked later in the week when I entered the kitchen.

I turned toward Kate, whose hair was combed away from her face and swept up into a flattering pompadour and curls. She appeared ladylike in a soft blue dress, lace collar, and string of pearls.

"So, you approve of my handiwork?" Nana radiated confidence. "It's Kate's birthday, and we're going to celebrate."

"Don't make such a fuss, Alice."

"She's the queen of broken hearts." Agnes, who had been mulling in the corner, broke into singsong.

"Stop it," Nana shot back. "This is Kate's day and you're not to spoil it."

"She's the queen of broken spades. . . . She's the queen of broken clubs, and of diamonds, and of rubies. Who can find a virtuous woman, for her price is beyond rubies? And of emeralds. When was she born? August, a Leo. Born to lead. Like Julius Caesar. See that mane of hair. What has she done with her hair? Hair, her ornament." Agnes had begun to harangue; the women coaxed her gently back to her room, promising her cake or pudding if she behaved.

A gale of activity swept through the house as Nana prepared the fixings for a Sunday dinner, chicken with cornbread, biscuits, and gravy. Swallowing resentment that my birthday had no similar celebration, that no such fuss was made over me, I raced with a handful of change from Nana for birthday candles, dinner mints, and Kate's favorite—Jordan almonds.

These small extravagances were meant to serve Nana's larger plan, to induce Kate to think better of herself, to give her a boost of confidence. She would first urge Kate out of the house and condition her in stages with a turn around the neighborhood in Uncle Ed's car. If that worked, even reuniting Kate and Ed was an eventual possibility.

I waited for the plan to backfire. Kate would be defiant and insist she could not leave Agnes. Or, once home, Ed would cut loose with a hateful remark that would reduce Kate to tears. Nana would berate him for losing his temper, or Agnes might launch another tirade. Finally, the antiquated Ford might fail at the last minute.

Nothing of the sort happened. Upon arrival, Ed was at first taken aback and puzzled, perhaps even moved to see Kate surprisingly outfitted, and he bowed deeply from the waist as to an honored guest.

"My compliments, milady. What is the occasion?"

"It's Kate's birthday, Ed, and I wanted to make a little to-do about it. I prepared dinner, and thought that after we eat, you, Kate, and I could take a little spin in the car." Serene in one of Ruthie's commandeered print dresses, Nana was all purrs and smiles.

Just before dark, I watched from the porch as they crossed the small front lawn with Nana in the lead. Wearing a jacket, likely at Nana's bidding, Ed steered a hesitant Kate on his arm toward the car. She looked piteously back at the house but continued heading toward the car. Kate would not be Lot's wife. The sisters took the back seat, and I could almost hear Nana order: "To the pahk pulease, James," as if she were addressing the church ladies.

Matters came apart later. The screen door banged and loud voices vented in the parlor. Nana furiously pulled pins out of her hair, scowled, and allowed she had given up trying to improve people's lives because they didn't appreciate it. She had better things to do with her time, and what was I staring at? None of this was any of my concern. "And you should be glad you have no living relatives, since family is nothing but trouble."

In the weeks that flew by, Kate drew a streak of red across her lips. A new bottle of almond-scented hand lotion—Nana's touch, no doubt—was installed over the sink. She applied it during the day, releasing a honeyed scent in the air that struggled with the odor of boiling corn. And although she resumed her nocturnal dusting, she ceased interfering with Uncle Ed and me and our games and music. From what Nana later revealed, the drive in and around the city would be Kate's last outing.

Toward the end of the summer of 1941, Bill and Mary Joan reconciled, and a pregnant Luisa and her husband returned to Mexico with pesos from a generous severance check bulging in their pockets.

During summers to come in Cleveland, air-raid wardens in white helmets would patrol our streets, and I pulled down the shades and doused the lights when I heard sirens. In the pitch-dark kitchen, I listened to radio talk about shortages of sugar, gasoline, butter, and meat, and of what to save for the war effort: coffee cans to fill with chicken fat and bacon grease, tin foil from cigarette packs, and rubber bands.

Rocking on the doorstep with arms across my chest, I overheard katydids debating in the dark and tried to comfort myself with the cups of warm milk and melted butter Uncle Ed prepared when it was too warm to sleep, how he once found me, a fellow insomniac, reading: "The night shall be filled with music and the cares that infest the day, shall fold their tents like the Arabs and as silently steal away."

"You can't beat Longfellow's cadence," Ed took a deep breath and walked with me to his patch of flowers on that night of stars he believed were far off worlds not unlike ours.

"You lied to me, you son of a bitch, you told me you'd get rid of them. You said you'd put the brat in boarding school and that shrew was going to get her walking papers." I heard Dee at full volume through my bedroom wall.

"Don't talk about my mother, and you just watch your mouth, lady. I can put *your* ass on the street any time I want. Who do you think pays the bills around here so you can sit on your duff all day and bellyache." A well-oiled Ray was in fighting prime.

"Are you threatening me? I can walk out of this shit hole anytime I feel like it."

"Oh yeah, let's see you."

During such clamors I heard the din of chairs and lamps being heaved, glass breaking against the wall, sometimes followed by the sounds of grunting bodies. Stirred out of her den of sleep, Nana would rap at their door, and shout, "Stop that racket." This was the third or fourth clash since we returned, and I hadn't yet adjusted to it.

"Mind your own business, you old hag," Dee shouted through the door.

"Slut," Nana hissed under her breath, returning to her room.

I ran downstairs with hands over my ears and unhooked the screen door, alongside which the milkman placed our daily order of three quarts.

10

On my blue bicycle, carrying Nana's white bread and Crisco sandwich along with my gym suit, sneakers, and books, I turned left, then right, slowly wheeling towards Nancy's house. I stopped and peered through the kitchen window. Would they invite me in again for toast and cereal? It was late, and I would catch Nancy at school, where we were learning bank interest and percentages, reviewing compound words and parts of speech.

At the moment I padlocked my bike and dashed to my class, Dee was spread-eagled across the bed, exhausted from last night's melee.

I pictured Ray on the train to the city, redolent with cologne and turning the pages of his paper. Worried about his dwindling bank account, he would smoke a half-pack of Camels and spout to a fellow passenger, "What a head I have on me. My mouth tastes like the bottom of a bird cage."

In my theater of the imagination, he was in his New York office scribbling notes in an account book that tracked his sales, figuring percentages and commissions. He would relay jokes over the telephone, join clients for a three-martini lunch, laugh, slap people on their backs, grip his head in his hands, feel his eyes and stomach burn, call Dee in the afternoon and say, "You Irish devil, let Pappy make it up to you."

In that same theater, Nana slipped on a violet chenille robe that matched her bedspread, squinted in the mirror, snapped in her dentures, rubbed her red-lidded eyes, and arranged her white mound of hair with combs and pins. She would descend the stairs, back ramrod straight, to the green and white kitchen nook, where she would pour the creamy top of the milk into a bowl of cornflakes, lick her lips, scratch under her arms, and switch on her white Emerson radio.

She would slowly swab the dishes with a damp towel, despite Mary Joan's advice that wiping them was unsanitary. As usual, Dee would sleep until noon and their confrontation was yet to come. Nana was convinced Dee was dangerous and had to be watched.

While Ray and Dee's scraps intensified, Dee and her mother had settled their differences and were in touch by telephone; a plan was made to have her mother come out by train for an afternoon.

"A boring house in the boring suburbs. Can you picture me as Mrs. Normal Housewife?" Dee in skin-tight slacks and bare midriff cradled the receiver to her ear and lit a cigarette. I had not seen her in the nude since Nana and I returned, and I guessed the outfit was worn for Ray, who thought nothing of patting and pinching her backside before me.

"No flab. This is a packed posterior, what I call a nifty arse," he cracked. "Down, boy, down." Dee rolled her eyes and gulped the residue in her glass.

I met Dee's mother several days later and decided her face resembled a ruined bell tower like some I had seen in a library picture book of English abbeys. I almost expected birds to fly from her mouth. Black, sunken eyes ringed with grey shadows gazed emptily through granny glasses.

Her smile exposed crooked teeth stained as if soaked in tea bags. Her shoulders and huge bosoms were augmented with bits of lace and flounces, and a short strand of jet beads was partially lost in the folds of her neck. She was imposing in a chair, filling it fully.

It was hard to accept that she had once been a beauty. A quiet woman, she was uncomfortable in the presence of her daughter, not looking at her, jumping a bit when addressed, as if in fear. Her halting table conversation was composed of gossipy shreds and recollections. So and so finally married, this one moved away, another was engaged to the brother of that other man. She had difficulty remembering names. Dee's sister was pregnant again; someone else had gotten an annulment from the church and was free to marry a titled somebody from Italy, or was it Spain?

In an obliging mood, Dee allowed me to serve lunch and satisfy my curiosity about the guest. In the time I emptied the ashtray, removed the half-eaten sandwiches, fetched her mother coffee and a dish of canned peaches in syrup, Dee had downed another Cuba Libre and was in the first stages of an alcoholic fog.

"Hahv one, you know you like it." Her synthetic English accent began to surface.

"You know I'm in recovery." Her mother's thin, whiny voice rose out of an impressive chest.

"Recovery? We all need to recover from the monster you're married to. What's new with the old son of a bitch? Are you still waiting on him hand and foot?"

"That is no way to talk about your father."

"My *fahthuh*? You mean the Ice Man. You mean Mr. High and Mighty. You mean Mr. Justice of the Peace who beat the shit out of us with a strap. I hope he roasts in hell."

"Not in front of the girl." She looked stricken.

"Get out." Dee discharged me with a wave of her hand. I ran to Nana's room and tried the door, which was bolted shut. She was either incommunicado or had departed for a card game with Mrs. Hamlin, a neighbor who modeled Stylish Stouts at the Arnold Constable store in Garden City. Was she visiting next door? Mrs. Cullen shook her head, asked if anything was amiss, and I said no. As it turned out, Nana had gone without a word for a short visit with a lady friend in Connecticut.

Nana was no fount of consolation, but I couldn't help wanting to be with her on this particular day. In sharing a common adversary, we had become allies of a sort, mocking Dee's theatrics, exchanging reports of restlessness. "I give this marriage a few more months and she'll pack her things and hightail it back to Queens," Nana predicted, wishing it were true. I was less certain.

After Dee drove her mother to the train station, I heard her banging about upstairs and the slam of the car door soon after. With Ray away, Dee drove alone to one of the local "gin mills," as Nana called them. I feared I would be the target of her explosive rage when she returned.

Dee had left her bedroom door open, and I was drawn in by the lure of her things tempting to be dabbed and stroked against my skin. I entered the display of her colognes and perfumes arranged in a row, her Tweed Lentherique, Tabu, Heaven Scent, her Chanel Number 5, the props of makeup.

I wanted to fondle the jars of eye cream, astringents, lip balm, rouge and mascara, eye shadow, the canister of eyebrow pencils, gold-stenciled boxes of mascara. I yearned for her glamour, her perfect posture, her boldness. My heart pounded with the fear of discovery, the danger of provoking her as I sprayed on cologne and perfume, darkened my eyebrows with short strokes, draped gold chains around my neck and rouged my cheeks.

In the middle of the night I was awakened by her shriek: "How dare you use my things! Do you hear me?"

How could she know? I'd used so little, just a spritz on the pulse points of my throat, wrists, and backs of knees, as did Ruthie. How could Dee have known? Did she measure the contents of her perfume bottles each day the way Nana had kept track of her medicinal brandy to discover whether Grandpa Burt had broken his vows of sobriety?

Years later, Nana disclosed that Dee had sprinkled talcum powder on the rug to mark my illicit footprints leading their hapless path to her vanity table. Why hadn't I noticed that? "Your head is in the clouds," Nana asserted.

"Answer me!" Dee's eyes bulged. She transformed into a huge and venomous frog, her wide shoulders looming over me, her freckled skin as green as pond scum.

I said nothing. She lurched toward me and rained blows on my face and chest. I covered my head to parry the swing of her open hands whose rings nicked my skin and drew blood.

"Get out of this house, right now!"

Her face smelled faintly of powder, and her breath reeked. We were staggering at the head of the landing when she grabbed my shoulders and pushed. I clung desperately to a newel post, let go, and she pursued me down the stairs. Stumbling and slowly treading backwards, I faced the oncoming Dee, almost convinced she would kill me. And for what? A spray of Heaven Scent, a dab of powdered blush? She leapt at me again, punched me in the chest. I gasped and fled, and how I was escaped through the front door into the street I can't remember.

That night, I slept fitfully in our garage, woke, dusted myself off, and rode my bicycle the mile to school. On other nights, when she was too drunk to lock doors, I would slip back into the house, but would remain rigidly awake, alert to every sound, vigilant, petrified she would find me.

I learned to sleep in unlocked parked cars near the railroad station and stored extra clothes, keys, papers, and toiletries in my book bag and locker, tidied up in the school bathroom, checked my bruises behind the toilet door and assessed the damages of the night before. The morning roll call in my homeroom reassured me that the world away from home was orderly, arranged alphabetically in accord with seating charts our teachers organized at the start of every term.

At about the same time early in the war, I began periodically yanking out my hair, strand-by-strand. When unobserved in class, I would slowly probe for a root, hold a hair taut with a forefinger and thumb, and evict it with the fingers of the other hand. I chose for annihilation coarse hairs that grew at the crown of my head, while the smoother curls at the front of my scalp and at the temples avoided attack. If others spotted my nervous plucking, they kept silent.

When I informed Nana that Dee had thrown me out of the house she alarmed me by not being outraged.

"*You* had no right to go into her room."

"But I had to sleep in the garage."

"You don't look any the worse for wear," Nana replied.

Lately, her moods and alliances again began to change. She had quarreled with one of her women friends; I knew only the barest details concerning accusations of her cheating at cards. Nana hated losing at games.

With growing panic, I sensed Nana could no longer be counted on to come to my aid. Yet weeks later, after scorching Dee's pajamas with a hot iron—explaining I was daydreaming, and expecting an eruption of physical violence—Dee merely expressed disgust and called me "stupid, a clumsy ox," before locking me in my room. It was the last time she would trust me with her laundry, she declared, as if washing and ironing her undies were a privilege.

Had Nana intervened, or had she spoken to Ray? When asked, Nana dismissed the idea, insisting she kept her nose out of other people's business, as should I.

During the second year of the war, Ray left New York for extended trips to southern textile mills. On the road for weeks, and flush with high commissions, he would sometimes travel with Dee, who was relieved to escape the house on Bayview Avenue. According to Nana, Ray had divulged what we already knew: Dee had difficulty in accepting her mother-in-law as well as a stranger's child under her roof, and we should respect her feelings.

"Her feelings," Nana harrumphed, "what about ours? Who does she think she is, royalty?"

"A stranger's child." The phrase caught my ear, recalling that my own mother, who carried me in a sack in her stomach, was a stranger. Where in France was she buried? Ruthie's body was interred in Hempstead's Greenlawn Cemetery, and her name and birth and death dates were engraved in stone. Was that also true for my mother? Nobody was saying, and, meanwhile, I disclaimed the impression of others that Dee and I were related.

"Oh, your mother is gorgeous. She looks just like a movie star," someone would gush as if her looks merited reverence. "She is not my real mother. My *real* mother is in paradise." I would raise my eyes heavenward and press my hands together as if in prayer.

Ray and Dee's absence was joyful. The ominous cloud of Dee's anger drifted away, as had the conflicts and clamorous reconciliations of a couple bonded by a passion for the bottle. Nana was restored to good humor. Despite rationing and shortages, by squeezing pennies and some finagling with black-market transactions, she procured her sugar, Crisco, and eggs, the ingredients that mellowed those days with her cookies, cakes, and pies.

To assist the war effort and economize on cleaning products, Nana made laundry soap. I stirred huge pots of foul-smelling lye in the kitchen, in time with the radio's steady babble of soap operas and war news—bulletins about enemy planes spiraling in smoke into the Pacific, and our valiant allies toughing it out for a safer world. Such jumbled reports and pop-tune lyrics invaded our lives. We were enjoined on the home front to salvage newspapers, which I hauled in my bicycle basket to a collection point at school; for what purpose I was unsure, but I brought natural fervor to the duty.

"Tell Aunt Kate to give your pile of *Cleveland Plain Dealer*s to the war effort," I wrote to Uncle Ed, "and could you grow a Victory Garden instead of zinnias and petunias, which we can't eat?" My appeal to his patriotism fell on reluctant ears. When I arrived later that summer, the house on Columbia Street was increasingly choked with yellowing newspapers, while perennials still bloomed in colorful profusion.

I planted my own Victory Garden in a vacant lot between Bayview and Hewlett Avenues. The ladies auxiliary, knitting navy blue scarves, socks, and sweaters for Bundles for Britain, kept Nana engaged and distracted. And Dee had adopted bingo and the horses when not on the road with Ray. Apart from after-school errands for the women, I was free to nurture tomatoes, red and white radishes, string beans, corn, and carrots. During that spring, I learned to value the heady smell of dirt and the gritty feel of it under my fingernails. I became a responsible parent to my patch of earth, nourishing its plants with pails of water and a weekly mix of cracked eggshells and fish bones from Mrs. Cullen's garbage.

"Children have no patience for gardening," Mrs. Cullen claimed. "They want everything at once. What's gotten into you?"

"Soldiers and sailors will have more to eat if we all pull together." I took quite seriously our teachers' pep talks about our role in defeating the enemy. The image of exploding Nazi storm troopers and goggled kamikaze pilots filled me equally with glee and revulsion.

I had recently befriended Barbara, an only child doted on by working parents living on Merrick Avenue. While their home was not quite as grand as that of Nancy's, just three long blocks away, the welcome mat was out for schoolmates like me, who descended on it after classes for peanut butter and jelly sandwiches or cookies and milk.

Owners of a fruit and vegetable store, Barbara's parents were minutes away from home while at work, and Barbara had the run of the house. Raiding the refrigerator and spinning records on the phonograph were usual amusements, but eventually we indulged in spinning the bottle with boys straggling home from school.

I learned to distinguish between three kinds of kisses—prunes, prisms, and alfalfa—best practiced to the harmonies of the Andrews Sisters, Nat King Cole, and Jo Stafford. And then I found a basis for judging Ray's kisses as definitely alfalfas.

A postcard from North Carolina addressed to me in Ray's oversized and curly script arrived one day. "Darling, having a swell old time. Love, Daddy." Despite its phony endearment, the gesture and message astonished and moved me. Father. Daddy. I had asked him to send me a card during his travels, and I was astonished that he kept his word.

A week after Ray's return, the Mills Brothers were crooning one of the year's hit tunes, "Paper Doll," on radio station WEAF. Nana had joined a neighbor at the local movie theater to see *Shadow of a Doubt* featuring Theresa Wright and Joseph Cotton. The living image of a snub-nosed Hedy Lamarr with hair parted down the center, Dee was strutting her uniformed figure to good effect at Mitchell Field, where she volunteered as a motor-pool driver.

I was alone in the house with Ray, idly studying a full-length mirror that reflected a mature twelve-year old with pointy breasts and slightly disheveled moon face with frazzled curls. I glanced at my feet, shod with run down heels and paper-thin soles.

"Honey!" Ray's slurry call echoed up from the basement bar, "What are you doing up there? This place is like a morgue." Hesitantly, I turned off the radio and joined him. Natty in a lightweight double-breasted glen-plaid suit, he was jiggling a cocktail shaker held over his head in rhythm to a Latin beat. The few times I saw him without a jacket and tie, he was wearing a print silk robe opened to gray hairs sprouting from his chest.

He poured an elaborate mixed drink and rolled his shoulders like the Latin dancers in the movies; he was early on his way to drunkenness, the customary start of a weekend evening in the Whoopee Room.

Experience told me shoe money might be only a drink or two away. "A Shirley Temple, please." I curtsied to him, my finger pressing my lower lip the way the dimpled curly head did so fetchingly in her film roles. He poured out a ginger ale on ice, fished out a maraschino cherry from a jar and handed me the drink.

I envied my schoolmates who were rewarded weekly allowances by their parents. I was often empty-handed when friends doled out nickels and dimes for candy, after-school sodas, movies, or donations to the war chest during solemn breaks when teachers made patriotic speeches and passed around collection cups. Conspicuously emptying my pockets or dumping out my school bag's contents, with a shrug I claimed losing the coins I had brought to school. Better to be thought a scatterbrain than admit I had nothing to give.

I couldn't remember the last time Ray had handed me a princely dollar. Did I dance for it a month or two ago? Why did I forget?

With Dee away, he would call me downstairs for a dance. Every penny was long gone. Must I show him the holes my shoes had sprouted? I distracted him with chatter: What was the New York Yankee score? Did he like Joseph Cotton and Theresa Wright? How was a Singapore Sling mixed? After he described the right brand of gin, how much pineapple and sugar to use and the techniques of the lemon twist, I decided Ray was approachable.

I politely requested seventy-five cents to replace my leather soles. He exploded. What kind of question is that? Why the hell are you asking me for chicken feed? I want you to get all the goddamned shoes your heart desires. Stuff your closet with them. Do you hear me? You ought to own more shoes than anyone in your little school over there—what's its name, the one near the bus stop?" He emptied his drink and set up another, pouring a jigger of Lord Calvert over ice cubes. Adding a squirt of soda from a seltzer bottle, he winked at me, the red veins under the surface of his cheeks and the skin of his nose curled like tiny worms.

Would I like a rumba lesson? I drew back when he licked his lips and widened his eyes. Evading his gaze, I scanned the high polish of his sleek, pointed shoes with admiration. Nana reported Ray began every working day with a nickel shoe shine at Pennsylvania Station. To look spiffy was part of his job, a matter of pride that salesmen must cultivate, since they're in the public eye, she insisted, proud of Ray's trim tailoring, his pale, small-boned good looks; so like her own, she enjoyed saying.

Ray's bloodshot eyes followed his fingers as they stirred a fourth or fifth drink. I'd lost count. His favorite song was "The Peanut Vendor." Dah duh de dun de duh de duh . . . from the Victrola in the corner of our basement. Dance lessons, he called them, gripping my hand and twirling me in circles across the newly laid linoleum floor. He squeezed me tightly around the waist, his sour lips ridged against my clenched mouth shut to his probing tongue.

Leading me around barstools, he pressed his thighs into mine. Dah duh de dun de day, boom de boom boom. Hearing his wheeze and gasp, I reached for thoughts to distract me from the odd, plantlike smell of the oily wetness that spread from his pants front onto my dress. I was to learn it issued from the thing that hardened and bulged as we spun.

I had seen it before. How unlike the shriveled pee-pees that hung from boys shivering on line during Saturday bath night at the institute. Naked and erect, Ray sometimes paraded downstairs past me hunched over a book, knowing that I looked at it. Did he presume my admiration of what resembled a joint from the butcher shop swelling from his thighs? I shuddered at what seemed its abnormally large size for a scrawny body. Was that what men plunged into women? How would it ever fit?

End of record. He removed the disk and flipped it over. "Souse of the borer, down Mehico way. That's where I fell in luff when stars zabuv came out to pray." Ray's slurred lyric echoed the words of the singer. I closed my eyes as the needle etched out music I blindly followed to his staggering cadences.

It wasn't nearly as bad when I was pretending, when I was imagining he was neither old nor drunk, just a boyfriend playing spin-the-bottle, or when I was yielding to his seductive whisper, "You've got a cute shape, nice curly hair." As long as I shut my eyes and averted my face. Dee and Nana had declared my hair out of control, my full breasts unnatural, my early period freaky. Nana had compared my precocity to that of a Peruvian girl in the news who years ago had delivered a baby at age seven. "Her father was *its* father," Nana repeated, shaking her head and clicking her tongue. "And you had no father," she added.

Ray disagreed, once remarking I was a bastard sired by a priest and nun. Although he had a storyteller's flair for spinning yarns, never before had he ventured such an original twist; I construed it as just another of his anti-Catholic rants. Certainly, I was acceptable to Ray as he grew bolder with booze and loud music, stroked my nipples, cupped a whole breast in his hand. He was the first to touch me there, and I felt dizzy and confused. Even queasy. When I tried squirming from his embrace by inventing a new rumba step, his fingers persisted, sometimes sliding along my thighs and under the elastic of my panties.

We barely spoke, the moment taut with his loud breathing, the sweet stench of whisky, the mingling of spicy cologne and scent of sticky hair cream. Our closeness, a secret.

If I had chosen to tell, who would listen or understand? Teachers? Pinch-lipped Miss Harbill or somber Miss Crayton, who lost her fiancé in the war? I could envision the shrill, rebuking voice of our redoubtable school nurse: "You've made up every single word of that. Admit it; say you lied." What of grandmotherly Mrs. Cullen, who baked us ginger snaps, chatted, and smoothed our hair? She was unable to keep a confidence, and Nana would be told. No, there was no one.

Ray purchased these basement favors for a dollar bill, dangling it before me, or tucking it in a pants pocket or under his belt, snickering as I fumbled for my reward. A dollar, sometimes two. It was a fortune at a time a jar of maraschino cherries was bought for a nickel, a double-dip ice cream cone for a dime, a double-feature movie for twenty-five cents. Yet a dollar was small change for Ray, who prospered by selling bolts of raw nylon to Southern factories during the war.

Dee had returned from the motor pool with her habitual migraine, her woozy slow speech greeting us reluctantly as she stumbled up the stairs. Nana revealed the twists and turns of the film story over a cup of Postum. Ray had passed out in the bar. And I later penciled the outlines of my feet on a cardboard stiffener removed from one of his newly purchased shirts. Scissoring out the patterns, I slipped them into my shoes.

11

At school, poetry seemed bland. We were obliged to memorize poems for class recitation, an undertaking I detested. I ventured an *A*-to-*Z* journey through the poetry shelves of the Merrick Public Library. "You'll never get to Sandburg or Whitman that way, and you don't want to miss those guys," remarked Floyd, when I confessed reaching only the *L*s. He belonged to the interfaith choral group I had joined with Nancy and Barbara. During air-raid drills and neighborhood blackouts I read poetry by flashlight under a blanket. Books were life rafts and, like my cherished blue bicycle, were vehicles for flight and freedom.

I continued to forge Ray's signature on report cards and write notes in his name, as requested by our school for various permissions. By now adept at using cardboard to stopple holes in my shoes. I was also apprenticed at pulling teeth cinched with strings wound around doorknobs. I never visited a dentist during my years on Bayview Avenue, although I prompted Nana to have Ray consider braces for my teeth, having seen the wired mouths of classmates eventually transform into flashing smiles. I longed for such miracles.

"How is Colette's smile like the prairies?" Someone piped aboard the school bus. "Wide open spaces." I covered my mouth while joining in the general laughter.

"Well, what did he say?" I asked Nana after asking her to intercede with Raymond about my dental needs. "He's too busy now," she replied, but I urged her to speak to him later. "Stop badgering me, I've told you over and over again that Raymond is not Santa Claus."

In June 1944, Nana saw to it that I appeared in a white dress and shoes for my eighth-grade class graduation. Buttoned down the front, the garment was fashioned with a square-cut neck over which I hung a miniature coral rose necklace Nana gave me as a combined birthday-graduation gift, a valuable necklace that she, in turn, received from her niece, Elizabeth. To her chagrin, I lost it within the year. "You can't hold on to anything. Things run through your fingers like water through a sieve." It was true; I had somehow mislaid a new coat only that winter.

"A coat, nobody loses a coat." Nana was nonplussed. A search of my usual haunts turned up nothing, and I speculated it was swallowed by high tides or buried by wild dogs.

"There are no wild dogs in Merrick. You made that up. You will simply have to do without," Nana declared in her campaign to convince me that carelessness was not to be rewarded. There would be no replacement for the lost coat; a heavy sweater under a jacket would serve for the rest of the winter.

"Your hair looks nice," Nancy confirmed. I had smoothed the frizz with rag curlers the night before, and I covered a small bare patch at the back of my head with a large white bow. "And I like your necklace." We squeezed hands before entering the auditorium stage, and took our places with the other girls for the ceremony; my friend Barbara was class valedictorian. Hair slicked down, the boys were oddly solemn in dark jackets and white trousers. Ranked according to height, we waited for our names to be called.

What quirk of fate brought Dee and Ray to my graduation? They had never attended any function, such as my eighth-grade school play, *The Scarab* (in which Mrs. Cullen's grandson, Jack, played a professor of Egyptology, and I portrayed a black mammy padded with pillows at the chest and rump). They ignored my confirmation service and the Christmas oratorios directed by our choirmaster, Mr. Carn. They missed the public-speaking contest in which I won first prize, a twenty-five dollar war bond Nana hastily deposited in her bank account before Dee "got her paws on it."

My name was called midway in the ceremonies, and they wove to their seats: Dee in elbow length white gloves, jeweled wedgies; a white turban; and a tawdry red, white, and blue dress that mocked the flag. Wolf whistles.

Ray, a diminutive George Sanders, was outfitted in a blue blazer and white flannel pants. Except for a foulard and a Panama hat, he was costumed much like the boys in our class of '44. Seated next to Mrs. Cullen, Nana disregarded the commotion and looked grimly ahead, and ashamed to introduce Ray and Dee to my teachers, I hid in a school closet, slinking out after the graduates dispersed.

I would have fled through the back exit, but they blocked my escape. Dee slapped me sharply across the face during our drive home. I said nothing, lest I be flung from the car to my death, which Dee would declare an accident. I was unnerved by the screech of tires as Ray tooled the Caddie through stop signs, bawling "Phrase the laud and pass the admonition," distorting the lyrics of another popular war tune he claimed to have written: "Gumming in on a Wing and a Dare."

When time arrived for my summer escape, I again packed a brown bag with hard-boiled eggs, jelly sandwiches, bananas and a thermos of milk, and took off on a bus trip with Nana. Her annual Chicago visit with Elizabeth was deferred, since her niece, accompanied by her husband and son, was planning a New York excursion, and we were to join them for Thanksgiving dinner at the Plaza Hotel.

That summer in Cleveland, I found part-time work as an underage waitress in a neighborhood tearoom frequented by elderly ladies who rewarded me with nickel tips for orders of ladyfingers, macaroons, and pitchers of iced tea.

"I'm off to the library," I announced to Nana and Kate after lunch. Scant attention was paid to my comings and goings. Ed was readying the house for overdue painting and papering. At long last, the mountain of *Cleveland Plain Dealer*s would find some purpose.

"Business is slow. I won't need you," the tea-shop manager grumbled after some weeks, but I found substitute employment reading personal letters for illiterate women, charging a nickel for each. I climbed walkups on hot afternoons, a wielder of words in musty rooms that gave off fumes of garlic and cabbage, witch hazel, vinegar, and liniment. I sipped tap water or tepid soda pop while immigrant women proudly flourished framed photographs of children and grandchildren now safely thriving in America. Partly out of curiosity about other lives, I reread their letters without extra charge, reaching for the pleasure of language in a dance of words I might articulate and share. I had come from Belgium speaking nothing but French, I told the women, but within five years the nationality of my brain turned American.

Disregarding the increasing disorder—cloth-draped furniture, curling flowered wallpaper, brushes, cans of fragrant paste, and buckets of paint and thinners making obstacle courses of the hallways—Uncle Ed and I played checkers on the kitchen table, read poems and the evening paper aloud, enjoyed footbaths, and shared hushed talks on the front-porch swing. He drove me in his decrepit Ford to Lake Erie to enjoy the sunset descending in a red splash of water.

Perched on stools, we slurped chocolate sodas at the local drug store and, as in summers past, Ed yanked off his shoes for a stretch on the living room floor, his hands behind his neck, eyes seeking phantoms on the ceiling. Believing myself too mature for reclining barefoot on the floor, I sat cross-legged alongside of him. "You've become a young lady," Ed had observed, huffing while he had lugged our suitcases up the stairs, and appeared more stooped than ever, his hands palsied with age.

"I don't know why I let Alice talk me into fixing up the place," he mused one night on the front porch swing. "I feel every one of my eighty years." He sighed as we gazed listlessly out toward Columbia Avenue, whose lights were dimmed for yet another air-raid drill. The Pacific war raged; in a year President Truman would unleash atomic disaster on Hiroshima and Nagasaki.

I did not return to Cleveland. A startling succession of letters and calls during the summer of 1946 informed Nana of Ed's sudden death by stroke, an end that she called merciful, followed in a month by Kate's fatal heart attack. By summer's close, Agnes had also departed and the entire generation ended with dirt in their mouths, Nana's phrase. If she lamented their going, it was in secret. I did not grieve for the women but mourned my loss of Uncle Ed, who had tempered my view of adults as adversaries with a warmth and tolerance he reserved for few others. For many months after, I carried his gift of the velvet-lined, gold-painted ring box in a pocket of my blouse; in private moments, I removed it to create a surge of Cleveland memories.

Since Ray and I left early, we shared the dining room table spread with his morning papers. He held the glass unsteadily, gulping his hangover tonic of raw eggs, tomato juice, cayenne, Worcestershire sauce, and whisky straight. I had been instructed by Nana not to annoy him. He needed to "get the cobwebs out of his head," Nana mentioned, as if I were ignorant of his morning habits, as well as of hers. She almost always woke rested, ready to attack her bowl of dry cereal.

"I'm in high school now." I broke the vow of morning silence, hopeful for acknowledgment. He gazed at me vacantly with popping eyes, his red face puffed like an ocean creature in a Jules Verne story, and said nothing. I guessed his thoughts were awash in a tide of financial concerns. According to Nana, Ray suffered business reversals, had changed jobs and now worked as a salesman for another New York fabric company. Trips south were few and far between.

In months to come, he appeared more eager to talk than dance and spoke heatedly about baseball scores, championship golf, football heroes. I squirmed when his haranguing turned to politics, choking down my anger at his charge that Roosevelt was in league with the Jews and had surrendered Eastern Europe to the Commies, and that Democrats were turning the country into a Bolshevik camp. It was fruitless to challenge him; I was a compliant audience, waiting for that state of inebriation that assured a cash handout free of grabby hands.

My now voluptuous teenage body held no more enticement for him than did Dee's broad shouldered, lean hipped, leggy frame. At times, when he trembled and sweated profusely, I was less guarded out of pity for his condition; here was someone in the house I no longer feared. "You're going to the best goddamned college in the whole country. I'll send you to one of those upper-crust all-girls schools. I can buy the goddamned bank in this burg, you know." More of Ray's promises ballooned and then burst before me.

As Ray's drinking hardened, Dee tried going on the wagon, cold turkey. "Get me a Virgin Mary" she yelled from her room, and after I delivered tomato juice straight to a jittery Dee, she conscripted me to listen as she talked. I shied away as best I could from talk of her wanting a baby, that her baby machine was going to rust and ruin if old Pappy didn't get a move on. "Guess who'll be the babysitter?" Nana chortled. Dee had quit her post with the motor corps and, in a fling at domesticity, decided to redecorate the master bedroom. Ruthie's dusty rose chaise lounge was upholstered blue. White organdy curtains matched the bedspread draped over a powder blue taffeta coverlet ruffled at the hem.

In December, Ray informed Nana and me that Dee wished to decorate the Christmas tree herself, and we were not to interfere. Shortly afterward a domestic quarrel exploded, leaving only Nana and me on speaking terms with each other. There would be no Christmas that year on Bayview Avenue, and Dee's tree glittered blue and white in our drab living room for months, a lonely icon of our failure to negotiate "peace on earth and mercy mild." "Happy New Year," I proclaimed to the embattled pair as they stumbled noisily through their door. “Mind your own goddamned business,” Ray retorted. “Who the hell was that?” Dee wove past me in the dark with a throaty laugh.

Her flirtation with sobriety soon over, she returned to the bottle with a vengeance, to bingo, to afternoons and evenings at Al’s Club House. The frilly bedroom, its door temptingly left open, seemed more suitable to a southern belle than an unruly and hard-drinking couple.

One night in mid-sleep, I woke to a shower of punches. Dee cursed me for failing to empty the garbage. I was yanked from bed, shoved downstairs, and locked out. Nana later offered me space to sleep at the end of her bed, next to her horny feet and beside a buzzing crescendo of her snores. I continued to sleep lightly, prepared for eviction at any time, and was ready to seek shelter in our garage or in neighbors’ parked cars.

“It’s not right for that banshee to wake up the whole house with her drunken binges. I’m going to give Raymond a piece of my mind.” Nana was an ally once more. She had received a postcard from Elizabeth about her family’s pending visit to New York next fall and the promise of Thanksgiving dinner at Manhattan’s Plaza Hotel. During the months that followed, Nana pried what money she needed from Ray to buy me a new dress: a melon-colored wool with three-quarter sleeves. My shoes were resoled and heeled. I borrowed Nana’s pearls, and, at my urging, she wore her amber beads to offset a smart purple suit. We left for the city in good spirits, Nana answering my “How do I look?” with “You’ll pass in a crowd.”

Even in a ankle-length fur coat, Elizabeth resembled her twenty-year old photo on Nana’s dresser. There was no mistaking the features, nor the bearing of someone accustomed to service. In the lobby, she snapped her fingers for a bellboy. “Have my husband, Mr. Henry Conlon, paged in the cocktail lounge.”

“He’s struggling to interest Hank junior in football, to which they’re listening over the bar radio. My husband worships the pigskin.” She wrinkled her elegant nose.

"I'm ready for some Thanksgiving turkey skin, myself." In a purple suede hat which Elizabeth complimented, Nana was all cordiality. Would she soon be dropping her *r*s, again speaking through clenched jaws in the manner of "people of breeding?" She seldom took interest in such matters, but had coached me during our train ride on how to behave in a high-class hotel: keep legs crossed, wait to be spoken to before entering a conversation, and never bolt down food.

"Yes, of course, we'll dine as soon as my boys arrive. And you, are you hungry?" Elizabeth searched my face, seemingly expecting a half-starved waif, a ragamuffin.

"So you're the little French girl." I concealed my irritation at being called "little" since I was as tall as she. I was at least spared the embarrassment of being greeted as the orphan Ray had taken from Europe, the fiction that I was snatched from the jaws of the war by a generous American family.

No amount of fine tailoring could disguise the man's heft, which he maneuvered with unexpected grace as he sat between Elizabeth and their son. The teenager pored over the Oak Room's menu as if memorizing the dishes.

"Soup to nuts. We'll have the whole shebang. What do you say?" He displayed none of his wife's fastidiousness nor his son's single-mindedness at the prospect of food.

I followed his hands after dinner arrived, the dexterity of slim, tapered fingers tying a napkin around his neck, spooning sauce from a gravy boat, gesturing in air and signing the check without studying it. Such delicate hands and his melodious high voice were at odds with his girth and wobbly pink jowls.

Wispy clouds of small talk hovered and dissolved above the table: the Democratic party in the Midwest, F.D.R. and the war, real estate deals, the polio scare, and how he couldn't whip up much enthusiasm for Elizabeth's purebred Dalmatians or Scotties. "But I like to let her have her way."

"I brought Yuki, who they won't allow in the dining room, even though my Pomeranian is better behaved than some of these patrons. The management is so unreasonable." Her eyes upraised, Elizabeth resembled a saint in torment.

"God help that pooch if it got into the kitchen. Steak Pomer-you-know what, grilled to a turn."

"You're being horrid, stop it." She plucked at her strand of pearls with a forced titter. I was asked what I thought of Cleveland, of school, of America. "Fine, fine, fine," I answered to all three, brief enough for Nana who, like the nuns, discouraged my attracting attention since no one cared for my opinions. Nonetheless, Hank senior examined me with warmth, perhaps recognizing my exuberance as a quality we had in common.

His son, scarcely looking up from his crowded plate, grunting "yes" or "no" when addressed, as if he wished to be invisible, but only until the end of the meal. "Will there be anything else?" asked the waiter after dessert. "Yes, I'll have another dinner," he demanded. Elizabeth was stunned. "Oh honey, you don't want to eat all that food." Turning to her husband, she urged, "Tell your son he can't be a glutton. Make junior obey you." Her voice quavered. The authority required to teach her dogs to stay and heel was nowhere in evidence.

"Yes, I do, I want another dinner." He was unshakable, a runty despot.

"All right. Waiter, bring my son another dinner." Behind a nimbus of cigar smoke, Conlon's face was quietly determined. "And you, my boy, will finish everything on your plate, even if you puke or we sit here all night." It was a scene whose ordeal was an uneasy replay of my times at the refectory, but to my astonishment the boy doggedly devoured all four courses, during which time his father and I broke away to the hotel's entrance overlooking the horse carriages parked on Central Park South.

"Now don't tell Aunt Alice I gave you this, she's a skinflint." He folded a crisp dollar bill into my palm, money I didn't have to dance for, a pure gift as exhilarating as the unexpected snowfall that began covering the city before our good-byes. On our return by train,

Nana felt duty-bound to extract meaning from our meeting and junior's behavior. "Let that be a lesson to you," she retorted. "You must be prepared to finish what you start."

Two months later, following Dee and Ray's fourth wedding anniversary, Nana slipped on a patch of driveway ice and fractured her hip. I was accused of ignoring orders to clear the snow and blamed myself for forgetting to spread salt leading to the back door steps. Corrective surgery at Nana's age was ruled out, and she was confined to a bed set up in Ray's den off the living room, her torso elevated by a brace of heavy sandbags. I was assigned the tasks of feeding and bathing her, of scrubbing bedpans of an irascible patient who deeply resented the loss of her treasured independence. Her infirmity would influence my life until her death.

After convalescing, Nana was fitted with a large corrective shoe. "Witch!" the neighborhood children taunted as she hobbled by on crutches in baggy stockings, thrift shop clothes, wisps of white hair escaping from a high-brimmed hat. "Snot-nosed brats," she countered; I admired her spunk and stoicism.

Even as blindness encroached with the onset of diabetes, Nana rarely complained about her health. But she endlessly berated me for the slightest infractions: too little or too much milk in her cereal, the tea too weak or too strong, too hot or too cold. Always more salt. "It's hopeless, you can't do anything right." I fought back the impulse to dump the contents of the bedpan on her head.

I often walked home from school with Nancy, and we dawdled alongside her hedge to swap impressions of boys, teachers, and books. While we were chatting on a mild April afternoon, Nancy's sister dashed from the house, face red with tears, and spluttered, "President Roosevelt is dead!" I raced home to find Nana glued to her Emerson. "I voted for him during the Depression," her voice grew hazy when admitting her covert switch in party loyalties.

"To celebrate the extinction of that S.O.B." Ray gloated, "I'm going to throw the biggest party Al's Club House has ever seen."

Barbara had moved to a larger, modern house on Quincy Avenue. I met her in town at her parents' grocery store and also visited her mother, who preferred friends of her daughter's age. Sometimes I lingered, perched on a vegetable crate with kindly, birdlike Syl, flattered at her accepting me as a confidante.

"No, sit and talk, it'll make the time pass," she insisted when I offered to help her stack the potatoes. Like Nancy's grandmother, Syl praised my complexion and naturally curled hair which, she observed, would save me from the ordeal of frying it when getting permanents. Her own neck-length bobbed hair fell straight as nature intended. Uncomfortable about my looks, and eager for dance and party dates as the school year closed, I tried without much success to ignore Nana's slights.

"Your lips are too thick, your eyes too small. I don't trust people with deep-set eyes," Nana leveled at me one evening over plates of boiled corn soaked in milk. While I was furious enough to respond, "Your lips are too thin, and I don't trust pop-eyed people," it was futile to answer back. But I finally stopped yanking strands of hair from my scalp, although a decade would pass before I ceased biting my nails.

A small annuity from her late husband netted Nana several hundred dollars, a few pennies of which she allotted for our suppers of lavishly salted boiled onions, potatoes, and carrots. She was never one to praise me for accomplishments, but as we huddled over bowls of steaming vegetables, I sensed she valued me as a confederate in league against Dee, who recently padlocked the refrigerator in fierce response to my nibbling at a cup of coleslaw set aside for her late-night snack. "This is the last time you will ever take my food," she wrote in a note tacked on the door.

During that year, I took part-time work in the high school cafeteria, chopped "celery boats" to load with cream cheese, and mashed hard-boiled eggs into mayonnaise for egg-salad sandwich spreads. Hot lunches and some leftover change at week's end were my wages. As my class's milk monitor, I pilfered a few nickels and dimes for pocket money, added to an occasional quarter plucked out of Nana's purse; no one would note my trivial thefts, I rationalized, and the Episcopal Church of the Redeemer had no confessional booth.

Following Nana's example of thrift, I practiced setting aside and tucking money I gathered into the toe of an old shoe at the back of my closet. Thankfully, there were books, always books, and I strongly believed in the power of language to change my reality. Even as my leisure time waned, I read three or four books a week—some required for school, and most prized, those borrowed from the Merrick Library, carted like vital cargo in my bicycle's wire basket.

Acting on Floyd's tip to read books from the end of the alphabet, I discovered Thomas Wolfe's *Look Homeward, Angel* and conscientiously copied out lists of splendid new words: stertorous, lambent, ptotic, rodomontade, apocrypha, plangent, pervasive. I memorized these and others as unfamiliar and invented paragraphs for them to work and live in. In this way, I could appropriate some of the wealth of the author's language and be enriched by an expanding vocabulary. In a sometimes chaotic life over which I had little control, I craved word power.

Curiosity about other lives led me to biography and to the encyclopedia as a source book for knowledge. I researched Pablo Picasso, James Joyce, Virginia Woolf, and literary lights mentioned in Wolfe's novels featuring Eugene Gant, his hungry Gulliver. I began recording the names of writers and artists in a notebook, listing their accomplishments, places and dates of birth: William Butler Yeats, Paul Cezanne, Joan Miro, H. G. Wells, Marcel Proust, Jane Austen, George Eliot, and Anatole France.

I normally pleased my French class teacher by fluently pronouncing the words of my mother tongue, but her admiration flagged with my lateness in turning in assignments, dozing in class, or wistfully gazing out the window. I was thoroughly sleep-deprived. "You are as distracted as the proverbial professor." She glared at me impatiently over steel-rimmed eyeglasses set low on her pinched nose. "But you can do *A* work if you put your mind to it." Properly chastened, I resolved to write a report on Alphonse Daudet's *Le Chèvre de Monsieur*

Séguin. "Bravo, mademoiselle, you have given us a thoughtful analysis. May we be favored with more?"

I had long ceased dreaming of the institute or falling back on French numbers and letters. Except in French class, I spoke English exclusively, with barely a trace of an accent—now peering in the mirror to apply lipstick, I would not rehearse "th" by extending my tongue.

Yet I was pleased with my French name, shared with that of writer Sidonie Gabrielle Colette, and remained persuaded in the superiority of all things French. Sister Henri's praise of French as the most elegant language in the civilized world had left its mark. And if I could edge the remark into everyday conversation, I volunteered that my real mother was French and buried in France.

I imagined her heart-shaped face and manageable curls were like those of the Breck girl in shampoo ads or Miss Lux Soap. I colored her downcast eyes French blue with violet crescents beneath her lower lids, and dressed her in a lace collar and pearls. But the image was misleading; she was too young to be the progenitor of my also-imagined North African French brother, the mustachioed policeman or army officer (I would change his careers) who would send for me after the war.

12

Genuine or not, my offenses seemed to multiply. Was it sinful to escape out the window down a rope of tied sheets when Dee locked me in my room? How did she discover I had worn her orange crepe blouse with balloon sleeves at a beach party, after returning it to its hanger? A telltale underarm stain, grains of sand in the cuffs? Nana pronounced: "You can't even be a good cheat. You always leave a trail a mile wide."

"Liar! Thief!" Dee burst into my room, like the wild dog I suspected lurked in a wooded neighborhood lot—teeth bared, eyes glittering, and body tensed for a leap at its prey's throat. I backed off, intending to leap through my window to the adjacent roof below. But she intercepted my flight and dragged me to the bed, her body sprawled over mine, hands choking me to near senselessness. With one free hand, I swept a lamp off the night table, praying the noise would alert Nana, whose shriek for the police would release Dee's grip. And it did.

Hurled again out of the house, I bicycled for miles, numb with rage and fear. I later whistled and hummed while pedaling, reassured by the drift of my voice that I was alive, that I could tap a wellspring of dignity Dee could not despoil. After a night in a parked car, I freshened up in the school lavatory, changed to the extra blouse stored in my locker, tied a kerchief around my neck to hide the bruise, and reported for homeroom at the sound of the bell. During a library study period, I tried to absorb the insights of Dale Carnegie's *How to Win Friends and Influence People,* while musing on the equally useful existence of another book, titled *How to Commit Murder and Not Get Caught.*

My faith in a biblical, benevolent God and the assuagements of daily prayer had come to an end. In its place I found consolation in a sort of pantheism, believing that a walk through the woods was more divine and real than the clutter of organized religion.

Turning sixteen I quit the choir amid cruel gossip of our reverend's supposed love affair with the town librarian. Why didn't church attendance make people better? I was aware of my own moral decline, but I expected better of adults. I was learning to negotiate several lives: the private, concealed one in a depraved house where I was alternately neglected and despised, the life of intermittent weekends in Freeport and Hempstead shoplifting gifts and party clothes I claimed to have sewn at school.

And on the other hand, I embraced a public, extraverted life among others at fairs, the county glee club, tea and Sadie Hawkins Day dances, the French Club, picnics and parties at Jones Beach. Through it all, I spun my fantasies and composed poems in a looseleaf notebook hidden in a vestibule-closet drawer.

Out flew a plate, a cup, a bowl, a tureen. Legs parted, eyes two sockets of fury, Dee emptied several shelves of crockery. What had I done this time? I didn't dare ask. How does one placate an erupting volcano? Flame seemed to spew from the orifices of her face. The kitchen floor resembled a lunar crater littered with debris.

"I want each and every piece picked up, do you hear?" Nana, who now maneuvered about on two canes, had reoccupied her upstairs bedroom. Ray was in the city or away; I did not know. I scuttled through the pool of splintered glass, hummed pop tunes from the Hit Parade, picking up the shards as thoroughly as I could to satisfy the whims of Madame Hellfire.

"And be quick about it!" She planted a sharp kick on my rear with her gold-studded wedgie, size five and a half, double-A width, toenails painted dragon's blood red. "And one for good measure." Another stab of pain. Her voice hissed above my shattered glass pond. I pretended not to care. Deep in my sparkling swamp, I was a fish or magic frog that could leap away on sensing danger.

I wove in an out of these reveries until she retired to the doorway and lit a filter tip. Boredom slackened her mouth, from which smoke spewed. Another glance while I swept the last shard into the dustpan, and she had disappeared. An appointment with a Cuba Libre in the Whoopee Room was my best guess.

A week later I found a note in a pale pink envelope on my bed. "See me at once," signed *D* in her thin, vertical script. My throat tightened and stomach knotted. I tapped on her door. Preparing for a night of bar-hopping, she had slipped on cocktail pajamas with rows of metallic chips along the neck and sleeves. Her eyes blazed.

"You'll learn what it means to disobey." She spat out each syllable, thick with English intonations. A bad sign. Ray was straddled across the bed in a deep, snoring slumber.

"I thought you knew about the beach party," I stammered. How I loathed the randomness of her bullying cruelty.

"You thought what? What?" Her voice tightened a noose around each word. Unthinking, I answered back bravely this time, my words edged with ill-concealed rage, at which she kicked my shin and cracked my front tooth with the heel of the shoe she held in her hand. Blood in my mouth. I screamed with pain, waking Ray, who grumbled about the hopelessness of getting some goddamned shut-eye around here and padded off to the hall toilet.

"Your own mother didn't want you." Dee saved this for last before shoving me out the door into the street. "Stay away if you know what's good for you." I was more convinced than ever that she meant to kill me. Even Nana, brooding in the bed we now shared, had cautioned against consuming food or beverages I didn't prepare myself. "Do you mean she's trying to poison us?"

"I'm not saying that. I'm saying stay on your toes. That hellion wants both of us out of the house, dead or alive."

The family of a school friend, Inge, had protectively taken me in twice before, and I turned to them again. Barbara's mother had earlier regretfully refused to let me occupy her store's couch, since business people such as she must avoid intruding in family quarrels. I said I understood.

The following week, I shared Inge's clothes, her mother's kugels and sauerbraten, and slept in a small room where clothes to be ironed were piled near the door. The hall cuckoo clock hooted every fifteen minutes while I restlessly twisted and turned through the nights.

Mortified, I spoke nothing of my troubles at home and was never asked. I had hoped Nana would call my school for a report on my well-being, but the secretary received no such messages.

Babysitting gave me a measure of independence—a job Inge's mother found for me, two evenings weekly at twenty-cents an hour, a fair rate for the times. Even so, I would stare at the telephone when the toddlers slept, poised to ring Freeport 8-3495, poised to hang up if anyone but Nana spoke. But no one ever answered.

Studying my features in Inge's dressing-table mirror at night, I despised the cracked-lipped face, the all too ripe body in borrowed clothes. But even in that miasma of self loathing, I donned a cheerful facade while I slivered olives into cream cheese spread for sandwiches at the school cafeteria. The masquerade went on during after-class dance committee meetings, while I helped plan an international theme for the Harvest Moon Ball.

My refuge at Inge's home could not last. The modest means of a family of five could hardly support another. "We can't put you up anymore, and you'll have to solve your problems somewhere else. You know we wish you luck." Inge's compassionate mother stroked my cheek. Tall and queenly, her hair in a coronet of braids, she kissed me good-bye. My first published poem which would appear fourteen years later in the *New York Herald Tribune,* was dedicated to her.

I left and walked aimlessly along a highway, a cold November wind penetrating my skimpy clothes. I recalled my bicycle, considered fetching it from home and speeding along the deserted stretch between Fly Beach and the tackle and bait store on the south bay. I would recreate myself as Amelia Earhart before she crashed and vanished on a remote Pacific island during the war, and would fly past dune grass while gulls wheeled above me.

Then why was I heading in the wrong direction, walking toward Freeport, not Bellmore and Bayview Avenue? Relentlessly, my body willed me forward as cars streamed toward me like phosphorescent sea creatures. I heard a siren's piercing note. Confused and mesmerized, I dove into the headlights of a moving presence that in the darkness seemed to scream and wail, and was struck by a police car on call.

The groans of women in labor punctuated the long, insomniac hours of my first night in the charity ward of the Meadowbrook Hospital. Diagnosis: concussion, fractures of the spine and collarbone, and whiplash injuries. I meditated for days on those parts of me that did not hurt, on toes, ankles, calves, and knees. I entered my body parts through an act of will and discovered that such distractions could subdue pain. My face was raw, the skin ripped off.

Mirrors were as rare at the hospital as in the institute, and I met my blurred and distorted image in cutlery and metal trays. Clamped into a body cast shaped like a strapless bathing suit, and later placed among poor and disfigured women in an amputee ward, I was oddly elated to at last find a haven with regular hours and meals. Bouts of pain and a few cracked bones seemed a reasonable sacrifice for the safety of the hospital—which I envisioned as an orphanage for adults, simply substituting doctors and nurses for priests and nuns.

In an underworld of memory, a nun swam to my bed, waving the fins of her white cap over a pan of water into which she dipped a cloth, wrung it out, and smoothed it over my forehead. Repeating the motion, she baptized my fever in the name of Mother Mary and the roster of saints who watch over childhood ills. How old was I then? No more than five or six.

Enforced privacy. I felt privileged to be alone in the center of a room, though fearful of being ill and set apart from the others. My body fluttered from hot to cold, from dry to moist. Between spells of drowsiness I was visited by angels and saints, the ones to whom I was taught to pray daily.

Slippery recollections. Black leaves shaken loose from a tree. Night. Who was that on the gravel path? Who was in the middle of the circle beyond my window? Anne, with her rope of blond braids? Jean-Pierre, with his limp, pink worm jouncing from unbuttoned pants? Marc, with his farty smells? Chantal, with damp palms and dreamy eyes?

And in my childhood reveries, longer and brighter afternoons arrived as warmth flowed through the window. Spring. I smelled groundwater odors—muddy, clean, and pungent. The sweet-sour bite of citrus on my tongue lingered after eating the daily orange permitted to the bedridden. What I had was more than a disorder and more grave than a cold. The tall doctor came daily to squint at me through pince-nez glasses. My arms were strapped to the bedposts to prevent me from scratching the rashes, the rose spots strewn across my stomach and chest. I saw the doctor's huge eye peering down my throat through a magnifying glass.

"The worst has passed," he must have announced. Or, "The typhus fever subsides." I would be rescued from the cliff's edge, the abyss children slip into with their coughs, fevers, pustules and aches.

The next day, soon after the doctor's visit, a nun balancing a bowl of soup floated into the room and freed me from my bonds. My thin wrists were as gray as wax candles at Mass, and I must have stared at them in disbelief. Had I grown so lean? A celery stalk . . . a string bean? I dipped into the sludgelike pea soup, bit lightly into the spoon, and licked it clean.

At the hospital I soon befriended Catherine, a gaunt, chestnut-brown teenager with unspecified stomach problems, whose bed was catty-corner to mine. We paired when I gained enough strength to walk about. "We're brown and white, like Christmas pudding and hard sauce," I remarked to her slightly mocking, winsome smile. We sang hymns in two-part harmony and visited with her relatives and with patients in other wards.

Her aunt, who was hospitalized for jaundice, knitted afghans by the yard and told of her travels north to Harlem and of various marriages to restless, abandoning men. I met several of her cousins who suffered from heart troubles or asthma, one of whom resembled film star Anna May Wong, courting starvation through a rice diet. Catherine recounted she was rich with relations, a fact I noted wistfully when visiting hours arrived. Her bed was circled with well-wishers.

"You can take on my brother; he's nothing new to me." Catherine waved a plump, shy boy, some years my junior, toward my bed. But glancing over his head, I caught sight of a familiar figure. "Nana, Nana, you came." I was touched by her effort, cadging a ride with neighbors and hobbling on canes. She would visit weekly, bringing homemade cookies and personal essentials and scolding me for my carelessness. "Look at the mess you made. You never look where you're going."

Get-well cards arrived, and I was visited by Nancy, Barbara, and others who brought our school paper and reading material: *The Life of Sister Kenney,* copies of *Junior Miss* and *The Buccaneer*. Among these was a collection of erotic poems by Walter Benton called *This Is My Beloved,* which caused a stir in the wards when I declaimed: "pubic hairs like crisp lettuce."

I felt guarded by angels who directed visitor traffic in the heady days before Christmas. Volunteer carolers sang for us, and gifts came from a local church, included a jigsaw puzzle that reminded me of the one I received from the Burts before Ruthie's death.

Nana appeared with homemade fudge and letters that I read

aloud to her; she had been declared legally blind at the onset of late stage diabetes. The brisk, erect woman of days past had mutated into a stooped hag with disheveled hair tucked under peaked or pie-plate hats. "If anyone is fool enough to get fresh with me, he'll feel this where it'll do the most good." She had lost none of her spunk, and brandished a hat pin, stabbing it in the air.

I too had changed. In weeks I vaulted from desperation to near happiness. Remorse seized me only when Inge's mother visited and dabbed tearful eyes. "How could you do this to yourself?" She repeated her reasons for asking me to leave and sought my pardon. Dee and Ray never came.

"Where will I go after I'm discharged?" I dreaded my day of departure. "Home," Nana said stiffly, "it's the law."

"But what about you-know-who?" I asked.

"That strumpet isn't about to become a jailbird. She'll toe the line." I was self-conscious about the red patches and scars on my face. When I had timidly peeked in the mirror Nana brought to the hospital, I shuddered and shook with tears, but Catherine traced her fingers along my injuries and soothingly announced, "Now this bad one is going to heal up real nice, and that one, too, and in no time you'll be looking fine again. You wait and see." A doctor agreed that my skin would mend like new. I was puzzled by Catherine's pensive look as she printed her Glen Cove address in my notebook, and by her barely audible "all right" when I promised to bicycle up for a visit once I disposed of my cast. Living in the rampant apartheid of the times, she grasped better than I the stresses imposed on interracial bonds. "I don't want to ever forget you," I gushed before Catherine left for home, a smart, straight slip of a girl with solicitous kin.

I wrote letters to her with sketches of the hatchet-faced head nurse, of interns with whom we jested and flirted, and recalled her aunt's words as a button-nosed intern walked in. "You can always tell the size of man's thing by the size of his nose." No replies by mail ever came from Catherine.

"You look like an alley cat who lost the fight." Dee's opinion of my battered face on returning home was delivered without malice and was her way of making temporary peace. We were on speaking terms for a while, and I had no choice other than to accept her olive branch. But I vowed to tread lightly in the future, *never* to touch her belongings, certainly not her food.

My days normalized. Lunch in the school cafeteria, then cupcakes or oatmeal cookies after school at Nancy's home or peanut butter sandwiches at Barbara's. Supper with Nana would feature canned soup and boiled vegetables. Or she might dine exclusively on a pint of vanilla or coffee ice cream.

A mildly tipsy Dee invited me to the Whoopee Room where her favorite tune, "Only Make Believe," spun on the phonograph. "How about this?" She modeled a pair of tight jodhpurs, sashayed along the bar, and introduced me to a neighborhood guest: Maureen, whom I knew by sight, a schoolmate's glamorous mother whose husband was often away. Dee zigzagged behind the bar.

"One tall gin and tonic, bartender. Love those pants. Where's your riding crop?" asked Maureen. Both were geared for an afternoon of earnest drinking. Uneasy, yet hypnotized by the women's Hollywood lacquered looks and easy banter, I sought invisibility in a corner, wanting to disappear into the marbled linoleum and wood panel decor. But still in my body cast, over which I had thrown a loose shirt, I could hardly evade Maureen's searching eyes. "What happened to your face?" She seemed concerned.

"An automobile accident." Dee slipped from behind the bar like a carnivore stalking prey. "Your face disgusts me. It's ugly. Get out." I ran up the stairs, gasping as if punched in the stomach, and later plumped up some pillows on Nana's bed, sitting dazedly next to her as she closed her eyes in real or feigned sleep. Radio voices filled our ears with the tribulations and woes of fictional widows and long-suffering wives.

In my daydream, I wore a soft white blouse and jodhpurs and rode a palomino bareback through the clouds, cantering above the cramped yards on our street, past the Caddie in our driveway, past Maureen's orange-shuttered house across the street.

Dee stepped through our front entrance and glanced upward the moment I aimed a streak of lightning at her head with all my might. I gazed contentedly at the distant fire of her burning hair while soaring like a goddess above the library where I no longer selected poetry books alphabetically but borrowed them in any order like an adult.

A brisk tap at our door, and Dee led me to the master bedroom for a little talk, she exclaimed. I inspected her face for danger signs: strained neck muscles, curled upper lip, bared gums or distended eyes. Her expression seemed neutral.

She stretched out on the blue chaise lounge and began forcing up the cuticles of her maroon-colored nails with a file. I declined an offered drink. "Maureen said I was sadistic." I paused while she made her point. "Well, I'm waiting for an answer; was I or was I not sadistic? You heard, answer me." Her eyes burned into mine, and I supposed she drew me into this uncomfortable charade for reassurance. "No, you told the truth. It's okay, I don't mind," I lied.

"I told Maureen I am not a phony and don't pull punches." She wore the air of the vindicated, and I was dismissed.

Something funny is going on there. A good-looking young woman with two growing boys carrying on with Her Nibs every day. She can't walk a straight line home. Besides, I don't like the way they look at each other. Too moony!"

Nana half-listened through the window to street sounds, children at potsy games singsonging "onesy, twosy," skip-rope chants, boys at stickball being called home for supper.

"Nana, who are you going to vote for?" I had been listening to pre-election talk at school. "Well, I won't vote for a man who looks like he belongs on a wedding cake. Someone should tell him to shave off that moustache. It makes him look like Hitler."

"Who are you going to vote for?" I asked Ray at the breakfast table the following week, "Dewey or Truman?" No reply. He had taken final flight to Planet Drunko, among aliens with sweaty bodies that shook as they slugged their morning fifths, booze dribbling down their chins.

Spiders and scorpions scuttled out of shadows or hissed and rattled in shaggy nests. Giving up his hair of the dog, he abandoned breakfasts. Ended were the greasy bacon and egg kisses I had wiped away with the back of my hand. Beyond the bottle, his only recreation was the newspaper he scanned like a robot, stiffly turning the pages.

Dee's relationship with Maureen had soured, and her disposition again grew foul. I heard her stomping, cursing, and kicking furniture. She shouted at my figure fleeing out the back door: "You, where do you think you're going? God, I hate sneaks." I resolutely wished she and Maureen could reconcile and toyed with the notion of forging a letter of appeasement from *D.* to *M.* I could fake her capital *M*s, big-bellied *D*s and small circle eye dots. I dismissed the idea.

After their nightly round of bars, which expanded to roadhouses on Sunrise Highway, Dee's brawls with Ray were more violent than ever. I was yanked out of bed to clean up a spill. The ogre with lipstick on its teeth loomed over me as I mopped up a sticky red substance riddled with chips of glass, her strawberry jam. Had she flung it at Ray? The body cast inhibited me from crouching on my knees as nimbly as she directed.

"Give it elbow grease, you idiot," she ordered, then turned and clopped up the stairs. Ray looked on, stunned, his ghostly face vacant. They were swamp creatures whose reign of terror had begun in the marshes where vats of toxic liquid emitted fumes I was forced to inhale.

I slept fitfully and fully clothed in Nana's room. Ray customarily avoided showdowns with his mother, but he now began cursing at her closed door, jiggling its knob, trying to force it open. I wondered why he waited all these years to vent his anger as vividly as this; her age, near blindness, and disability did not dampen his rage, and even seemed to kindle it.

"You fucking old bitch, I wish you were dead. Open the goddamned door. Do you hear me?" He was ignored, and I rooted for Nana to show her tormentor she remained in command.

Days passed. Dee made more ominous announcements: the family had run out of money, and Ray was seeking a new position. We were not to annoy him. On no account could I answer the doorbell or telephone, for fear of bill collectors.

"They have money enough to spend at gin mills," Nana observed. Since I no longer danced with a besotted Ray, whatever his dwindling resources, they needn't be threatened by my needs. But I worried about a cutoff of electricity: Nana's silent Emerson, reading at night, and how would I iron my dirndl skirt for the prom?

Other reasons for apprehension. A report on Lope de Vega's *La Vida es Sueno* for my Spanish class was soon due. I was to hand in a paper for Social Studies next week. A quiz on uses of the subjunctive in French could be sprung at any moment. Less critical was a reading of *Lady Windermere's Fan;* I felt confident of coasting through the English class discussion, having a knack for intuiting what teachers wanted to hear.

And I must also arrange a ride to the hospital. My body cast, adorned with inscriptions, weighed me down like a bulky second skin, and was ready to be zipped off with a power tool. Nana persuaded a lady friend from the Church of the Redeemer to drive us to the hospital. Zreep, zrip, and it was gone, the plaster cast dumped unceremoniously in a mound on the floor. My skin felt gritty and itchy, and gone were the curves of my milkmaid figure.

I weighed slightly more than a hundred pounds, and being a featherweight alarmed me. I needed more muscle and heft for the tests of strength before me: finishing high school and finding a full-time job. I avoided thinking about or discussing my prospects with friends who brandished letters of admission from colleges and spoke excitedly of their futures.

In the late spring of my senior year, the spiraling frenzy of our skewed household spun into still another calamity. "Bitch, I'm going to kill you. You've ruined my goddamned life" bawled a besotted Ray, pounding on his mother's locked door. Nana bolted upright in bed, arms folded. She would not knuckle under a barbarian at the gate. I am fashioned out of steel, announced her look of no retreat.

But Ray's was not an idle threat. An axe slammed into the door, again and again, then there was a sharp crack as he splintered his way into the room. I crouched at the window, ready to leap out onto an adjoining rooftop just below the window ledge. In a state of disbelief, I was undecided whether to run for help or let the rampage take its course. Nana stood, teetering on two canes to full height. He withdrew without a word under her icy stare.

In the eerie quiet that followed the storm—its memento, a gaping wound in the door—I was mystified by Ray's civility at the breakfast table. Contrite after his surge of violence, perhaps augmented by an encounter with spiders on the wall, he replaced his morning whisky with a pot of coffee.

"Have some java?" he offered as if to members of a traditional household waking up to bird song. I disliked myself for welcoming his attention as would any eager twit. I tried unsuccessfully to harden my eyes into a malevolent glare and felt foolish as I displayed a copy of my yearbook picture, meekly asking his opinion. "You look intelligent," he noted. It seemed as futile to ask him if he thought me pretty, as it would to plead for money to pay the photographer.

His flirtation with sobriety was brief. I came upon him later in the week, loaded. And he repeated his earlier claim more emphatically: "You're the fucking bastard of a priest and a nun." It was an eccentric charge that again held my attention. Why would he name two religious figures as my true parents? If he intended to offend me, why not as the bastard of a pimp and his slut, or a gangster and his moll which was more his style? But a priest and a nun? It was too outlandish for his confined imagination, so I wondered . . .

I had since placed the anguishing puzzles of life in separate compartments I constructed for ordering the world that I inherited nine years earlier, and Ray's accusation might conceal a clue.

I returned one afternoon from a senior-prom committee meeting, cheered that I was asked to the event, but also irked at not transcending such banal concerns as allure and popularity. Since meeting my date at my house was out of the question, he would join me at the school on prom night.

By habit, I opened the vestibule closet, which stored most of my poems, letters, books and keepsakes. It was empty. I raced up the stairs in panic; my clothing and other belongings were gone, everything was stripped away. Dee strode through the hallway, eyes popping. "If you're looking for your things, you'll find them in the back lot. I want you out."

Behind our house, beyond the parcel of land on which I nurtured vegetables a few years earlier, was a mound of smoking ashes. My writings, diaries, letters from Cecil and Uncle Ed, and from Mr. Carn inviting members of the choir to a feast of banana splits in Freeport, letters from a French pen pal, Claude from Auvergne, photos of the Cleveland house on Columbia Avenue, of Bill and Mary Joan in Parma Heights, my walnut ring box, Mrs. Morse's prayer card, valentines from grade school, Nancy's gift of a beaded bracelet woven by the Cheyenne with whom she had lived in Wyoming—all gone.

I drew small comfort from what remained, items stored in Nana's wardrobe and a collection of postcards she set aside to steam off uncanceled stamps. Fortunately, I kept a few valuables in my school locker, among them an outfit for the prom, textbooks, a class notebook and yearbook, some snapshots, and a *Cassell's French Dictionary,* my few surviving artifacts of those times.

The next day would be my last in the house, and I barely recall my dazed state while I waited for the clunk of Dee's wedgies down the stairs. "She's not human," I cried to Nana when the footfalls neared, "She's an *it*!" I spat the word out. She leapt at me, punched me in the stomach and face. I bit down on her fingers, jabbed her in whatever soft places my knuckles found.

We struggled, staggered to the kitchen and fell in a squirming heap. I hammered her head against the floor until she rolled over me with pummeling fists, her puffed face and red-streaked protruding eyes as surreal as those of an extraterrestrial. This was my final vision of her: the jellylike glisten of damp skin, the shiny pink pores of her nose, the bristling black hairs in her nostrils, the thin ridged streaks of pointed lips. Nana limped toward us, lashing our legs and backs with a cane until we rolled apart in exhaustion.

It was my last day at 242 East Bayview Avenue. I nursed my wounds and prepared to leave while the monarch of the Whoopee Room was uncorking another bottle of Jim Beam.

I soon after took employment as a telephone operator in Freeport, Long Island, and to attend my graduation, I swapped schedules with someone who also worked split shifts. Tight-lipped and grim, Nana came to the ceremony, having hopped a ride with one of the church ladies.

"I will not be slobbered over," she countered when I tried to embrace her. A year later, I chanced catching my last glimpse of Ray in a packed commuter train, his face the color of boiled ham. "I'm just the grandson of an Iowa coalminer," he blustered in a loud slur to a passenger while I hunkered down in a nearby seat.

13

The wad of dollar bills from babysitting savings stuffed in a shoe at the back of my closet was now stashed in a pouch attached to my bicycle. I borrowed what I needed from a schoolmate, and for fifteen dollars a week, gas and electric included, rented a room on the second floor, complete with kitchen privileges and a toilet down the hall.

Miss Hoppen's boarding house on Wantagh Avenue was a block from the railroad station, a nearness that proved handy in the years I commuted to the city. But to save carfare during the year after graduation, I bicycled or hitchhiked to my job as an operator manning the B-board during day or split shifts, just before the arrival of automatic dialing. My weekly paycheck totaled twenty-eight dollars.

By then almost blind, Nana joined me several months later, banging her way up the stairs with her cane, filling the room with a clutter of boxes, jamming the closet with a lifetime of belongings.

"That banshee has put a spell on my son," she claimed when asked why she left the house. Nana held to her belief that Ray's dereliction rested in his choice of women and in the shortcomings of his gender. "Men are weak as water," she retorted.

We slept head-to-foot in a double bed, prepared modest meals on Sundays in a small kitchen at the end of the hall, and shared the bathroom with a short-order cook working at the Blue Mill Cafe. A large, quiet woman, she quarreled loudly with her only son during weekly visits, his calling card an odor of beer and whisky wafted through the hallway.

Nana began a contentious alliance with our landlady, on whom she depended for favors in my absence. At night I stuffed my ears with wads of toilet paper to shut out Nana's fuming at Miss Hoppen's recent willfulness. More often her diatribes were aimed at me and my failings to measure up. Soon enough, her sleep arrived, filling our room with snores that swelled and subsided like the tides. But the commotion seemed bearable enough. I could now sleep without fear of being yanked out of bed, kicked, slapped or ejected from the house in the small hours of the night.

I continued to read Nana's mail aloud: letters from her niece, Elizabeth, and from friends at the ladies' auxiliary who wrote how they missed her company on Sundays. Some offered to drive her to services, but Nana insisted she was done with the church, and God had better accept her absence. Full of youthful condescension, I prodded her with questions.

"Do you believe in heaven and hell? What does God look like? Do you really think Jesus is his son? What do you believe in?"

"I believe in not pestering people with damn fool questions." Nana closed my court of inquiry.

I ordered recordings of books that came in large black leatherette boxes marked Library for the Blind, Washington, D.C. Peaceful evenings passed as I, too, listened while Nana, with cane at her side, often dozed to the lilt of cultivated voices reading the classics: *Jean Christophe; Lorna Doone; The Last of the Mohicans;* and *Ivanhoe,* whose escapades in medieval England had been required reading in grade school.

When not tuned into these recordings, I read five or more books a week selected from the Freeport Library shelves, authored by John P. Marquand, F. Scott Fitzgerald, John Steinbeck, Upton Sinclair—whose *The Jungle* made me shun meat for a month—and poetry of all descriptions. During lulls at the switchboard, while in the woods behind Wantagh Avenue after work, or at the local library, I transported myself to other worlds: Long Island upper crust, European or mid-American.

Ray had not yet sold the house on Bayview Avenue nor had he disappeared as he would the following year, leaving a trail of unpaid bills and rumors of wrongdoing. About that time, Nana received a visit from an investigator who plied her with questions. Had he come with evidence of my shoplifting at Arnold Constable? Had I been secretly photographed pinching seamed nylon stockings from their boxes? Did he plan to trap me in a lie? "Are you or are you not in this photograph?"

"You've been caught red-handed stealing," Nana would gasp. It's reform school for you, just what Her Nibs is counting on." Thankfully, it was not I who was under suspicion. While eavesdropping, I heard charges of "embezzlement . . . defrauding the company," accusations that further shadowed Ray's already shaky reputation. I repeated the indictments I overheard to Nana and braced myself for a tirade on born sneaks who can't be trusted to keep their noses out of other people's business. To my surprise, she took me into her confidence.

"They've no hard proof he's done anything, but don't breathe a word of this to anyone." She need not have worried; my silence was guaranteed. I was too ashamed to reveal such charges to anyone. Nothing more on the subject was ever mentioned, and "jailbird" was never added to Ray's list of occupations: boozer, blowhard, fitful job seeker, or man-at-large with delirium tremens in the morning. Whether he had vanished into the junk lot of drunken men or was drawn to missions for the saved, I would never know.

Reports drifted back of a solitary Dee occasionally seen with a younger woman hitting the roadhouses and bars along Sunrise Highway and Merrick Road. At times on the B-board, I exacted a small revenge by ringing their number, my heart constricted with elation and alarm at the fury in their voices when I cut them off. I kept in touch with Barbara's parents, Syl and Joe, who entertained their daughter's friends at weekly dinners, even when she was away at college.

I exulted in sampling exotic foods from their fruit and vegetable store: Bermuda onions, avocados, persimmons, figs, quinces, and joined the family tradition of preparing a California salad, a revelation after subsisting on canned peaches on iceberg lettuce that Nana served on holidays. I had revealed an early enthusiasm for meals made by others than myself.

"I'm a gifted eater," I would say after bringing filched gifts: handkerchiefs, colognes for Syl, herbal teas or cheeses for Joe, easing a guilty conscience by unloading my loot, vaguely disappointed that no one suspected. And I displayed a talent for gratitude when accepting Barbara's cast-off dresses and old winter coat, a square-shouldered mouton that fit me perfectly.

In Wantagh, newfound friends from lands as distant as Hungary and Switzerland moved in next door. Suave Jeno from Budapest introduced me to Ernst, a Swiss engineer working in Manhattan, and to lively and artistic sisters Marilla and Suzie. At the time, the former *au pair* girls hand-painted teacups and translated German and French into English for extra cash. My nearby colony of transplanted Europeans was of solace and diversion during years of dull office jobs following that with the phone company.

Having absorbed some of Nana's pinchpenny ways, her Scottish frugality, I painstakingly set aside $1.25 a week for a Modern Library classic. One year and fifty books later, a well-thumbed volume became companion to my brown-bag lunch at a new and better paying job as file clerk with the Textile Banking Company on Madison Avenue. I was pleased to be fired after less than a year; habitual tardiness

Colette with Alex Scotti, 1950

was a chronic flaw inflamed by tedious work. I hardly missed my office uniform of white gloves; seamed hose; hats; and the high-heeled, steel-tipped pumps I cheerfully exchanged for sneakers at the start of summer.

Buoyed by unemployment checks, I scanned want ads; kept late hours; improvised music on Miss Hoppen's parlor piano; and rode my bicycle, sometimes to Jones Beach where I idled until sunset with Marilla, Suzie, and their circle of friends. I continued signing out books from the library, especially poetry, and remained faithful to French literature—reciting Baudelaire, Rimbaud, and Mallarme to the incoming waves of Jones Beach as high-summer clouds drifted over the dunes, or to trains clattering by Miss Hoppen's sagging porch. Happy at detachment from the swarming commuter cargo delivered to and from the city.

Attracted to Rockefeller Center, its proximity to bookstores and to Fifth Avenue and Central Park, in which I lunched on sandwiches in good weather, I accepted work organizing files at the American Cyanamid Company with offices on the sixty-second floor of the RCA building.

What did I foresee in life? The idea of owning a bookstore café on a ferry boat docking at river towns along the Hudson River beguiled me, although I had neither assets nor a head for business. I also fancied myself a proprietor of a Greenwich Village coffee shop, with an invisible partner to handle the irksome details of taxes and bills.

In one fantasy I plunked a young Colette in a Parisian cafe, scribbling poems eagerly praised by a prominent agent who invites her to dine at Maxim's and sells her work at high price to a leading New York publisher. She is adorably photographed at her typewriter for feature articles in *Harper's* and the *New Yorker,* followed by radio interviews with Tex and Jinx Falkenburg as well as Dorothy Kilgallen.

"No man in his right mind is going to want to marry you, so you might as well learn stenography." Nana commented. I despised the idea of taking dictation and wanted no part of Pittman's or Gregg's shorthand schemes. I pined for a livelihood graced with a wealth of bright talk and opinions from people in the arts, citizens in a shining country of books, concerts, paintings, and theater. How I might obtain a passport for such Edens was unclear, and I viewed them as eagle nests remote from my anthill of nine-to-five toil.

During the 1950s, Levittown houses mushroomed where cabbage fields had once found me heatedly petting and necking in near occasions of sin with Frank, a super-bright high school boy with whom I shared distrust in the power of prayer and the existence of a personal God. I was now attending his wedding and those of other friends—a bridesmaid floating down the aisle at Barbara's teenage marriage to Ivan, a troubled bond of several years.

I was invited to, but for vague reasons did not attend, Nancy's wedding to Al, a Freeport boy who sang in the Church of the Redeemer choir. Marriage seemed to me like a coat that did not come in my size. I could never accept the role of caretaker mired in daily domesticity: egg-smeared kisses in the morning, preparing hot meals from sensible cookbooks for a harried husband commuting on the Long Island Railroad.

As a government contractor, the American Cyanamid Company ran routine security checks of all employees. One morning I was called into the personnel department and informed of my citizenship status: formally that of an illegal alien. Ray had neglected filing papers as required by the Alien Registration Acts of 1940 and 1948. In the government's view I was officially subject to deportation. In the company's view, I was at risk of losing my job unless the right documents were secured.

Nana recalled that until Ruthie's death, the attorney, Bale, had mailed yearly Christmas cards from somewhere in the south. Her boxes of postcards saved for recycling had been stored in Miss Hoppen's basement. I pored over them for something, anything, that might technically anchor me in America. Eventually I found it, a greeting card from the Bale family and an attached photograph of a kneeling couple with two children swept up in their embrace. The envelope bore a Richmond, Virginia, postmark.

I tracked the name and address in an out-of-state phone book, borrowed fare from a coworker and boarded a bus for an unannounced visit to Bale's law offices. I believed my immigration problems stood a better chance of solution face-to-face, fearing Bale's outright rejection over the telephone.

It was recognizably him, the well-defined hairline unchanged, his square-jawed good looks intact. At first bewildered, he smiled in recognition when I identified myself and insisted I spend a few days with Sue and his family.

A stylish and perfumed Sue greeted us at the door of their affluent suburban home, introduced me to the children, and ushered me into the study that would double as a guest room. It was filled with books and family pictures: snorkeling in the Caribbean, skiing in Vermont, touring the monuments of the Capitol, Christmas and New Year's Eve parties with beribboned bottles of champagne in hand. Had Sue and Bob adopted me, I would have appeared in such photographs as their grown daughter. They would pridefully declare: "Here, she's just home from college, that's her composing stories at her desk. In this one, she's in Amherst in front of the home of Emily Dickinson, her favorite poet."

I wondered why they had stopped sending cards, why they had not inquired after me. Nana claimed they didn't want to butt into other people's business. And besides, I was not the Bales' responsibility.

After the others retired, Sue confided that her husband had recently passed through a crisis and stopped drinking. She did not elaborate, and I did not recount my personal history, but hinted at what she guessed: I had been less than lucky in the parental lottery. I now needed help only Bob could provide, I explained to a moist-eyed Sue who patted me on the shoulder and kissed me goodnight.

The next evening, after driving Sue to a church bingo game, Bale and I remained in the car and discussed my predicament. He offered me a cigarette and lit one for himself.

"Your California-born father was a Roman Catholic priest ordained a monsignor the year you were born. He died when you were three or four and living with the Belgian sisters. I had been his student at Catholic University in Washington, and when he called, he pledged me to secrecy and told your story. Later, he arranged to pay for your passage here. I can never reveal his name, do you understand that?"

I didn't entirely; I wondered why I had remained in Belgium four years after my father's death. Bale said nothing about the oncoming war in Europe, that I needed to be removed from the institute for my safety. I wasn't completely satisfied. Had he and Branigan erased thoughts of me, preferring not to be reminded of the monsignor's lapse? No answer came. I nodded, recalling Ray's odd charge that I was the bastard of a priest and nun, and how I had suspected some truth to that claim.

"You resemble your father, and that became a problem. Another former student of his agreed to take you to California, but you looked so much like him, she felt the resemblance might be detected and compromise her." Bale paused to light another cigarette. "But your walk, your gestures are like those of your mother, a scholar who probably still lives in France."

My birth certificate, stamped "illégitime," was in his files, and he would soon process citizenship papers. He reaffirmed that as my father's daughter I was deemed a U.S. citizen, but since his name would never be divulged, papers must be drawn as if I were a newly arrived immigrant.

"I know a judge in New York who might speed up this whole process," he reassured me. "Your father was an American chaplain shell-shocked in World War I. He remained in France and was never quite himself after that."

Bale spoke slowly, seeming to probe his own thoughts for explanations of my father's broken vows. The idea that I was conceived while my father languished in delirium thirteen years after the war was outlandish, but I withheld my question.

My mother was alive in France, and I must find her. I would look for her as she must have sought me. She would insist I stay with her. Wasn't a mother supposed to love her child? Perhaps she was married and I had brothers and sisters, a family. The words throbbed in my head, and above the drone of voices from the church basement, I thought I heard someone call out, "Bingo!"

France seemed a fortune away, and my savings were almost depleted. More scrimping, as I cut back on food and books, bought clothes at thrift shops and church bazaars, sold Christmas cards on consignment door-to-door, spent nights after work addressing bank envelopes for extra income. Marilla and Suzie kept my spirits afloat by supplying addresses of parents and friends in Switzerland for stay-overs and donating hours of language practice with suppers and walks conducted in French. Barbara's parents were also encouraging, providing an international membership list of the Rotary, to which Joe belonged.

Nana, too, took notice, although she doubted that my mother had any intention of seeking me out. "If she'd wanted to find you, she would have found you." Her taunt echoed my own wavering doubts. Yet in the ensuing days, her feelings toward me softened and I became the unaccustomed object of her good will before my departure. Despite her failing sight, she borrowed a Singer and with my help sewed a small take-along wardrobe for me from Simplicity pattern cutouts: seersucker pajamas and a navy blue princess-line dress with a zip-up front, practical duds for my journey.

I also declared peace with the bellicose Miss Hoppen, who one evening produced her collection of European postcards dating to a turn-of-the-century tour with her parents. When asked for her impressions, she asserted all those countries could do with a fresh coat of paint.

Visiting with Syl at the store one afternoon, I met Carmen, a young Peruvian woman from Lima now living with a sister married to a naval officer from Merrick. Two years older than I, once plush in wealth, Carmen was now obliged to economize. Like me, she was orphaned—having lost her mother to illness, her father to an accident—and commuted to an office job.

Her search for her Spanish origins coincided with my own

pilgrimage. "Carmen is looking for her mother country and I for my mother," I would say when people asked for reasons behind our quest. We plotted a backpacking trip to Europe, prepared provisional lists, checked maps, and marked up calendar pages.

Tall, with a long neck and aristocratic good looks, Carmen spoke fluent, but heavily accented English studded with quaint slang. "What the Dickens," she would say in her soft, husky voice, "let's do it, what the heck." She was a welcome guest at Joe and Syl's Tuesday-night dinners, and I introduced her to friends. We seemed to attract cheering sections everywhere as the departure date approached. My citizenship papers were issued two years after I had gone to see Bale, in the spring of 1952, before our July sailing.

Another seeker was swept up in the tumult of our family odyssey and joined us at the last moment. Sondra, Carmen's nightschool Hunter College friend, planned to meet her maternal grandmother in Germany. Artistic and exuberant, Sondra wore earnest dark-rimmed glasses and dressed with flair, scarves tied at just the right angle, belts cinched to highlight a narrow waist. Her hands fluttered when she spoke in a high-pitched voice with opinions that left little room for debate.

I gazed warily at her blond ponytail swishing back and forth, distrusting her sudden entry into my established partnership with gentle Carmen. But I would come to value Sondra's flamboyance and resourcefulness when renting rooms in a grubby dollar-a-day Parisian hotel on rue Monsieur le Prince. Carmen had left for Spain and sent letters that reflected her lively diction: *Dearios, I'm here in Madrid, almost broke, going nuts, but by hook or crook I've found a job. It's fantastic . . . Cheerio and Love, C.*

That winter, time and money were eroding like the scuffed steps Sondra and I climbed to our fifth floor quarters—like the rain-soaked stones along the Seine whose shores I traced in long walks contemplating Valéry's *Poèmes;* Henri Michaux's *l'Espace du Dedans;* or turning over lines of a newcomer, Welsh poet Dylan Thomas; and rearranging stanzas of my own increasingly despondent verses.

I fretted about finding my mother. Would she deny I was her daughter? Since I was told I favored my father, would she be upset or indifferent at the resemblance? I feared the coldness that women in my life had slammed down with heedless disregard, like cards at a game of solitaire. Hesitantly and to no avail, I searched for her at the Sorbonne and in the town of Meudon outside of Paris, where Bale had reported she once lodged.

One afternoon later that autumn, I traveled to Brussels and also sought out the institute on rue Chant d'Oiseaux. Although given clear directions to the outskirts of the city where my children's home had stood, I became hopelessly lost and panicky as darkness fell. Circling about on foot, turning wrong corners, I finally happened upon the familiar iron fence through which I had passed fifteen years earlier, exultantly waving good-bye to Anne, Chantal, *le petit* Jean-Pierre, and the Sisters who raised me from infancy. The Institute de Puériculture was no more, and the buildings, remodeled beyond recognition into a series of offices or a private school, were shut tight behind the locked gate in an abandoned neighborhood.

How might I find my way back to where I was staying in the city? Alone and overcome with tears, I called out to the first rare passerby, a well-dressed elderly man who escorted me to a bus stop with comforting phrases in English and French. It was pointless for me to ever return. Years later, an American archeology student, brought me her photos of Sint Martins, a research center at the Chant d'Oiseaux location. The fence was gone, but I recognized the flat contours of the land from my childhood.

Sondra and I read the *Herald Tribune* at the Café Danton, smoked Gauloises pulled from blue packets, looked erratically for work with the forced gaiety we thought appropriate to our semi-Bohemian, down-at-the-heels existence on the Left Bank. Days of gray light gave way to blue skies pierced by sun and clouds. Snow arrived and hurried off. Jazz riffs and blues, streaming out of our street's nightclubs heightened my sense of isolation much like a fugitive note searching for its score.

We dated American and French Fulbright students who had sailed with us on the Ile de France. Sondra designed a festive calendar she taped to the wall to track our social engagements. I checked it daily while eyeing the clock; both jeered at me. Who am I: what do I want?

I secured a job as an *au pair* on the Right Bank but was hardly the person to care for a colicky baby and two children who endlessly whined, "When is Mama coming home?" as I stirred boiled diapers and infant formula. To the astonishment of the youngsters, I sometimes wept in shared frustration and helplessness when the baby bawled, refusing comfort. During the all-too-few moments of idleness, *Mama* handed me knitting needles and *Papa* stared hard, licking his lips, sizing me up. I left as I came, down the servant staircase, resolved to make a final effort to regain my mother.

From my birth certificate, which listed her own place of birth, I traced my mother to Nérac, an agreeable Gascon river town, the site of the summer palace of Henri de Navarre, a Sixteenth Century French king. On the train to Nérac's neighboring city of Agen, my compartment held discharged soldiers returning from Indochina after the army's defeat at Dien Bien Phu. Not much older than I, some could have been my French brothers, had sons been born to my mother, had other wombs housed my father's seed.

The soldiers reached into duffle bags for cigarettes, sausage, and wine to share with me, and as the train hurtled by fields and vineyards lying fallow in winter, I sang with them: "Chevalier de la Table Ronde," and from the ashes of an earlier war, "Auprès de Ma Blonde." Wine poured from bottles buried doubts and apprehensions on returning home to their mother country.

An official in the mayor's office in Nérac reported the family river house overlooked the old bridge into town, and I was guided to its location on the crest of a steep road. Its door was opened by a benign, white-haired elderly couple appointed as custodians following the recent death of my grandparents. I introduced myself as the daughter of an American professor who had known Marthe Dulong through university friends. The couple knew nothing of her whereabouts; she had not attended her mother's funeral last year, a curious absence, they agreed.

Marthe was an infrequent visitor, known to accept scholarly assignments, and was perhaps out of the country. They sought reasons to excuse her. I was invited to share their midday meal, and after coffee I received the Paris address of her sister, my aunt Jeanne, who lived no more than twenty minutes from my current hotel near the République.

I slightly altered my invented story when writing to Jeanne. My new identity: a friend of American professors who wished to contact her sister, Marthe. Might I stop for a brief visit?

Jeanne greeted me at the door. A small, vivacious woman, she was enviably poised in a well-cut suit, pearls, and stylishly curled short hair. I caught a whiff of her floral perfume when offered a martini she had learned to fix while a Fulbright scholar at the University of Kansas in the mid-twenties. Her American-accented English was as smooth as the cocktails we sipped from chilled glasses.

Jeanne withdrew from a box photographs of her year in heartland America, and these pictures were passed along to me in quick succession as she spun stories of toppling from a horse while riding near Topeka, Kansas; of motor trips to Chicago; and sightseeing in New York. She adored excursions and annually toured exotic countries such as Yemen, Korea, and Senegal. This year? Perhaps Tunisia and Morocco. She brightened when I described my backpacking travels through Europe with Carmen and Sondra.

Jeanne freely divulged Marthe's Oxford address, revealing a snapshot of her sister in a hat, which framed her face like a helmet. Eyes tilted upward, bare of makeup, the woman in the picture resembled a saint.

"Sad to say, we don't get on." Jeanne mentioned her sister's piety and conservative politics, and criticized her for not settling into a steady teaching post.

"She has what Americans call a master's degree, is fluent in several languages, is an excellent Latinist and a trained archivist. I tried to obtain a position for her with the Bibliothèque Nationale, but she would have none of it. Would you like another drink?"

Mildly tipsy from the alcohol and these revelations, I politely refused as she continued. Was I acquainted with such and such an American professor? I shook my head. Was I enrolled in a university? Night courses at a city college, I responded.

Their father, she added, motioning to a large framed photo of a man with a full mustache, was a professor with advanced ideas on female emancipation. He educated his daughters to have a sense of purpose, and they were encouraged to pursue meaningful, successful careers. Jeanne spoke with familiarity and ease in English, obviously proud of her fluency in a second language.

I studied her animated face, musing how it might collapse in amazement at the announcement: "I'm Marthe's daughter . . . your niece." I trembled while shaking her hand and saying good-bye at the door. When I glanced up at her window from the street, I glimpsed her peering at me heading toward the Métro station.

Returning to Oxford, England, I lodged with Geoffrey, a tall, long-limbed, previous fellow-well-met. It was the previous summer in Cornwall when he and his friend Tod invited us three hitchhikers and our bulky rucksacks to jam into his MG outside of Truro. Both were on holiday: choice companions who demonstrated the fine points of shooting darts and ordering ale at local pubs. As automotive comrades over a span of days, we rode and hiked through abandoned mining towns, past uncrowded tourist villages, and along a craggy coast of dazzling prospects—views of the strand and sea in the calm of early August. We vowed to stay in touch, to meet again.

"Ring me up when you're in Oxford." Uncomfortable with farewells, Geoff placed his card in my outstretched palm. I telephoned him six months later, explaining that I needed to locate a party who might put me in touch with my family: "The person was in Oxford." The detailed truth seemed too complex to divulge and might invite unwanted questions, but the naturally discreet Geoff assured

Aunt Jeanne

me he was only eager to revive memories of our recent Cornish idyll. The next day we drove together over a snow-covered road to my mother's address on the outskirts of town. "I'll pick you up when you're ready to leave." His large, comforting hand rested lightly on my shoulder as I stepped from the car.

Her face reforms itself in the doorway of a modest cottage set back from the road—the glint of a gold front tooth sets awhirl recollections of the gloomy woman at the institute, the woman who pretended to be my aunt and had me kneel with her in prayer. Her wide eyes are level with mine. She is not the virginal woman in Jeanne's photograph, but one heavyset with white-streaked disheveled hair, loose strands at the neck.

Full breasts swell under a threadbare sweater and elbows poke through the holes. A North Sea wind drives late winter snow across the streets and fields of the gray hamlet in which I have arrived unannounced in the afternoon. I say my name, but she does not recognize me, appears puzzled. Who is this girl come to trespass on her twelfth-century devotions, Saint Marcellin, Hugh of Saint Cher, the medieval tracts, the study of Petrus Pictaviensis, Distinctiones super Psalterium?

I speak in French and then in English. "I am Colette, your daughter." Her long, oval face grows pale. A wedge of lines deepens between her wide, gold-brown eyes. She motions for me to follow her, and we take the stairs to her rented rooms. Does she walk like me? I study her as she climbs, her rumpled hose, baggy skirt, unlaced brogues. The hunched shoulders are those of one older than her forty-eight years. Disheartened, I had hoped to find a less humble-looking parent, one modeled more like Jeanne, whose bearing and style, even in her fifties, would impress my friends.

I stare at my mother's hips, transfixed by her flesh, my first protective shell, her blood and milk my early nourishment. We are in her furnished rooms; a sputtering grate, fringed lampshades, and knickknacks of English vintage blur in the landscape of two people tenuously together at arm's length, seated opposite one another amidst a clutter of papers and books.

I vainly look for signs that she has remembered me. Pictures. Sentimental objects: bronzed baby shoes, a silver cup engraved with my name, gifts for the beloved child. I tell her the family members to which she entrusted me are dead or have disappeared. She accepts my brief chronicle without comment. We prattle about her arcane labors, the professors for whom she works sporadically for meager pay, and about my recent meeting with her sister.

"We do not see eye to eye on many subjects." Her thin voice is dry and expressionless. We speak of the family's river house in Gascony and of her sister's fashionable Parisian apartment and high-ranking post in the French government, of Jeanne's published French translations of Dickens and Thackeray. My mother does not wish to share this worldly wealth, has turned her back on family life as if in penance for a guilt that I inflicted with my birth.

She agrees that I take after my father, but says, "We will not speak of him." Her tone is firm. Stories about my father must remain locked away like a box of rare coins. I accept her injunctions without murmur, fearful of tipping over the frail structure of our meeting.

I strain to find our physical likenesses. A temple vein pulses blue like mine; there's a similarity in the smooth line of her neck, around which clings a crucifix on a slender chain. At my urging we touch once, back-to-back, to compare heights. I stroke the tops of our heads; the nest of my mother's soft hair, my short, cropped curls. Marthe and Colette, five foot three. There was nothing more to measure; what mattered went mute. A turning of the page a little less illegible than before.

"I have no money to give you." Only these words pierce the flat and tentative conversation. Colette, the avenger, the blackmailer, a dark presence that is never fully erased from her apprehensions of a Catholic purgatory. I promise to keep the twenty-two-year secret from prying minds. She fears scandal will blemish her already fragile career as scholar-archivist. She will be mocked by colleagues and friends. No one in her circle or in her family must know I exist.

"Did Jeanne suspect anything?" Her frown carves a deep *V* between her eyes. I reassure her. Her somber, withdrawn face bares the gold tooth in an effortful smile.

Fantasies collapse. She does not want me, she does not want to know me. I have blundered into a scrupulously censored and solitary life that will not yield to my desires. Yet she leaves the door ajar when it might have been closed; I am given permission to write her without reference to our true relationship. I leave her buttressed by

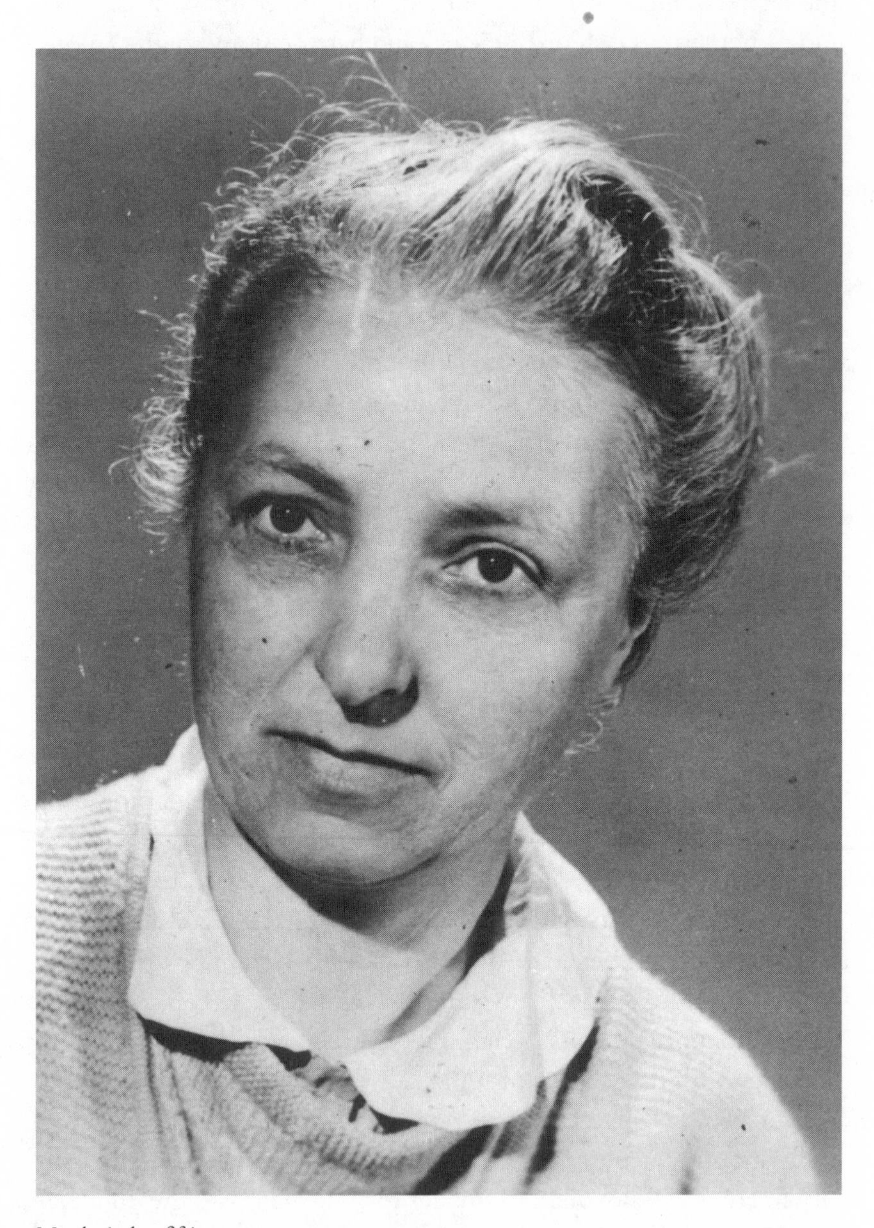

Marthe in her fifties

feudal indices and elisions of time in which she will recall her daughter and wonder what God has in store for the child conceived in the dim light of private rooms, my father's pink flesh, his cassock, crested by an unsnapped collar, flung on the floor.

Geoff's parents, a well-meaning don and his wife, asked over supper, "Did it go well?" Was I given clues to locate my family? Does the person to whom I spoke teach at one of the colleges here? Their gentle queries and my evasive replies dropped in eddies and swirls like the snow gathering in their garden.

"Colette may not wish to be cross-examined," Geoff said in agitation. "Please excuse me." As my voice trailed off, I rubbed my eyes with my knuckles, giddy with fatigue.

Later that night Geoff tapped at the door, stooping as he entered the attic. "Here's a little book of poems to distract you," he stammered. *Pomes Penyeach,* bound in red leather and written by a youthful James Joyce, remains today in my collection of prized editions.

14

I returned home two months later, only a little less disenfranchised than before. Nana, now supported by checks from her niece, Elizabeth, in Chicago, had grown increasingly frail and with snarled hair and stained clothes took on a frazzled, almost deranged appearance.

At American Express mail drops in Europe, I had opened barely legible one-page notes from a vintage Nana: amusing, gossipy, joking at another's expense, and tough as a boot. But the correspondence varied, and I would find myself unnerved by a scratchily written "I will never forgive you for . . . blah . . . blah," wandering off into an unreadable scrawl.

Another in childlike print, rather than in her standard angular script, ended: "You will have to answer for this." Still others: "You are nothing . . ." with words fading into incomprehensible blather. Hate mail aimed at me, but why? Since I had ceased being a captive audience for her spiteful words, were these messages another means of venting grievances? What did these broken bits of scribbled fury augur for our lives?

I hated myself for continuing to curry Nana's favor, believing myself a weakling for wanting it, for not transcending my need for her appreciation and regard. She had respected my European voyage, the gumption she thought it took. But I was now an object of her disdain, a "nothing" come home to roost without a mother's backing or love, without money or a job.

Miss Hoppen shook her head, alluding to death announcements that arrived with greater regularity. Members of the ladies auxiliary, women with whom Nana had played cards, had begun to enter a country of minus signs—transported by coffins and funerary urns.

At eighty-three, Nana was the lone survivor of her family's generation. Was she sliding off the precipice to looniness? Her younger sister, Agnes, had lurked in hallways, crooked a bony finger toward us, asked our names, and threatened to report us to the authorities. But Nana seemed perfectly sane, even imperious as she cocked her head in what I recognized as the Grand Duchess look now residing in a diminished frame. She promptly announced there was no need for my "measly contribution."

"You may as well move out right away and take those infernal books with you." She repeated her fixed opinion that reading, in any case, was an unnatural act. As I packed the last of my belongings, Nana hobbled into the room, cane thumping.

"You can't do anything right." She had pulled a favorite phrase from her bag of disparagements and was about to haul out others. I moved toward her so we stood eye to eye, for a close-up of the wreckage that age had bequeathed, the pouches and spots, the spidery maze and patches of red veins on her long nose and heavy lids. In the upheaval of moving I had discovered my backbone and stood erect.

"In all our years," I exclaimed, my voice tipped in steel, "you have never, not once, praised me. Is there nothing right about me, not one solitary thing?" Nana did not interrupt, and I waited for the usual dismissive remark. She paused wearily, seemingly lost in reflection. "Yes," she paused. "Yes, there is something." I watched her milky blue eyes lift toward the ceiling in her Church of the Redeemer pose. "You have a good disposition. Now don't try to wheedle anything more out of me. I'm too old for these fishing-for-compliments games."

The answer and Nana's apparent sincerity surprised me but ultimately left me frustrated; didn't my "good disposition" permit me to be browbeaten, bullied, and led around by the nose? I distrusted her judgment, especially this compliment, extracted from her like a stubborn tooth.

Tom, a literate engineer I had dated the year before and whose steady flow of letters cheered me in Europe, helped me settle into a furnished third-floor walk-up in the shadow of the elevated train on East 17th Street. I now had a city apartment with a single bed, a hot plate, a toilet down the hall and a popular pay phone on the ground floor.

I was preoccupied with and dazed by change. No longer compelled to catch the commuter special, I slept late and blocked my ears to the din of passing trains. I filled out forms in a daily round of employment agencies. At the same time, I fought off crying jags; incomprehensible inertia followed manic eruptions.

Nana seemed as indifferent to my activities as was my distant mother, who had written to me but once: a cool, brief letter in answer to mine. "Do not write often," she admonished, "I do not want to arouse suspicion on my sister's part, and so will be obliged to destroy whatever you send." In a fit of pique, I ripped up her letter. More nights gave way to insomnia.

A downtown Belgian banking company hired me as a clerk-typist, but I was ill-suited for typing and spent hours over my Remington or Royal brushing away the detritus of innumerable erasures before the days of white-out. One of the managers reported me flopped over my desk, asleep. Another employer accused me of wearing long earrings inappropriate for office work. Other jobs followed, as did tardiness, inattention, and pink slips at the end of the week or month.

"Unemployment's a lark, it's not having money that gives me the jitters," I'd repeat to whomever might ask about my fortunes. I assumed no one understood my predicament, hardly understanding it myself: the fear that had begun to gnaw at me that I was losing my boundaries, losing the familiar identity I had cultivated as a blithe and literary spirit fated to work in gray offices. The anxious face reflected back from public mirrors seemed to belong to an angry other-person, and that alarmed me. Who was I? Did it matter that I often felt invisible?

Sondra and I shared our separate letters from Carmen, who had discovered and embraced her mother country and was engaged to marry the son of an ex-marquis, an artist in Madrid. Sondra headed up a textile design company with a midtown office. My travel mates had secured proper passports and were settling down to purposeful pursuits.

A September 1953 heat wave wilted the city and surrounding countryside. At the same Meadowbrook Hospital where I was fitted with a body cast six years previously, a toothless Nana brushed flies from her emaciated face. Escorted by Tom, who would soon marry one of Miss Hoppen's new tenants, I had purchased a bouquet of red carnations, flowers Nana admired when they were ordered as altar decorations by the ladies auxiliary.

"I brought you flowers, Nana," I imitated the soothing voice of visitors bearing gifts amid doctors and nurses with thermometers, prescriptions and charts, briskly consulted even in that numbing, unbroken heat wave of late summer.

"They bring on bugs, you fool." She knocked them to the floor with surprising strength. I stared at her collapsed mouth, the skin flaps at her throat, curious that words shaped in those withering places still carried the power to hurt.

"I did my best," I sighed, faintly nauseated from the odors of rubbing alcohol and disinfectant. In answer, her terminal words: "Your best was never good enough."

Was it a quarrel that made me late to her funeral? I was then living with Bill, a handsome and tempestuous left-wing artist in Greenwich Village, spent evenings at jazz spots: the Village Vanguard, Nick Condon's, or retreated to the Cedar Tavern, listening to painters debate the merits of abstract expressionism. During days I worked as a file clerk for Office Temporaries.

With help from Tom, I had purchased a pine box and supplied a burial outfit from Nana's closet, a favored blue dress and matching slip. Before she was primped and laid out in the coffin, I removed her diamond rings—tugging at them as they clung stubbornly to her knuckles—the engagement and wedding rings selected with care in Clinton or Ames, Iowa, by her violin-playing suitor and husband, Arthur. Within the week, I managed to lose the jewelry she had safeguarded for more than sixty years. Where . . . how? While washing my hands in a public toilet? I couldn't remember.

Raymond did not attend the funeral. and I wondered if he knew she was dead. A few church friends came to pay their respects, and most left before my arrival. Hot and breathless, unsuitably dressed in a see-through, speckled print, I half expected a resurrected Nana lift the coffin lid and reprimand, "You never do anything right."

I continued to work for Office Temporaries and later as a clerk-typist for a music company, taking dictation in longhand or at the typewriter from composers of rhythm and blues and early rock and roll songs. At the mid-morning coffee break, a dealer came with a white powdery substance in glassine envelopes. I was once offered a snort but declined, while enjoying our clients' faith in my silence and the thrill of the illicit.

I later accepted a job as gal Friday for the New York correspondent of *Le Figaro*. Luckily, I could keep my French in good repair and once again haunt Rockefeller Center near to my beloved bookstores and Central Park. Wraith-like Francoise Sagan, then the teenage author of *Bonjour Tristesse,* floated through the door of our office in an ankle-length fur coat; I envied her aplomb, longed for that same barrage of attention and the respectful questions that trailed her American tour.

In the fall of 1955, at the close of our stormy years together in a Greenwich Village flat once occupied by Marlon Brando and his sister, I left Bill and ventured into self-betterment. A night course in Speed Writing promised ten more dollars a week in secretarial wages.

Supported by the therapist Bill had encouraged me to see at a New York University clinic, our split was amicable. Now I could detach myself without bitter wrangling or fear, find my own place, and carve out a future.

I found another job as an office factotum for *IT,* a short-lived magazine of contemporary theater whose premier issue featured Swedish film star-director Mai Zetterling on its cover. *IT* was headquartered on the first floor of 77 St. Mark's Place, a building that housed the illustrious poet W. H. Auden. His face creased like an old leather jacket, he would pop into our offices, often in pajamas and a rumpled robe, to discuss the state of our shared mice. Our staff and W. H. had agreed to forgo spring traps—the thought of broken rodent bones was too gruesome—but to install devices that imprisoned them for later release to their uncertain fates on the streets of the Lower East Side.

Through a housing tip from Charlie Marowitz, an energetic would-be director and journalist-at-large, *IT* writer and eventual theater reviewer for the newborn *Village Voice,* I relocated to a West 23rd Street walk-up with high ceilings, a view of London Terrace, a tub in the kitchen and toilet down the hall.

I resumed writing to my mother, explained my engagement to an artist had broken off, and asked her to understand my silence. Her response was courteous and noncommittal. Bland accounts of her life as a scholar-at-large sometimes lifted the curtain on a fact or two. At my repeated appeals to learn more, she acknowledged to feeling only admiration and pity toward my father. Not love. Her motive for leaving me in an austere orphanage? To endow me with Catholic virtues and purity. Why had I stayed in the orphanage four years after my father's death? It was God's will.

Marthe let drop astonishing word that she had not entirely abandoned thoughts of marriage, that she longed for someone named Johnny, an elderly English historian and Catholic, an Oxford don for whom she felt a certain fondness, although she had seen him but once and they never met. She would wait for a sign from God.

I wondered if my father were somehow resurrected in Johnny, as a shadow of the monsignor. But her fondness for him made no demands. As might Dear Abby, I exhorted her to write to him and arrange a meeting through scholarly friends. An account of her painful reticence appeared in a letter sent to my new address:

> I hoped he would come to the library, but he did not. I saw him in the street and I think he expected me to talk or go in the same direction, but I don't know what seized me. I felt terribly shocked somehow, and suddenly so shy I could not move.
>
> He must have been hurt. I must explain that on top of that he is extremely tall and I am short. Perhaps someday if God wants it, all will be well . . .

Almost twenty years later, she would write wistfully in her firm and methodical script of visiting the library or the British Museum in hopes of seeing her historian. They still had not met, but friends advised her he "might" be there, and God would give her courage. Her lack of worldliness, her adolescent yearnings touched and exasperated me.

A clerical job for the Louis Dreyfus Company, near Battery Park, brought me a fatter pay check and an unexpected yearend bonus, which I lavished on a used piano, drawing a street crowd as it was hoisted by crane through my window. "Why couldn't you get a spinet?" my landlady squawked from the bottom of the stairs. Buying sheet music, rippling arpeggios on the keyboard after work, I recalled Uncle Ed's injunction, "Practice makes mastery," and sent his spirit form my allegiance through the air.

"Am I college material?" I asked my therapist at one of our weekly visits, and discussed the possibility of taking classes for credit. "Look at it as an adventure," he advised. His answer roused me, and in the spring of 1956 I began my climb up what seemed like Mount Everest: a night-school degree at Hunter College. I registered for nine or twelve credits each semester and six each summer from City College, all the while working daytime jobs.

From outside the window of an English composition class at Hunter, I heard crowds demonstrating before the Russian embassy on Park Avenue. Soviet tanks had rolled into Hungary. "COMMUNIST BETRAYAL AND TREACHERY," the headlines charged. And where was Bill? He had spoken of escaping the city for the woods of Tennessee, but when I asked a mutual friend, he recounted that Bill had quit the Communist Party and moved to Westport, Connecticut.

"He's married and the father of a son, and become respectable." A twinge of regret swept through me that I continued to remain an outsider to the complex country of wedlock, where so many I knew had taken residence.

A fellow night-school B.A. aspirant enlivened those intense and purposeful years with her wit and street smarts. Sunny taught me how to shop for seven-dollar dresses, preferably black with good lines, at S. Klein on Union Square or Orbach's on 34th Street.

As confidantes during late-night calls between my Chelsea and her Morton Street apartments, we soothed one another at the end of failed romances, shared textbooks, holidays, folk songs (with Sunny on guitar), several vacations, and clothing. Our waist and hip measurements were alike, although willowy Sunny was almost six inches taller than I. Moody, sometimes difficult, but instinctively generous, she became the sister I had sometimes wished for myself. I would be maid of honor at her wedding soon after graduation.

My 1961 B.A. degree in English Literature and Creative Writing was a latchkey to the euphoria and exhaustion of teaching in some of the city's backwater schools. Not an early riser, sleep-deprived and stunned, I made my first foray by crosstown bus and elevated subway to an east Bronx junior high school, where I taught so-called adjustment classes. But the adjustment was mine, as I learned the custodial skills of public school education, mediating among and consoling a hodgepodge of foreign-born, hyperactive, and passive or hostile students.

I left the hair-raising, surreal world of junior high school for calmer precincts at year's end to teach English as a Second Language at New York University's American Language Institute. Being foreign-born, I empathized with the dislocation and confusions of my adult students; their struggles at adapting to the unfamiliar had been mine as well. It was an awareness I clung to during the next decade of teaching newcomers to America.

Despite my mother's and Bale's refusal to name him, I had not given up hopes of identifying my father. Another avenue was Branigan, my other escort to America. Do you keep in touch with Branigan? my mother inquired in a letter. They had been acquaintances in Paris with scholarly interests in common. I wrote to his still-active university address in Massachusetts and enclosed my photograph. We agreed to meet in the Algonquin Hotel lounge in Manhattan.

Unlike Bale, his appearance had distinctively altered during the years: red hair and moustache had gone gray, and his body fleshed out. His most recognizable feature was his small blue eyes and their penetrating gaze. We spoke of Bale's battle with alcohol and pledge to stay sober; the men had lost touch with one another. I asked about his field of study and, eager to make a good impression, mentioned coursework in ancient history at Hunter, for which I earned an A.

I expressed admiration for Dorothy Parker's stories, Robert Benchley's essays, and the works of other literary lights who frequented the Algonquin Round Table. I hoped to put Branigan at ease, who in an unguarded and amiable mood might disclose what was rightly mine: my father's name. I was Mata Hari lulling a suspicious agent into revealing state secrets.

"No," I lied over drinks at his clear concern about protecting my father's reputation, "I'm only interested in what you can tell me about his character, his looks."

"The monsignor had auburn hair, what little there was of it, and was of average height. He was a good talker and enjoyed the pleasures of the table. Of course, he was also a prodigious scholar." Branigan was forthcoming with these innocent details, and had softened his familiar blunt and irascible manner I remembered when we sailed from Europe to New York. Was it twenty years ago? Yes. I did not interrupt, hoping he might inadvertently drop a clue.

"The monsignor often dined with Jacques Maritain in Paris of the 1920s and was friendly with John Meng, now president of Hunter College, your college." Those were the details I sought. My carefully penned letter to Meng, contrived as a heartfelt appeal from a former student, made note of my college prizes and honors, and asked for the name of the "American priest" described by Branigan. The ruse: my search for an anonymous priest who might lead me, an orphan, to lost parents whom the parish priest had once counseled.

I trembled while opening Meng's reply weeks later. "Undoubtedly," the letter began, "the man whose name you want was Monsignor L." I chose not to reply to Meng's question, "How did you learn of my friendship with the Monsignor?"

My father's name appeared in a library edition of the *New Catholic Encyclopedia*. The entry read:

> Historian of medieval philosophy whose writing and participation in international historical societies stimulated basic research into the history of medieval thought. (Born San Francisco 1/1/86, died, Paris 11/1/34.)
>
> Born to a pioneer California family (of French descent), he attended St. Patrick's Seminary, Menlo Park, and was ordained 6/21/10. While a parish priest in Mayfield, he became a chaplain with the U.S. Army, World War I.
>
> After the war, he earned his Ph.D. from Stanford University (1921) with a thesis on *The German Origins of the Modernist Movement.* His archbishop, Edward Hanna of San Francisco, sent him to École de Chartes in Paris 1923. . . . His thesis was published as *La Vie et les Oevres de Prévostin* (Le Saul Choir, Belgium). Living in Paris, Msgr. L. soon became the European representative to the American Council of Learned Societies of the International Academic Union, and the delegate of American universities to the International Committee of Historical Sciences.
>
> He himself undertook to prepare a catalog of all the medieval Latin mss. of Aristotle's works. The first of the two-volume catalog,

Colette's father, the monsignor

Codicum Aristotelicorum Latinorum, was published in 1935, shortly after his death.

Posing as a scholar engaged in assembling materials for a monograph, I wrote to publishers and chancery offices, to Stanford and to his colleagues, accumulating a stack of descriptive papers that bore witness to my father's extroverted personality and gargantuan energy.

My mother's response to the outpouring of information about the monsignor was understated: "I see that you have learned quite a bit." At my prodding, she confessed to being his associate in assembling a catalog of Aristotle manuscripts, but she typically dismissed her role in the project. "It was all so long ago, I can hardly recall the work. Besides, it would be too tedious to describe."

Proud of my persistence, eager to show that I had prevailed despite his discouragement, I informed Bale I had uncovered my father's name, but reassured him I would neither misuse nor malign it. Informing Branigan was obviously too cheeky, but I confessed to trickery. I never heard from either of them again.

15

My years of therapy were drawing to a close. As my psychologist's parting prescription, he recommended an aesthetic and affordable getaway to Monhegan Island, Maine. In the summer of 1962, bracketed between two lusty painters in the lobby of the New Monhegan House, I glimpsed a tall, attractive freelance writer entertaining nearby vacationers with a dazzling array of statistics about the Sane Nuclear Policy and strontium 90. Saul Stadtmauer's high forehead and boyish grin brightened an otherwise melancholy face.

While drawn to him, his dry wit and basso profundo voice, I was erratically involved with Phil Rosen, a jazz clarinetist, social worker, postman, playwright, English teacher, and poet then traveling in Europe. Phil had entered my life some years before in Washington Square Park, where he indulged his passion for chess; I enjoyed following the players and their moves. One Sunday in spring, I joined the onlookers while toting a collection of poems: *The Blue Hen's Chickens* by Vincent McHugh.

"What the hell kind of title is that?" Phil's tough guy mien, his wiry, blond Steve McQueen looks excited me. When we discovered our shared appreciation of books, jazz, and poetry; that we spoke in metaphors; liked dancing, were hungry for mothering; and mostly shunned commitment, we gradually became intense and unstable friends, and lovers shuttling from my room in Chelsea to his studio apartment on the Lower East Side.

While on Monhegan, Saul and I fed hamburger to the rock-pool anemones, slogged through moonlit marsh water in our walks around the island, stretched out on flat rocks near the sea to study the stars. "The work of the universe is never done," he philosophized, reaching for my hand as I sighed, mesmerized by his deep voice. We flung wildflowers from the prow of the *Balmy Days* ferrying us to the mainland and home. By tradition, if the cast-off flowers floated back to the island's shore, so would we. Both happened, with a few detours between.

I met Phil at the airport on his return from the Continent. My heart hammered when he ambled through customs: tanned, eyebrows and hair bleached by the sun, his sharp-boned face a study in cool preoccupation. He asked for breathing room, which was cheerfully filled by Saul, who helped me rearrange bookshelves, framed and hung pictures and posters, revealing a much-welcomed domestic facet to his sensitive nature. Phil, who scooped food out of paper containers and littered his floor with clothing, suffered in comparison.

During the last hot gasp of summer and into autumn, I returned to teaching and began taking graduate courses at New York University. A congenital bachelor adept in the kitchen, Saul wooed me with gourmet cheeses, canned anchovies, olives, and pimientos from his father's Connecticut supermarket.

We were amiable talkers and agnostics, he, a former Yeshiva student who also rebelled against the rigors of organized religion. We were stargazers, word- and book-lovers, politically liberal, bound by our histories of childhood losses and by the dreams we struggled to interpret during years of psychotherapy.

Through an unconscious calculation, I became pregnant at the same age my mother had been when she conceived me: thirty-two or so, I thought. (I later computed she was younger than I by five years, and eighteen years my father's junior when I was born.) Our child would have arrived in late June, coinciding with my birthday.

For a day or more after the news, I was in the grips of a mystifying joy, suddenly sharing with all my gender what Plato defined as the lowest level of creativity. Careless with birth control for a decade or more, sometimes trusting in Vatican Roulette, the rhythm method, I believed myself barren. I was now with child, as the quaint phrase put it, feeling like a sailing ship with a freight of riches in its hold. My headiness was destined to go aground; neither of us was prepared for parenthood, and Saul, a writer then with modest prospects, was at an emotional as well as a financial arm's length from marriage.

In that time before its legalization, clandestine abortion was the rule. "I have not been feeling well for six weeks, and must make an appointment as soon as possible," I wrote to a doctor recommended by a friend of a friend. I had earlier phoned from pay booths and waited in parking lots for connections that never showed. At last, I received an answer from Dr. Spencer, at the time the Dr. DeBakey of abortionists located in Ashland, Pennsylvania.

Saul honorably drove me on Thanksgiving week to a grim mining town three hours from New York City. We split the cost of the procedure. But angry and remorseful, I turned for solace to Phil, who unexpectedly proposed. Perhaps the knowledge that I was fertile provoked his matrimonial longings. Spending little time analyzing his motives, I instead chose to immerse myself in the tumult of planning. Sunny would be my maid of honor. I must select a dress, shoes, compose a guest list, mail invitations, order flowers. With each day, the chores kept pace with my resolve to bring off the wedding.

I harbored an unformed but inflexible idea that marrying might make amends for my lost pregnancy. Despite Phil's last-minute forebodings and entreaties to cancel the event—which I ascribed to an understandable case of nerves—we married in January on St. Agnes's Eve, during the week of Robert Frost's death.

Colette and Saul at their wedding, 1964

A poem that appeared in the *Nation* brought little comfort during days of desertions and shaky reunions, misery followed by eager lovemaking as Phil shifted his scant belongings to and from our apartments. After untold late-night calls and cabs, after fruitless visits to counselors and therapists, toward the end of the year, by mutual agreement I was served with annulment papers, my husband claiming fraud for my refusing to bear his children. A witness was brought in to swear overhearing a conversation to that effect. Mr. and Mrs. Rosen were legally unknotted.

"I give their marriage less than a year, don't give up," my friend Gerry had earlier consoled Saul, who continued to pine for me. It was also he who alerted Saul the following summer that I would visit

Monhegan Island to heal my battered psyche. We met unexpectedly, or so I thought, on the path to White Head, the island's tallest cliff, and resumed our moonlit walks, but more guardedly than before. "I'm not marriage material," I told Saul, who responded, "Then let's live together." He persisted and I agreed.

Sharing a sublet on East 87th Street, and geared for adversity, we learned that our affinities also included Tom Lehrer records, Feiffer cartoons, and comedic shticks by Mike Nichols and Elaine May—seasoned by Sunday brunches of grape leaves and baba ganoush on Atlantic Avenue in Brooklyn, followed by visits to Manhattan's Frick Gallery or time spent with invertebrates at the American Museum of Natural History.

Despite our usual flurry of doubts, we married in the summer of 1964 in the rabbi's study at Temple Beth Israel. Gerry was our best man, and Sunny, now married to Simon, was once again my maid of honor.

Saul's estranged parents did not speak to each other at the ceremony but were satisfied that their offspring had not strayed from the faith by marrying a shiksa. Before the wedding, I had converted to Reform Judaism after six weeks of instruction at Temple Rodeph Sholom and was proud to add my name to a faith I equated with high IQs and spectacular exploits in the arts and sciences. And although I continued to pray To Whom It May Concern, it was undeniably kosher to print *Colette Nehamah bat Avraham* on the wedding invitations, the second such issued within a year and a half.

Saul and I honeymooned on Monhegan Island, where in a reverie I informed my ghost priest father that I now held a second father to my bosom, the venerable Abraham. "I am *bat Avraham,* the daughter of Abraham." I asked him to bless us from whatever realm in which his spirit lodged. The flowers we had cast overboard from the stern of the *Balmy Days* had been as resolute as before; Saul and I sailed from the island into Port Clyde and embarked for home.

More deception followed a year later in my passion to learn about my father, his family, and their history. Again posing as a scholar, I wrote to my Aunt Elizabeth, whose California address was divulged by her lawyer cousin. Would she supply details for a monograph I proposed writing about the monsignor? Her positive response, delayed by a trip around the world, was cordial and self-contained.

In an exchange of letters I inflated my project from a monograph to a biography, in the hope of extending our contact and gleaning more information. Her replies were flushed with pride at her older brother's accomplishments; she spoke of his illustrious career and death in Paris, struck down by a heart attack at age forty-eight.

Other letters praised their mother as a strong-minded woman of Irish stock from County Cork, the lone Celt in a Gallic American family proud of its history as Californian pioneers. I learned my grandmother had visited Paris for her son's ordination as monsignor during my birth year, and that she outlived him by more than three decades.

The monsignor's paternal great-grandfather, an adventurer from Bordeaux, had fought with Emperor Maximillian in Mexico, but escaped the consequent disasters and struck out for California at rumors of gold. She glowingly mentioned her nephew, a Jesuit novitiate enrolled nearby at Saint Joseph's College. The last born and only surviving member in a family of five college graduates, Elizabeth described her father as a successful hatter and haberdasher whose business was located in the Palace Hotel around the turn of the century. He died before his sixtieth birthday, as had the monsignor's two younger brothers. Heart disease felled the male line.

She idealized what she believed were my father's saintliness and probity, his modest posthumous fame, and even suggested we might meet when she visited New York friends or boarded ship for a European trip. Revealing my origins would be a cruel shock to an aging lady, or so it seemed, a cause célèbre within a conservative Catholic family that would hardly countenance a priest's bastard.

From Aunt Elizabeth I received my only photograph of the monsignor, taken some months before his death: a fringe of white at his temples, hair receding along a broad forehead, lower lip slightly clenched as if holding his appetites in check, clothed in a clerical collar and cassock, and appearing older than his years. I was surely his daughter. Our resemblance was unmistakable, evident in the full mouth and squarish chin. Hovering over the picture, I brushed his lips with mine—so like his—imagining my kiss might somehow bring my erudite and sensual father back to life.

Collecting papers, perusing biographies of learned Catholic men, I earnestly tried easing my guilt by turning subterfuge into fact and even attempted to compose my father's biography, but lost heart after drafting a first chapter. And I had neither the scholarly temperament nor the training to research his field of medieval history. Pleading ill health, I forwarded my excuses and ended the correspondence with Aunt Elizabeth, my father's youngest sister, in 1966.

I had taught English to people who were illiterate in Operation Second Chance, a federal antipoverty program whose intimacies introduced me to the foment of my students' family lives, and caused me to mull further on the notion of family. As a secular Jew, Saul remained loosely engaged with, but spiritually disconnected from, most of his kin. Our circle of like-minded friends constituted a sort of extended family, a valued and dependable clan. But I ceaselessly yearned for what some of my friends were attempting to escape: a bond with blood relations. Family. How might I reclaim mine?

My mother's earlier comment on the news of my second marriage had been cool and vaguely critical: "Saul, I note, is not a Christian name." I had fruitlessly asked permission to visit her in England, where over the years she had taught Latin in a boys' school, translated *The Life of Mohammed* into French, the Latin Bible into English, and assisted sundry professors explicate eleventh- to thirteenth-century manuscripts.

More humbly, she also undertook housework for academic families, cleaned after their infants, cared for stroke victims, worked as a nurse's assistant in a mental hospital—moving from job to job while waiting for appearances by her aged historian, who was as tall as Charles de Gaulle, she once wrote. I wondered how a man of such impressive dimensions could remain so illusive.

Saul, 1975

"The time is not right. Maybe we can meet one day in Paris in a place far from the apartment of my sister," she replied when I pressed her again for a reunion.

Rereading dispatches sent over the years, I sensed her singularity. My mother, the stoical, principled, and self-abnegating soul, seemingly without a shred of vanity, unconcerned with the sensuous and voluptuous. My mother, scholarly, precise, joyless, dutiful, her letters to me were only in response to mine. I saw her martyred in a narrow life of few comforts, yet buoyed and assuaged by faith in

God's divine will, the power of prayer, and the promise of the hereafter. Studying the straight line of her methodical penmanship, her *t*s with short crosses, her *i*s dotted low near the letter's stem, I presumed her an independent spirit, pulsing faintly but steadfastly in her messages now and then poignantly signed "With Love."

In the late 1970s, now in her seventies, Marthe returned to her sister's apartment in Paris, a city she detested for its hubbub and smoke, taxi horns, and crowds. Irregular employment and the frailties of age had forced her to capitulate. Although it was a bitter move that compromised her cherished autonomy, I knew she would fare better with Jeanne, who had retired from government service and still pursued a life of intellectual pleasures and travel.

Once settled, my mother wrote that Jeanne had urged her to apply for social security, but she objected because she thought that working only fitfully in her native France did not entitle her to such assistance, and she was reluctant to answer personal questions. However docile she might appear, I gathered Marthe would not budge from resolute decisions, whatever they might be. I would never know if she was hiding something, and I respected her secretive ways and skills.

At one point in our correspondence, feeling the pressure of time, I pleaded with her to reveal me to Jeanne. "We are mature women with more than lineage to share," I wrote, "and your sister should be pleased to know she has a niece, someone educated and French-speaking." Months later, Marthe replied in a firm, even indignant tone: "How can you know the torment my sister might give me if she knew this secret? How can you know what I might suffer?"

Of course, I could not know. I could never enter into the nuances and intricacies of their relationship, nor understand the pattern of their long-held grievances. Not wishing to inflict pain, I let the matter rest and would wait for the death of one or the other. If it were Jeanne, there would be no impediment to visiting my mother; if it were Marthe, I would be free to announce myself to my aunt.

The Dulong family house in Nérac, 1986

Approaching their eighth decade, the women retired to Nérac, their childhood home in the southwest of France. They lived in the spacious, blue-shuttered house I had seen in my early twenties as a young woman searching for family. They settled into the book-filled rooms whose objects I had poked and prodded, squinting at family photographs and paintings.

They would stand in the gallery that faced the river Baise, a tributary of the Garonne, and merge their footsteps with the shadow of mine on the spot where I blinked back tears. Marthe's daughter, Colette, in her grandparents' house.

Likely, the women were also persuaded by the congenial climate and the slow, agreeable pace of southern life. Custodians supported by a family trust would permanently maintain the garden and upkeep of the property, and their offspring would run small errands in town. The family and the country my mother had forsaken in youth would provide for her old age.

Although much of her leisure was spent communing with medieval history books and reviews, my mother admitted to enjoying her subscription to the *National Geographic,* gifted to her in perpetuity by unnamed friends and scholars. Finding few incentives to leave the house, she became something of a recluse, while effervescent and well-connected Jeanne commuted to Paris, entertained family and friends, stayed active, and annually booked whirlwind tours to exotic places.

"She does not care what worry she gives me," my mother complained when Jeanne at eighty-four flew off to Borneo with companions. Jeanne suffered a stroke in 1983, which robbed her of speech and the full use of her right side. She was tended by Marthe, but the exertion of feeding, lifting, and bathing an invalid sister eventually proved too great.

Ranting and confused, Jeanne spent her last days tied to a wheelchair in a nearby nursing home. With a ferocity born of despair, she once broke loose of the straps and was found roaming the streets of her native town. Marthe wrote that she visited as often as possible, and I tried to envision the pain of those last meetings between the sisters: one mute, a nonbeliever and unresigned to dying, the other righteous in her immortal link to God and Christ.

After sending my condolences, I suggested to Marthe that the barrier to our meeting had been removed with Jeanne's death. Might I and my husband visit her in Nérac? Six months of anxious silence followed. Had she decided to end all contact with me? Did her sister's death liberate her in some inexplicable way from obligations to answer letters? I felt panicky, aware that no one remained to send word of my mother's death. I called the mayor's office in Nérac to make certain she was alive.

I was assured that my mother had not expired. Only ankylose, a stiffening disease of the joints, and hypertension, had brought about her late response. Our correspondence arced in slow motion, the trajectory of my letters, floating plumes, her answers shreds of silk from a torn parachute making its way in a season or two across the Atlantic, languorously dangling over the city before drifting into the proper zip code and the postman's bag.

I tended to forget she was in her eighties, a weathered snail making her way from the bed and down the hall to the commode, across to the kitchen, perhaps for a cup of cambric tea, sweet and weak, and to the salon, where bookshelves invited her to an afternoon of reading histories, articles, genealogies, dictionaries, gazetteers, and Baedekers.

I had feared the worst as I am inclined to do; she was taken by a wretched stroke like Jeanne, or by a heart attack. But, no. She wrote that none in her immediate family was prone to heart disease. What of my proposed trip to Nérac? She ignored it, let the thought of it ride like a bit of debris on the waves. Perhaps she had grown forgetful, and it was for me and Saul to take the initiative.

We flew to Paris, where I mailed a postcard announcing our arrival at such and such a time in Nérac. I did not include the return address of our hotel, reasoning she could not turn us away if we were to appear on her steps. We imagined catching sight of her standing behind the window, motioning us inside, her face a beacon guiding us to the door. I would see her again after a thirty-one year absence.

Seated in a brown wing chair, she was radiant, her topknot of thin white hair glistening in the warm light of a Gascon spring, tawny cheeks unlined, her body now gaunt under a loose, dark blue robe raveled at the sleeves. She did not directly meet my eyes, but Saul assured me later that during our three-hour visit she glanced at me whenever my eyes wandered.

"These are my American friends." How cool and self-possessed she looked when nodding to the gardener and his wife. Jehovah's Witnesses, they rented rooms in exchange for house and garden work. The hearty Mediterranean pair conversed in the rolling accent of the South and made their exits, the woman carrying away the remainder of my mother's lunch of puréed carrots and peas.

"I eat very little, my digestion is poor." She turned her head to the side; wide gold eyes and slender lips betrayed no emotion as she posed tourist questions: "Have you seen the palace, and the museum?" The region is filled with interesting ruins. How long is your holiday?" Her Oxonian English seemed at odds with the sigh of wind-blown palm leaves on the red tile roof. As she spoke, I noticed her flashing gold tooth had vanished, that large, shiny front tooth I remembered disliking as a child when she visited me at the institute. I commented on its disappearance.

"My dentist removed it—what a thing to remember." Did I detect a note of reproach in her voice? Poised, her head tilted back on the chair, she seemed remote from the often timid and fearful woman who had corresponded with me for all these years.

Intrigued at meeting his mother-in-law, Saul was his usual agreeable self, engaging her at one time in talk of the Vichy Government and World War II. "Marthe," he commented, "almost all of my mother's family died in the Holocaust." She acknowledged the revelation with widening eyes and pinched lips, but said nothing.

What was she thinking? "It would be better if Colette and Saul practiced the Catholic faith," or, "Tomorrow I will wake from this dream of my daughter come with her husband to Nérac." Could she have actually accepted as truth the fiction of me as an acquaintance from America here for a late morning chat?

My mouth was parched in the heat of the room; Marthe had offered us no refreshments. Had she, like many old people, begun losing sensations of thirst? I hesitated to embarrass her by asking for a drink and retreated to the bathroom where I splashed water from the faucet into my mouth. My face reflected in the streaked mirror peered back quizzically.

"What do you want? A reconciliation, an embrace?" Neither was possible in this theater of denial. I pulled at the tiny folds of loosening skin around my eyes. At fifty-two, I was older than my mother when in Oxford she pressed her back to mine while comparing our heights—long ago in her beloved England, a country of muted blues and grays, so unlike this red and yellow province of roses and saturated light.

"Next year Halley's Comet returns." A lull in our chatter found Saul injecting a new subject. She warmed instantly to the memory of the comet's immense glow and how she, a seven year old, tugged at her father's arm a decade after the century's turn, beside the river whose navigable waters were deep enough to ship barges of produce to townspeople gathered on the quays.

Watching her brighten as she spoke of the past, I transformed her into a romantic young woman, naked, pink-tipped, full breasts lolling from side to side as she waded into the river. In a shadowy cove, her compact body swam lazily, the wing of one arm raised, and then the other pulling her to the far shore, where my father scribbled notes on the margins of a manuscript. He hummed when he combed her wet hair. She closed her eyes to the glare of the sun. He kissed her shoulders, neck, arms.

Before I shook Marthe's small, limp hand and bid her good-bye, Saul and I snapped pictures of her on the gallery. She obeyed my directions. "A smile. Good. A little wider. Would you move to the right, left? You have a radiant smile. Yes, that's it."

Again I imagined her announcing me to her family, and how she might say, "Yes, I have a daughter. I want you to meet my brave Colette, who lives in the United States." She would drape her arm over my shoulders, her face flush with elation. My mother in the land of my invention.

The next day, a hard rain fell at the grave site in Espiens where my family of blood strangers reposed. I read Jeanne's freshly engraved dates of birth and death on the same tombstone as her mother, Marie. I was her only grandchild. She never guessed her younger daughter's anguish or fathomed her silences. Marie was laid next to my grandfather, the affable professor, and alongside him, his parents and their parents in a long line of Gascon men and women, all journeying with the pull of the earth in its sweep around the sun.

The second meeting with my mother would take place two years later during my 1986 Guggenheim year, when again I asked if we might see her. "If you are in the region, by all means stop by," she wrote while complimenting me on my award. She also spoke of increasing weakness in her legs and of an unnamed cousin from Paris who looked in on her every few months and was now present.

She praised another cousin from her mother's side, Paul, for his attentiveness. An economist in Bordeaux, he began to manage her affairs, arranging to pay taxes and to purchase a large television. She mentioned watching *Dynasty* at day's end, judging it "vulgar but amusing theater."

Fitful showers and scattered clouds trailed us as we drove the winding country roads to Nérac, but when we arrived the sun broke through the overcast, throwing bright light on narrow stone streets that circled the town. Just as Saul suggested we took a wrong turn, we were at her riverfront address, 1 rue Sederie. We had found our way again, stumbled onto it.

The house appeared shabbier, the wooden shutters a paler blue than I recollected, although the garden tended by her tenants was as luxuriant in calla lilies, roses, foxglove, and wisteria as it had been two springs ago. It was noon, the time of expected arrival I'd announced in a picture postcard of Notre Dame once again mailed to her from Paris. Noon, because I recalled she took her lunch at eleven and would by that time have finished her vegetables and tea.

I glanced up at the second-story window, which framed emptiness. At the last visit, Marthe leaned from it and beckoned us up the flight of stairs to her rooms. We now walked to the door, knocked, called out our names and were met by a tall, elderly man with a benign face and manner who introduced himself as Maurice, her cousin from Paris.

"You must be the American friends." He shook our hands and led us up the stairs. When I saw no one on the top landing, I feared he would tell us Marthe had died in her sleep. A stroke or a heart attack. Or that she had been hospitalized or carted off to a nursing home, such as they were in the venerable town of her birth.

My postcard had read, "Chère Marthe, we will be in the southwest of France next week and will come to call on you Wednesday noon. Paris is as beautiful as I remember, and we are taking in the usual tourist sights: the Eiffel Tower, the Louvre, Centre Pompidou, etc. Love, Colette and Saul."

Maurice whispered, *"Elle est fatiguée,"* and guided us into a spacious room, the salon, in which she appeared immensely frail, propped up in bed by huge white pillows; rose, maroon, and tan blankets in disorder; packets of medication scattered on a side table; and a white sanitary pot a step away. It would not be feasible to give her a rehearsed message asking her to divulge the news of my existence, to assure her the family would likely accept the announcement with sympathy.

She was limp as a cloth doll, her mouth crimped in an oval face now grown pale as that of an ivory figurine. She peered out through a tangle of heavy bedclothes as if it were midwinter instead of a fine mid-spring day.

Her knitted coverlets swirled and twined like a dessert of strawberry mousse, dark syrup, and crème anglaise. I had last seen her eating little whipped puffs of strained vegetables out of small porcelain bowls, this old woman who had hidden our secret as if it were a rare family recipe in a locked chest kept under the stairs. She pointed to a wheeled walker standing in the corner of the room, and Maurice explained she had suffered a badly bruised hip and arm during a recent fall.

She described her injury to us, where she fell, how she slipped and the nasty weakness in her legs. Her English had begun to falter and sometimes halted at the beginning of sentences, as if she were reluctant to make the dive into the abyss of half-remembered words. The bed now held her cargo of dreams, the hours of her old age in the house she was brought to when she was a baby; Jeanne was then five. Marthe had not left the house in two years.

"Everything I need is here," she insisted, "my books, magazines, papers, and look, a new television set. What idiotic things one sees there. Sometimes I sit on the porch to watch the river . . ."

Our words flew over her diminishing body, interrupted from time to time by her random questions: "What day is it? How long since my accident? When did you write?" She looked at me indifferently. I might have been a casual visitor come to idle away part of the afternoon.

"Entertaining guests is tiresome, but one must bear up and show what one is made of." Was she thinking that? She appeared self-contained and disoriented, both at once.

When Saul and I took a break from the vigil, Maurice proved a witty and informative guide to the house and garden, pointing out the tall palm tree planted the year he was born, showing us roses my grandfather had pruned, the hand-carved buffet that her mother had brought as part of her dowry, her cream-colored linen sheets, the family initials scrolled on the hems. With much enthusiasm, he described the fine points of a priceless chest left by an old priest, a curé, during the Revolution. We speculated whether he survived the guillotine.

When we resumed our places around the bed, I noticed Marthe had applied lipstick, a gash of dark pink at her mouth. I was startled by this gesture—my modest and pious mother in makeup—and supposed she chose to assume the appearance of a hostess receiving guests, even while discommoded. Perhaps TV had inspired her to reconsider her looks. Prior to the visit, I had certainly considered my own image and chose an optimistic pink linen suit rather than the funereal black I had worn years earlier.

She clasped my hand mechanically, offered a wan smile, anchored me for a moment with her yellow-brown eyes and asked the same incurious questions of two years ago. "Where will your holidays take you? Have you seen the Chateau of Henri de Navarre? Have you walked along the Garonne, seen the ruins in the province?"

We learned that Maurice, who spoke no English, was a retired professor of Latin and Greek, summoned from Paris to attend his ailing first cousin. We discussed the price of petrol here and in the United States, addressed the cost of car rentals in Bordeaux and Marseilles, the disaster at Chernobyl, terrorist attacks in airports, Hollywood film stars of the 1930s and 1940s—his favorites: Humphrey Bogart, Gary Cooper, Madeleine Carroll. And we talked further about student apathy and the problems of teaching in our separate countries.

In the coat and tie he had troubled to put on for our visit, Maurice struck me as a gentleman of the old school. He served us a pleasant wine of the region and seemed pleased to entertain us with family anecdotes.

"My son, Jean-Jacques is a lawyer," he attested with pride. We learned that Paul, the appointed guardian of the family estate, was associated with the city of Bordeaux's legislature, but I did not grasp every French word. The effortful hour moved forward. Sitting in the commodious room with its inlaid wood ceiling and beige wallpaper, translating French into English for Saul and into French for Maurice, I had little chance for reverie; nonetheless, I fixed my gaze on my mother, the delicate star in our constellation of talk.

Filtered through the occasional lapses in our conversation were recollections of Marthe's earlier letters, the rare confessions she offered, I so hungry for facts. I learned that my father, in civilian clothes, came to see me on one occasion when I was a infant, held me for a time, but I had cried. She, too, had visited me when I was a toddler, she had written, and claimed being "influenced" by him, which

I interpreted as being seduced, but could not be sure. Perhaps it meant he had prevailed upon her to give up her child.

Motioning to the half-circle we formed at bedside, I observed, "It's like the Société Précieuse of the eighteenth century. One receives guests while in bed to speak of philosophy, love, poetry and share court gossip." I was prattling, trying to make a good impression. He nodded and responded with remarks I interpreted for Saul while Marthe relinquished her fragile hold on the hours.

I saw her drift away. The withered stretch of day slumped toward midafternoon. Doors closed as Marthe's indisposition and age formed a shield I could not pierce. My proud and willful mother, an intellectual perfectionist, appeared, without knowing it, to have won a reprieve from the need to break our silence.

"Go with God or whatever you believe in." Were those her thoughts following us down the steps and into the garden my grandparents planted just a few years into the new and bright twentieth century? Episodes, large and small, are framed in God's will, she would say, holding firmly to her faith as I to my doubts.

Birth and alienation are to be endured. We are part of a blueprint, a celestial master plan; this was her credo. Whatever her belief, I was an ally in her strategy of denial, an accomplice, an actress in this melodrama that allowed her to pretend I was not who I am, her exiled daughter.

From a vase on her night table, Marthe handed me a rose before we left. It wilted during the long, hot drive to our distant hotel.

One of my mother's last letters to me reads:

August 31, 1986

Dear Colette,

I am late in answering you, but my health is not good. I can recover slowly with the help of God. I do not share your opinion about a religion that needs celibacy in its priesthood. It is a religion to which I have thoroughly adhered.

God does not want our happiness in this world, and Christ did not give us that example. Your father asked me to give him companionship so that he would have the strength to renounce the venal women he received regularly.

He realized it would lead to madness, as he could not renounce his early vows, and was grateful to me in the last period of his life to have saved him from suicide which he contemplated. Thanks to me, he died in peace in the bosom of the Catholic church, bringing no shame to his family.

As I wrote you once, you were to be adopted by Mrs. Inez L., who was satisfactory in every way, but someone told her or saw in person that you very much resembled your father, which was true, and she thought that as people knew she was a friend of your father, they would quickly guess where you came from.

She decided at the last minute not to take you, and since the American family wanted a child, it seemed a good solution.

I cannot make myself explain to my cousin, Maurice, who you really are. It would bring a lot of worry to him. I have already told you the fact of your birth, and those circumstances were entirely independent of my will.

I am trying to read your book of poems, *Eight Minutes from the Sun,* but I must admit I do not understand very much of it. I notice at the end of the book you invoke St. Francis. I wish it were true.

16

Correspondence with my mother thinned over the passing years. She alluded to insufficient postage, to difficulty transporting letters to the post office, to her increasingly weak legs.

"I am like a goose with a walking stick," she wrote with rare humor. Her once firm penmanship wobbled and slanted downward, her English stumbled and reeled.

Meanwhile, twenty-seven years after corresponding with my Aunt Elizabeth, I wrote to various members of my father's family listed in the San Francisco area phone books.

> July 1991
>
> It has taken me many years to summon up the courage to send this letter to you, for I am the daughter of the late Monsignor L. Of course, a brief history is called for.
>
> Twenty-five years ago, through the thoughtfulness of your family attorney, whose name was provided by the office of the

Archdiocese of San Francisco, I approached Elizabeth D., my father's youngest sister, with plans for writing a paper on the scholarly contributions of the monsignor. While that was a stratagem for gaining information about him, it seemed at the time the only discreet way to make innocent contact with my paternal family.

By putting together bits of revelatory facts furnished by the monsignor's American lawyer and ex-student (who kept his promise not to reveal the secret of his identity), I was eventually able to uncover my father's name.

In a series of letters to me, Elizabeth D. was gracious and generous with her help, and provided me with the only photograph I have of my father, taken shortly before his death in November of 1934. At some point in our exchange of letters, I realized that divulging my true relationship to her and the monsignor, who she greatly admired, might deeply shock and disillusion her. As you might understand, this reluctance to give pain, coupled with my own fear of being rejected by her, discouraged me from corresponding further.

I am fitfully in contact with my mother, now eighty-eight, bedridden and living in her ancestral home in France. Never married and fearing scandal, she continues to conceal the secret of my birth from her family. I first located her in Oxford, England, in 1953, two years after I was told of her existence by Father L.'s lawyer, who helped me obtain American citizenship.

As a young woman, a medievalist earning an advanced degree, my mother met Father L. at the École des Chartes in Paris, where they became colleagues and friends. With his approval, immediately after I was born, she placed me with the Catholic Sisters in the Belgian orphanage where I spent my early childhood.

It appears the monsignor wanted me to become an American, for he had covertly arranged and paid for my voyage to this country. It was the monsignor's hope that I might be adopted by a former student of his, perhaps at the San Francisco College for Women, which he was instrumental in founding, an Inez Cliff-Lundeborg, who then lived in California. But it was not to be, for Mrs. Lundeborg, either when she saw me in person or looked at my photograph, believed my resemblance to my father would compromise her.

For that reason, soon after my arrival, I was placed elsewhere, with a family in Long Island, New York, an unhappy choice, as it turned out, for it was an alcoholic household in the throes of decline. Despite early setbacks and discouragements, I managed to work my way through college and received a B.A. with English Honors in 1961. Since then I have gone on to distinguish myself as a teacher and to earn a national reputation as an award-winning poet.

I currently teach poetry at Columbia University and have been married to Saul Stadtmauer, a freelance business writer, for twenty-seven years. We have no children. I am enclosing a curricula vitae profiling my career and photographs of me taken at age eight and recently.

You may wonder what it is I ask of you. Certainly, it would mean a great deal to me if you were to share photographs of the family, especially those of the monsignor's generation, as well as pictures of my father's parents and grandparents.

Marthe in her early thirties

> Most important, and another reason I am writing this letter, is my need to know something of the family medical history, life spans, serious diseases, disabilities, and the like, whose inheritance could affect my own health and future.
>
> As you can imagine, I am eager for your response and for those of others in the family to whom I am also sending an identical request.

No replies were received, and I suspect the family's lawyer advised them there was nothing to lose by ignoring my inquiry.

I was also in contact with Maurice, whose elegantly phrased letters apprised me of his frequent visits to Nérac to tend to my ailing mother. In the late winter of 1991, he reported her death, which he assured me was peaceful. She would be buried in the family plot at Espiens, with its dazzling view of the Pyrenees. Being at long last relieved of my vow of silence, I composed this letter in French, announcing myself to Maurice and my family:

> April 29, 1992
>
> Dear Maurice,
>
> I thank you for your kind letter of last January, which told of the sad news of the death of your cousin, Marthe. As you say, at eighty-nine she was well on in years and I am consoled by knowing that her end was neither solitary nor painful. I am also content that Marthe reposes at the cemetery in the little village of Espiens, so close to Nérac. I visited it in 1986 with Saul, and was impressed by its beauty and calm.
>
> Surely you have reasons to believe that I am very moved by the death of Marthe. From time to time, were you perhaps curious about my earlier visits to Nérac, and my fidelity in sending postcards and letters to Marthe several times a year? Between

> Marthe and me, it was not a question, as you may have believed, of a distant friendship between Mademoiselle Dulong and the daughter of American professors. I hope you will not be too startled to know that I am the daughter of Marthe, Colette Inez, born in Brussels and placed just after my birth with Catholic Sisters in a children's home, where I spent my childhood before coming to the United State in 1938.
>
> As you can imagine, Marthe wanted very much to keep the secret of my birth and her friendship with a Catholic monsignor, my American father who died in Paris in 1934 at the age of forty-eight.
>
> In respecting the wishes of Marthe, I promised, when I saw her in Oxford in 1953, to maintain silence on this question until her death. Marthe's older sister, Jeanne, suspected nothing.
>
> Finally, having received your gracious letter, I am now free to tell the truth of my identity. I hope with all my heart that you will accept this news with the intelligent and generous spirit I recognized in you when we met in Nérac almost seven years ago.

Two years and a month after I sent the letter, I arrived at the doorway of his Paris apartment. Maurice insisted that I resembled my mother around eyes: "The right eyebrow." He urged his older brother, Marcel, to share that opinion. "Well, perhaps." While less convinced, he studied my face with interest. "But she is a good woman," he affirmed. I was pleased at this welcome, which finally admitted me, undisguised, into my mother's family.

I entered his third floor quarters at 4 rue Brochant, a museum of bric-a-brac, a floor-through crammed with china, statues, books, family mementoes, snapshots, tapestries, and antiques. Mirrors, elegant and cheap, large and small, adorned every room, and I imagined my mother as a young woman arranging her soft hair before the gold framed mirror in the salon. Maurice reported that she often came to his apartment for lunch or dinner while staying in Paris.

Living here periodically since 1938, Maurice identified pictures of his mother and his son Jean-Jacques, but it was the spirit of his late wife, Liliane, that haunted the space. Photographs of her were everywhere: her level, gray, intelligent gaze, her neck-length hair later shaved to pluck out a malignancy in her brain.

The brothers were animated and intrigued by my story, a chronicle beginning with Marthe and my father's meeting near the Sorbonne on the other side of the Seine, where I was conceived. At the table, we probed the mystery of Marthe, her motivations and secrets. Maurice, who had assumed he knew her well, exclaimed, "But what a pleasant surprise to uncover your existence, our cousin, Colette."

"We thought Marthe was a virgin," Marcel laughed, "but she must have suffered when she gave you away. It goes against nature to abandon one's child." At eighty-three, he was pink-cheeked with a moderately sized aquiline nose, quite unlike Maurice's long, thin nose, which cast a shadow on his upper lip, or my mother's nose, which curved bulbously at the tip. Long noses were distinguishing traits among the Dulongs. My own shorter, slightly upturned nose likely came from my father's side of the family.

I had not slept on the night flight from New York to Paris, and my heart raced when I was ushered into a small, crowded "guest" room next to the kitchen. On the wall above my bed were paintings by André Dulong, the oldest among four brothers, a successful artist deceased for fifteen years. On the opposite wall hung an autographed photo of Albert Camus, a childhood friend of Liliane, who grew up with her in Algeria and was best man at her marriage to Maurice.

Camus had been among my literary heroes at college; I doted on his novels and essays, their integrity and passion for justice, their commitment to human decency. Considering myself an existentialist, I took to heart his themes of man's responsibility in a world without meaning. In a taxi, I had heard news of his fatal automobile accident on the night of January 1960, and choked back tears.

We later watched TV at peak volume; the brothers were somewhat hard of hearing. *"Trop fort,"* very loud, I protested, and Maurice turned down the set. Maurice had learned to care for women: for his mother, who survived fourteen years after a massive stroke paralyzed her body and muted her speech; for Liliane, who battled with cancer; and for Marthe during her last years in Nérac. My mother was stoical, deeply reserved and made few demands.

Maurice now daily attended his sister, Suzanne, in a nearby nursing home. Marcel, in turn, would regularly visit his daughter, Michoux, in her Paris apartment. This was a family loyal to its members. A student of the piano with excellent technique, Marcel had hoped to play professionally, but lacking world-class artistry he entered academia. He spoke of Schumann and Schubert, whose piano pieces he favored, and I of Beethoven's sonatas and Chopin's preludes and ballades.

"Your mother was an accomplished pianist who played with great eagerness and charm when young. Jeanne, on the other hand, had no ear, much like Monsieur Maurice here." The brothers teased one another with affection. We were to drive down to Nérac next week.

Maurice's son arrived with a bottle of whiskey, which we sipped over ice. Jean-Jacques, tanned and wide-eyed, appeared younger than his forty-two years and exuded a nervous energy, chain smoked, and paced back and forth as he spoke. He assessed me. Not beautiful, I believed he thought. The men were obsessed with women's looks. "I like her face, but not her body," Jean-Jacques appraised a TV anchor woman. "She has had a face lift," Marcel commented, "maybe two or three." Maurice rolled his eyes and uttered, "O là."

Maurice's large, wide-set eyes resembled those of my mother and grandfather, Alfred. Aunt Jeanne inherited her mother's more deeply set, Mediterranean eyes and slightly hooded lids. "You have something of your mother's eye color." Maurice's glances took me in with sympathy. "Your mother could have brought you home," he speculated later that evening. "Our family is tolerant about such things, although they would have been startled. One would not expect this of Marthe, but you would have been brought up by our family in Nérac." "And Marthe's career, what about that?" I asked. "What better career than that of a mother caring for her child?"

I envisioned being introduced into this household; a story would be concocted. My father was killed in an automobile accident or fell fatally ill during a trip abroad. Cut off from her work as a medievalist, my mother would become more withdrawn. If I were exposed to her notions of Catholicism, conflicts would arise in her parents' largely agnostic household.

Children born out of wedlock were not cosseted in provincial families of that time, and my undemonstrative grandmother would not have cherished me. Likely, I would have seen Jeanne as someone to emulate and embrace—zestful Jeanne, an intellectual and an athlete who climbed mountains, skied, bicycled, and hiked. Maurice suggested that, having exhausted most of her affection on her husband, my grandmother had less in reserve for Jeanne and Marthe, although she *was* a conscientious mother. "Papa first and then us, we got the leftovers." Here he quoted Jeanne's summary of the mother-daughter alliance.

As TV watchers, we were compatible compatriots. My French cousins were as informed about riots in South Central Los Angeles as was I about problems an aging population presented to Western Europe. Among these cultivated men, one spoke comfortably of Inca culture, the Shining Path, rituals of sacrifice, and the pyramids in South America. As an immigration lawyer, Jean-Jacques was reputed to have said to a skilled Peruvian mason for whom he arranged political asylum, "Since your ancestors built pyramids, you can surely make me a tool shed."

Maurice recounted my mother's last days and repeated that she had a peaceful death without summoning a priest when her time came. He regarded such an action as a clue that religion had ceased to matter to her, but I was not persuaded. Her faith in an eternal existence with God and Christ needed no emissary. She believed profoundly in what Maurice and I denied: life everlasting.

It was dusk, and as my cousins watched the Paris-Monaco soccer match on TV, I studied a photograph of a long-haired Jean-Jacques at age sixteen joined in the student revolution of 1968. I thought Jean-Jacques might have also described me as "not bad for a woman of her age." Contrasted with "not beautiful," the opinion of the women on Bayview Avenue, emphasizing the failings of an awkward girl unconnected to them by blood.

A cloudless sky welcomed me as I sat in the dining room whose windows overlooked rue Brochant. The clamor of children's voices from a nearby school momentarily tugged me back to my childhood on rue Chant d'Oiseaux:

I was skipping rope or squatting alongside mud puddles to greet my reflected face and that of Anne's. We squeezed each other's hands and whispered I forget what, committing the venial sin of vanity as we consulted a mirror of rusty water. How divorced I was from those penitential and wistful years.

After lunch, Marcel left for the south and his home in Auxerre, rejoining his wife of fifty-five years. The couple slept apart, watched separate TVs, and dined each night without speaking. What was alienating them? I asked Maurice who shrugged, as if to say, "Who understands such things?" Marcel's two daughters sided with their father, and Maurice remarked, "When in Auxerre, I refuse to stay in the same house with her."

"But why?" I asked. "She is the jealous type, an ice palace. She has no friends; no one likes her." Of his own marriage, Maurice observed, "It was a love story."

The Villa Monceau nursing home was quartered in a house with shuttered windows facing a scraggly garden with tall shade trees, giving the place a countrified air of peacefulness. At eighty-eight, Suzanne was unwrinkled, rosy, and rather beautiful when smiling. Arched black eyebrows rose over astonished dark eyes. But her body was hideously deformed from osteoporosis, a disease that had so crippled her, she could barely hobble from place to place.

Maurice buttoned her clothes, lifted her to bed, fetched what she needed. She protested and sobbed; he was like a father to a querulous child. But when he left for a moment to summon a nurse, Suzanne's manner changed abruptly as she looked at me directly and began a refined conversation. She said my mother was "very intelligent and played Mozart's piano pieces especially well." They had shared a Parisian apartment for a year while my mother attended the Sorbonne. Both were about the same age and had flourished in their musical studies.

I supposed Suzanne accepted my illegitimacy, maybe too self-absorbed in her losses and indignities to care either way. But clearly I *was* embraced as Marthe's daughter without comment. It was, after all, a family with good manners. She later asked about my livelihood. "I am a professor of literature," an inexact answer that would have to serve. "Stay, stay," she pleaded when we prepared for good-byes.

Speaking of Suzanne, Maurice commented with unconcealed pride, "We are not a family of weepers." Better to grieve with tears, I thought, but, experienced in the arts of accommodation, and out of tactfulness, I chose not to challenge him. We toured his collection of books, and I was touched that he and Liliane, like me, were fond of Katherine Mansfield, whose journals and short stories they read in translation. I marveled that we were connected, after all, by literary and scholarly interests.

Now that Marcel had gone, I helped Maurice prepare dinner and set the table. He explained that other than Maxime (the son of his mother's first husband), the brothers were born to Emile Dulong, my grandfather's brother. He told a complicated story of his father's first marriage to Lucienne, who died giving birth to Suzanne, and of a second marriage to Lucienne's sister who, in effect, became her niece's mother. I was fascinated by these complex bloodline family stories from which, as an adopted child, I had been excluded.

Maurice showed me Marthe's translation of medieval lore from Latin into Occitan, the ancient language of Provence. She was also an accomplished Latinist who won prizes for her work at her lycée. It was the Latin my father needed for his Aristotle studies that began their collaboration.

Actually, Marthe was no Francophile, and she disliked things distinctively French: vintage wine, fine foods, fashion, abstract art, and, above all, Paris, which she characterized as "a great garage with no air." She preferred the sangfroid and boiled victuals of English life. Maurice recalled her repeated comment, "The English do not ask foolish questions."

At dinner, I learned more about Marcel, who lost a lung while a POW held by the Germans during World War II. The conversation drifted to their relationship with my grandfather, affectionately called Ton-Ton. With him they shared the masculine joys of hunting, fishing, playing cards and billiards. For a few months every year, the father of daughters could fantasize about being the father of sons.

To Maurice and his brothers, who lived in the industrial north, memories of Nérac and its childhood summers glowed in a sort of paradise. No doubt, it was less heavenly for the women confined to the kitchen and nursery. Even with the help of a maid, Grandmère Marie rarely sat idle and ran a well-ordered household. No matter where they had wandered, the men were obliged to return home in time to wash and dress for the evening meal. Maurice recalled it as an unbroken rule.

I slept late but felt more rested, even as my cold clung, producing a nasal voice. "Is my voice like that of my mother?" I asked Maurice, oddly not recalling precisely how Marthe sounded when we last met in Nérac.

"*Pas du tout,* no, she had a small high voice."

"But that was in her old age."

"She always had a small high voice, childlike and innocent." He imitated her calling sweetly, "Maurice . . . Maurice."

He produced more pictures, one of Jeanne in the German Alps, posed in jodhpurs and boots. Another captured Maurice as a boy, hair cut straight across his forehead in the style of Jeanne D'Arc. The adored youngest son appeared angelic. Marcel at twenty, in handsome profile, looked reflectively out into space; another photograph of his young wife, neatly coiffed and well turned-out, was flooded in the light of a summer afternoon.

A few late-1920s snapshots of my mother in Italy showed her stylishly attired in the close-fitting dresses and hats of the period. In one sultry pose, her hair was becomingly cut into long bangs that accentuated her large eyes. At what point had she begun to look frowzy and disheveled? Was it gradual neglect, a growing contempt for society's emphasis on appearance? Did she live anesthetized, fitfully moving through a fog of despondency and regret?

I immersed myself in family lore, consoled that I was no longer a piece of flotsam, but anchored on a natural shore settled by the Dulongs. It was my good fortune that Maurice served as the family genealogist and guardian of memories, that he maintained a passion for the past.

Maurice had lived in the same apartment with his mother during the war while studying for a doctorate in Latin and Greek, and at about the time Marcel joined the army. While officially in a government post, Jeanne worked covertly for the Maquis, the French underground. After the war, Charles De Gaulle awarded her a Legion of Honor award for heroism. "And where was Marthe?" I asked. "In Oxford. She had it easy compared to us under the Nazi boot."

"How I adored *ma mère,*" Maurice exclaimed. His mother's framed photos in the salon revealed a strong, square face whose eyes gleamed with vitality. Maurice read passages aloud from the works of philosopher Marcus Aurelius, quoted in his mother's "Pensees"—her collection of handwritten meditations on literature, social science, and art, including excerpts from the books she read and her critiques of them. I noticed that her penmanship revealed the same steadfast baseline and wedge-shaped m's and n's as those of Maurice.

We visited Suzanne's vacated apartment in the evening. Dark and small by American standards, it was attractively appointed with antique cabinets, buffets, and marble-topped tables. The knowledge that she would not return saddened me. All was in place: her clothes and her dead husband's; his pipes, tools, the kitchen utensils. "Give them to the poor," I urged Maurice, who nodded politely, confiding he was not one to dispose of family belongings.

Maurice would sell the apartment after Suzanne's death, the proceeds to be shared by the surviving brothers after the government collected almost half in taxes.

When asked about my mother-in-law, I described Saul's elderly mama in her youth as resembling a Merle Oberon of the shtetl, a movie star whose name Maurice instantly recognized. "Ah, Merle Oberon, *elle était belle,*" how beautiful she was. I discovered at our first meeting in Nérac that we had in common a love of vintage movie stars: Greta Garbo, Mary Astor, Carole Lombard. Maurice raised his eyes heavenward at the pleasure of recalling their glittering images on the screen.

We were also inveterate journal keepers, and at my request Maurice read a touching account from his daybook: the magical appearance of a finch perched on Liliane's tombstone on the morning of her burial, perhaps attracted to the floral arrangement. Later, in the Parc Batignolle, a pigeon landed on his shoulder—a first-time occurrence. Still later, a sparrow flew from the courtyard through the window and roosted on his kitchen table. Were they mystical message-bearers from Liliane's newly released spirit? I incorporated these incidents into notes for a poem.

Maurice drove me in his coffee-colored Citroën along the route past the Bois de Bologne, the Renault auto factories, the turn-off for the northern provinces and toward his son's weekend house in Dourdan. A careful driver and estimable guide, he named trees and flowers and related histories of villages that existed before the twenty-five-year-old highway system was built.

A village whose castle and buildings were constructed in the style of the Middle Ages, Dourdan was built of stone intended to last an eternity. Close to town, Jean-Jacques's house was being expanded; two more rooms would be added to its three bedrooms, the studio and modern bathroom.

We gathered in the kitchen to lunch on mackerel and trout sautéed in olive oil with a bit of lemon and fresh herbs—different from

Maurice's butter and flour preparation, but equally delicious. This was a family for whom dining well was a daily given, unlike the institute where I pushed mutton fat to the side of my plate, violating the rule that all plates be swept clean, and at a far remove from the boiled chicken and watery vegetables of later deprivations in Merrick.

17

Our talk continued as we drove back to Paris. At the age of eighty-some years, Marthe had visited a Nérac dentist who declared, "Madame, I salute you. Allow me to compliment you on your teeth." She brushed them carefully after every meal, Maurice recalled. Yet she cared nothing about her looks: cinched her thin hair with a few ancient combs, wore the same moth-eaten, shabby sweater day after day. Marthe had written that she never visited a doctor in all her years in England.

Maurice surprised me by claiming her teeth were too large for her face. He was usually more charitable in his description of family members. In any case, as I wistfully recalled during our few meetings, Marthe rarely smiled. I searched for the glint of Maurice's teeth, which were masked by the shadow of his nose and gray moustache. He confessed that the bridge his dentist constructed was so uncomfortable, even after many fittings, he had ceased wearing it. I encouraged him to be fitted again for new dentures. It is on my mind, he assured me.

Cousin Maurice in Nérac, 1994

I packed for the south, and looked forward to discovering villages named Boupat, St. Pé, Poudenas and Francescas, the dwelling places of my ancestors.

Arriving again in Nérac, I found a crib in the room I would occupy; the thought of sleeping next to it was unbearable. I was the baby *not* brought home by my parents, the baby parceled out to strangers, the child who shamed her father and mother. My early history went unrecorded; no pictures were taken of me before age seven. And although I was now a grown woman transported to my mother's house, I could not entirely overcome feelings of resentment at having been cast aside. These musings preoccupied me as I appealed to Maurice to remove the crib. He nodded sympathetically and rolled it into his room.

In a closet, I discovered my mother's limp clothes, likely washed countless times: an aged brown and orange check tam-o'-shanter, a roughly knit tan sweater, a shapeless brown plaid bathrobe, gray wool stockings, and thin white socks she probably wore with her one pair of battered felt slippers. Her correspondence, filed in sundry boxes and methodically arranged in proper envelopes, untouched since her death, had fallen into a torpor of unread words. I was their rescuer setting them free from confinement and neglect.

The few toiletries she allowed herself—cotton balls, toothpaste, toothbrush, mouth wash, rubbing alcohol, talcum powder—slept in the medicine cabinet as she had left them.

Later, descending into sleep, I recalled our long drive past fields of colza, safflower, pastures in the rain, past the Loire; Orléans; Tours; and Poitiers, the gateway to the southwest; and on to the outskirts of Bordeaux, which my father's ancestors called home. In memory, I glided past the river Garonne glittering in a light that warmed me as we sped along the southern auto routes.

Nérac in the rain was less charming than I remembered. Ugly new buildings had been added to the town. Factories rose where none had existed, yet the countryside had an air of spaciousness and houses were bordered by gardens filled with irises, calla lilies, and sumptuous roses in spring bloom.

My grandfather's garden in a stony courtyard clustered with yellow and pink tea roses, foxglove, lilac, lilies, and dianthus. But the rain prevented a leisurely discussion of who planted what and when, and which flowers were favored. Now seated in the kitchen, we spoke of my first meeting with Marthe in England, the long years of correspondence. I once more reflected with Maurice that she *did* leave the door ajar when it could easily have been slammed shut.

We tried again to better understand why the sisters did not get along. He guessed Jeanne may have resented her younger sister's more conventional good looks and seen her as a rival for her parents' attention. Jeanne reigned for five years as the only child. And Marthe may have felt overwhelmed by her sister's imposing memory and effortless brilliance. Unlike her sibling, Jeanne seemed to earn high grades without long hours of study. The younger sister could not successfully compete. We examined these motivations like detectives probing a persistent mystery.

I woke refreshed in a town I found noisier than rue Brochant. Sounds of motorcycles, scooters and low-flying aircraft (we were near a military air base) mingled with the whine of power tools. Our downstairs tenant-caretaker, a cabinet maker who worked at home, added his hammering to the racket.

All the same, the river house was large and airy, and I easily made my way through its rooms and corridors, inspected books and professional journals, examined the paintings and drawings on the salon walls. I was struck by a large pencil sketch of a demure Marthe in her early twenties drawn by a German painter, a friend of Jeanne's I was told. Proud of her family house, Jeanne had enjoyed entertaining friends here, some of whom were artists and writers from Paris, whose smoking and agitated talk Marthe likely found tiresome. *Tiresome* and *tired* were words that reoccurred in her letters. "Take it, it's yours." Maurice removed the picture from its frame and wrapped it in protective tissue.

Today we set out to visit my mother's grave. As the day cleared, we could make out the snow-clad Pyrenees to the south. I passed my fingers over her name, freshly incised in stone, satisfied that her last thirteen years in Nérac had passed quietly, that she died peacefully in the town of her birth. As we drove into Nérac, Maurice pointed to a window of a local hospital. "That's where she passed away," he shook his head sorrowfully. When we returned, he recounted a story of Marthe and her cousin Margot visiting the family grave site.

"They will dig a hole for you, too," she reported Margot as saying. Marthe did not reply, but later related the comment to Maurice, observing, "That remark was in very bad taste." I relished such anecdotes that revealed my mother's resentments, that made her seem more flesh and blood.

After leaving the deceased in Espiens, we dined well at the Hostelerie du Henri IV in Poudenas, the birth place of Ambroisine Pesquedoux, Marthe and Jeanne's maternal grandmother. We inspected her now-abandoned country estate at St. Pé near Poudenas. And we visited the old stone church set back in a field not far from the house. Ambroisine was comfortably well off for her day, and educated by a priest who taught her Latin, literature, music, and French history.

According to Maurice, my grandfather Alfred's sale of his large property at the start of World War II was disastrous. "Never sell land at the start of a war, never, never. It will always gain in value afterwards," Maurice contended. The house had fallen into disrepair, but it stood as an impressive reminder of the past, its solid stones unperturbed by change.

Maurice had kept Ambroisine's letters, which were well-composed in a good, clear style; he related these facts with the pride of a consummate professor. In a marriage arranged by the priest, she moved to the more isolated village of Espiens, where she bore two sons: my grandfather and Maurice's father.

Her photograph captured deep lines grooved into a well-modeled, almost startled face. Of a morose disposition, and profoundly reserved, she became increasingly catatonic after her husband's death. Garbed in black, gazing vacantly out the window, she spoke hardly a word and was stricken in old age by a cerebral accident while living in her son's home—the house Maurice and I now shared at the crest of the street above the river bank. Maurice was born in December 1917, the month and year of her death.

I asked whether my mother ever spoke of her grandmother, and he recalled Marthe's horror at the gloominess of Ambroisine, whom she avoided whenever possible. Touched by this evidence, I gathered that Marthe was not entirely a passive Goody Two-shoes. With the sting of sudden insight, I realized that she had not bonded well with any of the major female figures in her family: grandmother, mother, sister.

After dinner we watched purple martins in flight and absorbed the rich, pure notes of the blackbird in our courtyard's sycamore—a *plantaine* in French. The drone of traffic issued from the bridge my mother crossed daily on her way to the École Élémentaire. I later traced her route up the stone staircase to the street and along the short path bordering the river.

I tried entering the thoughts of the well cared for, dutiful child who was my mother, the child who never had to be reminded to practice the piano or to finish her homework, the girl who would head her class in every subject at the lycée in Agen, the same private school Jeanne had attended five years before.

Marcel and André, as well as Suzanne, pictured her as a sweet-natured child with excellent powers of concentration, a girl drawn to music and books. But my mother described her past differently. At my urging, she confided in a January 1966 letter:

> . . . I don't know what to say about myself. I did not have a specially happy girlhood. My father had studied in order to become a professor of literature. He married my mother only because she was richer than he, but she had little brains.
>
> My sister was enterprising and insisted on being sent as a boarder to a lycée at Agen, and then to the University of Paris to study English. Since then she has been a translator of some English novels and a

civil servant in the government (with a good pension).

It was my sister's idea that I enroll at the École des Chartes, where I met whom you know, and helped him with his studies. He had a strong power over me, as he confided in me and I pitied him. Later on I worked either for him or for a research group in which I was paid by him. He received money from several learned societies, but first and foremost, from a government pension paid through the American Legion, as he had some health trouble in 1917–18 in the First World War . . .

On the terrace, Maurice and I idly surveyed the birds and river barges and resumed our study of the family, a topic that wearied my mother but fascinated us. We were partners in a concern for heritage.

"Take what you want," offered Maurice, and I removed some postcards and a tender photograph of Marthe taken at age fifteen. Slender in a wool dress with square wooden buttons, smooth hair combed away from her face, lips parted, she was prettier by far than was I at that age, and less voluptuous. The picture confirmed our resemblance in the arch of our brows, although her eyes were wider and drowsier than mine.

She was not entirely solitary and unconnected. Scholarly acquaintances named Ursule, Edwige, and Edith sent her postcards and Christmas greetings illustrated with Gothic art, portraits of the Virgin Mother and child, and Pietas. Some wrote of meeting again in Oxford or Paris. Professors thanked her for her assistance and apologized about delayed or undeservedly meager payment for researching their medieval subjects of study. She corresponded with several American and Canadian scholars, but mainly with English acquaintances.

My mother was turning the pages of *Words for the Saints of God* and other religious tracts I discovered among her possessions, a dozen such books dated through the early and mid-1930s, while I

Jeanne and Marthe as young girls, 1908–9

was in Belgium kneeling at my prie-dieu and mouthing *"Marie Vierge, Écoutes Nos Prières."* During those mornings the wards rubbed their eyes awake; left their beds; formed a line that wound down a drafty corridor leading to another huge, white tiled bathroom with a long row of porcelain sinks. We rinsed our mouths, washed our faces, and patted them dry with rough cloths. I would touch my scalp and finger my hair for a part, which I arranged with a comb dipped in running water.

It was what the other children and I did year after year at dawn. Girls in one wash room, boys in another. Cold water gushed from the faucets. Gray light or winter dark. A touch of a wall switch lit up the chapel where we sang the *Sanctus,* prayed with bare knees on a cold stone floor for the forgiveness of our sins.

On this gray morning in Nérac I was in the kitchen mulling on my fate as an exiled daughter returned to home. What if, in an astonishing turn of events, my mother had willed me this house? Would Saul and I, as proprietors, have fretted over taxes and repairs to the veranda—would we have entertained American friends at cozy suppers, mulched my grandfather's roses, trimmed the calla lilies for a vase?

As if in an afterthought on arrival, Maurice had explained the rules of succession, the property's line of inheritance. It was registered as a trust whose ownership was conferred to the male line from grandfather to father to grandson. To no surprise, the illegitimate daughter was excluded from this plan. My legacy would be rich stories, memories of Paris and Nérac, and these dreamy hours in Gascony.

All who inhabited our conversations had lived in this province. All had walked these town and river paths on soft mornings and in the brightness of noon. All had watched hoopoes and magpies fly into the scattered woods and hills.

Others beside Ambroisine had died here. I was shown where my grandfather succumbed after a long-neglected prostate infection. In rooms now occupied by the caretaker and his wife, a year later, my grandmother, Marie, expired in her sleep, a familiar pattern among long-married, devoted couples.

This was my fourth trip to Nérac. On my first visit, in 1953, as a woman of twenty-two, I was dizzy with expectations that my mother wanted me and had vainly searched for me all these years. In 1984, I arrived in a rented car with Saul at the wheel and was sick with dread and anxiety. Would she open her door to us, and could I contain my feelings of longing and regret?

We came back two years later when Maurice appeared at the entrance, and I was too absorbed translating French into English to take the pulse of my feelings. But I was determined to let my mother know that I refused to remain obscure, a minuscule glyph in an intricate carving or an addenda in a hidden manuscript. I would announce myself after her death. I sent her this letter soon after our return home.

June 19, 1986

Chère Marthe:

I hope the bruises you suffered in your fall last month are on their way to being healed and that you have begun the exercises on your walker. Strengthening your leg muscles is important to recovery; your cousins Maurice and Paul must all say the same thing. No doubt, your strong faith will help your resolve to get well.

My journey to see you this time was not merely to speak about my travels in France with Saul. I had hoped to speak to you about more personal matters, of what is in my heart and has occupied my reveries and concerns these many years. But since your health was fragile, and Maurice was ignorant of our mother-daughter tie, I felt it inappropriate for me to ask for private time to speak to you.

I take that time now to tell you, first what you already know, that I have for thirty-three years been faithful to your wishes to keep the secret of our relationship intact. You can understand I was afraid to alienate my only living relative, the sole family member who recognizes me, knows that I exist. You.

Certainly, you have become aware of my longings for family acknowledgement, and know that through circumstances of my illegitimate birth, I am an outcast, a stranger to my relatives both in France and in California. As the monsignor's bastard daughter, and even that is a fact I can only prove circumstantially, my father's California family would likely shut their doors to me. I wrote to you about my correspondence with my California aunt twenty years ago, and my reluctance to reveal myself as her niece.

Perhaps the case will not be the same from the point of view of the Dulong family. I am your rightful daughter with proper papers. You know in my desire to shield you from professional embarrassment or humiliation at your sister's hand—situations that no longer require my silence—I have exiled myself, with your consent, from a family whose name I carried in childhood and on my birth certificate.

I don't need to explain how important it is to have the acceptance and respect of one's family, or to be given access to one's past. It is a consolation you must greatly value in your old age.

But to come to the point, this is what I wish: for you to finally let the secret out, to announce my existence to the family. Tell them I have no wish to legally challenge "la succession" [the inheritance], and would be pleased to visit them in Nérac, Paris, or Bordeaux when Saul and I are again in France, or to see them in New York if their travels take them here. You and they have every reason to be proud of my accomplishments as a poet and teacher. Without false modesty, I can say I would bring honor to the Dulong family.

If you still wish to keep your secret, then I hope you will understand that someday at a circumspect time I will feel free to reveal my presence to the Dulongs.

Needless to say, times have changed since you gave birth to me. With today's acceptance of offspring born out of wedlock, I can imagine only compassion for your plight as a young single woman with child in the early 1930s. Surely, the family will be understanding and curious to know your daughter shares their bloodline and professional standing as well.

If it is easier for you, no mention of my father need be made. You might say I went to live in America as a child, and later found you in England where our correspondence began. That story, however meager, would at least be truthful.

Chère Marthe, in the time left to us to make things right, I appeal to your sense of justice and look forward eagerly to your response.

With love, your daughter,
Colette

P.S. If you would choose to give me something your mother gave you, something of sentimental value, I would deeply appreciate it.

Seven years later, I was reconciled to her inactions and began to let go of the indictment. I felt tenderness for her high-mindedness, sympathized with her early rivalry with clever Jeanne, and came almost to accept the resolute passivity that deepened after her affair with the monsignor and my birth.

Maurice called her behavior a sort of passive resistance she practiced for unknown reasons. Again I communed with her pictures, moved that her grace was nourished and protected by the customs of a petit bourgeois life—in the town where she crossed the Pont Vieux on her way to École Élémentaire Pour les Filles, a school whose students still climb the stone steps to the sound of the bell, past the river and down the road.

We waited for the roofer to plaster our leaking roof. Thunder and lightning, and a heavy rain fell on the swollen and muddy Baise. Again, Maurice and I sat in the gallery under heavy clouds moving westward out to sea. We spoke of how Liliane shattered her thigh bone after spreading cancer eroded her femur. She collapsed into Maurice's arms; we agreed that to love well was a worthy feat in our short passage on earth. I savored the intimacy of these moments as we exchanged thoughts or shared poetry. He read Valéry aloud and discussed the poet's philosophic and scientific bent.

When the roofer finally arrived to replace a tile loosened by the storm or by nesting birds, I beamed as Maurice introduced me to him as *ma cousine.* Not *ma cousine Américaine,* but *ma cousine.*

On the trip back, I let Maurice do much of the talking as I posed questions. *"Parle moi de"* such and such, speak to me of the war years; your childhood; your travels; your experiences as a teacher, as father to a son, as a youngest brother.

We spoke in bursts, then fell back into an easy-fitting silence. At last I had adjusted to the dislocations of another country, to a man other than Saul, but with similarly long and well-shaped fingers on the steering wheel. Proud of his smooth, unmarked hands, Maurice modeled them on the table when we stopped at a *ruralarie* for lunch, "Good hands run in the family." I flexed my freckled but shapely fingers in the air.

"Sleep a little," he coaxed me, but I didn't want to miss anything fleeting past the car window.

"I'll sleep when I'm ninety years old."

"O là, what insomnia."

After we'd driven more than five hundred kilometers, warm Gascony sunlight gave way to a cold, slate-colored Parisian sky. I missed the extravagant roses, the ocher-colored river carrying debris from the spring rains. I missed the shabby though convivial air of Nérac, cold suppers on the porch, my tall, airy room with a wide, low bed, feather pillows, and antique yellow blankets.

When asked about the other residents in his apartment building, he spoke of his upstairs neighbor. "She is very Catholic, but belongs to the Catholic Left, which is much more tolerant of others than the Right, with whom Marthe sympathized. During her studies at the École des Chartes, your mother fell in with a group of monarchists, arch conservative and moneyed people of that sort. You know, Jeanne had heard that your father's people were very well off." Maurice drew slowly on his pipe.

I recalled that my father possibly first saw Marthe at that school in 1927 or earlier, when he retained her to research medieval Latin manuscripts. We calculated that she was twenty-four when they met, and he was forty-two. Their affair lasted three or more years and broke off after my birth. It was not clear to either of us just how many years had elapsed from the time of their meeting to her trip across the border into Belgium, where I was born.

I pressed Marthe for information, which she supplied with rare candor in 1966. My last letter mentioned reading an obituary of the monsignor in the *San Francisco Monitor*, a Catholic journal. She replied:

> Do not be deceived by what you read about our mutual friend in accounts made in reviews or newspapers after his death. A dead man's memory is always exalted. If he had volunteered as an army chaplain in the First World War, it was because he could not bear living with his mother who harassed him with reproaches about a tendency to like girls too much.

There was nothing much amiss then, but on his long sojourns in Europe and then with a scholarship, he gave up any fight (struggle) within himself about that sort of thing, and the disequilibrium caused by a double life brought him to deep despair, and the desire to destroy himself.

Of course, he did not confide in me immediately, but asked me to help him "find himself" again and to give him love and support in order to break with mercenary women. I did not want things to go as far as they did. Anyway, as he often said to me during his last illness, it was only my great devotion which saved him from destroying himself or from carrying on with less and less prudence and being found out by his superiors—that before you were born. After that his main worry was to prepare himself for death in a Christian way.

I should not say hard things about a dead person, but I see that you truly want to know. I must add that owing to the anonymous life of a great city like Paris, and that he mostly always wore civilian clothes, I more or less considered him as a mere civilian. Of course, except for brief and hidden moments, I was his assistant and we kept a respectable facade. What he wanted was for me to save him from madness.

Indeed he was grateful to me, warm hearted, unselfish and generous, studious and fond of hard work. So you see there were good things to be said of him. Be sure he died in the religion of his youth and wished you to be Catholic. It is also what I pray for, very often, although things have not turned out that way exactly, there is still time . . .

The time to leave for home had arrived too soon, and yet I was homesick for Saul and my life in New York. At dinner, we again broached the subject of my mother.

"I see her in your eyes," Maurice repeated my resemblance to Marthe, "but your character must belong to the paternal side. Your mother lacked your sense of life, your courage."

Maurice defined himself as somewhat of a *vélleitaire,* a person who wants to, but does not, consummate his or her wishes and ambitions. I believed he needed an ally to urge him to buy a hearing aid, a set of comfortable dentures, a new pair of glasses (his were cracked) and to repair his failed stereo. But the notion of a second marriage filled him with horror. Fate granted him an ideal partner as it did me; there was no proxy for Liliane or for Saul.

On this, my last morning, I woke too early and sipped coffee from a cup imprinted with *Bonjour* in blue letters. Like a child, I ate a soft banana and sliced bread smeared with raspberry jam.

Jean-Jacques was behind the wheel; Maurice and I climbed in.

Good-bye rue Brochant and Parc Batignolle. *Au revoir.* When Jean-Jacques moved to light a cigarette, Maurice again leapt to my aid. *"Il faut pas fumer dans la voiture."* You must not smoke in the car. I did not quite know how to say good-bye to Maurice when we reached the airport, and I swiftly brushed his cheek with a kiss and glimpsed a spark of warmth in his eyes as I squeezed his hands. "I have more to tell you, and you'll be back next year," he ventured. He patted my hand and turned his face away to hide his emotions. "Yes, I'd like that."

Jean-Jacques rolled my suitcase to the *Aerogare* door. I praised his father's charm. "*Ah oui,* but he lives too much in the past." I did not say it was that past whose highlights and shadowy corners I wanted to explore. My French faltered with Jean-Jacques, yet flourished with his father, who corrected my errors only when asked, *"C'est correct, Maurice?"* As the good pedant, he would elaborate on the word's usage and its Greek or Latin derivations.

I left knowing my presence cheered him and buoyed up his flagging spirits. More than just blood relatives, we were like-minded companions tracing the paths of our ancestors, whose mute photographs would now forever be accompanied with an aura of lively stories and anecdotes. My dear cousin, keeper of memories, had proved an excellent guide to the mother country.

18

During the year and a half of correspondence that followed, I learned that my cousin Suzanne died at age eighty-nine in the nursing home where her last years ebbed way. Her apartment had been sold, its belongings parceled out to family members.

A cousin from Bordeaux was alleged to have tricked my mother into signing away Jeanne's inheritance from the sale of her Paris apartment. Through power of attorney, he appropriated most of the proceeds and reportedly absconded to Switzerland.

"Your poor mother would have signed anything," Maurice wrote. I remembered that she had put her name to papers that signed me away to the American family. Had she even hesitated? Had she wondered about this smartly dressed couple and their easily given promises? No, she saw herself in others and placed her trust in their sincerity.

Although prodded by Jean-Jacques and Marcel, Maurice refused to press charges. "I cannot take a member of our family to court, I cannot have him spend one day in jail, even if he is a scoundrel."

Jean-Jacques had wed Béate in an outdoor ceremony in Dourdan in the summer of 1994, and Maurice forwarded photographs of the couple circled by family and friends. A multilingual dress designer employed by a French fashion house, Béate, a native German, had also worked in England, Korea, and Japan. They expected a child in January, and Maurice invited me again to Paris.

Looking more fit than when last I saw him, Maurice was waiting in front of the apartment house, and together we rode the narrow *l'ascenseur* to his floor.

Almost everything remained in its place, the mirrors and books, the hand-carved Louis XIV buffet and ornate cupboards, the paintings and photographs, the spinning wheel, Liliane's tapestries and bric-a-brac, porcelain ducks and small stuffed animals, brass pots and plates with hand-painted country scenes. Albert Camus gazed at me serenely from his photograph in the guest room as if set to reminisce about his childhood in Algiers.

The apartment appeared more cluttered now that some of Suzanne's furnishings were moved in. Maurice showed me her mink, a black fox and leather jacket. We pored over photographs, explored boxes of postcards mailed from European capitals and seaside resorts. Married to a successful businessman and childless, Suzanne had enjoyed well-tailored clothes and deluxe vacations.

Maurice kept to his schedule. At one o'clock we dined on steak, and I laughingly complained that he fed me like a Doberman Pincher. I learned that the next summer he would vacate his rented apartment and move to Jean-Jacques's Dourdan house, an hour from Paris. His son would relocate his law practice to a new apartment purchased near the Arc de Triumph, and would acquire some of the rue Brochant antiques and paintings for his residence. Maurice would hold on to what he valued most, and the rest was to be sold.

"It is more economical, more practical. And Jean-Jacques is right, this place has become a shrine to the past." Even so, I observed it would be a wrenching move. And although much less wrenching for me, I would lose Paris, walks in the neighboring park, a private room presided over by the spirit of Albert Camus. No longer Maurice's only guest, I would in future visits have to share the Dourdan house with a growing family.

I walked through my cousin's domain, a place now as familiar as a jigsaw puzzle I had completed, whose pieces I cherished all the more by knowing they could be reassembled in memory. Tomorrow we would drive to Dourdan. Marcel would join us, but the day and hour we three musketeers were to leave for Gascony had yet to be decided. I spoke briefly on the telephone with Béate, whose fluent English bore only faint German intonations.

Maurice paced about the rooms. "This place is a graveyard of memories. First, my mother, then my wife died here, fifty-six years of accumulated recollections and souvenirs."

We discussed the advantages of leaving. He would now have a country garden and two cats and goldfish to feed. He could save on rent and the monthly garage fees, and reduce the wear and tear of weekly visits. And since the house would be empty weekdays, visited by Jean-Jacques and his family only on weekends, he would have his privacy.

"All the same, I am terrified of losing my independence, of becoming an old dog, half deaf and half blind." I reminded him of the pleasures he would continue to enjoy: soccer matches and detective stories on TV, the daily paper, academic journals, and the traditional satisfactions of preparing classic French cuisine for which he shopped daily with an eye to quality.

"It is always worth paying more for quality," he often advised. I refrained from relating that Saul and I, intermittent dropouts from the school of thrift, were taught opposite lessons. Buy cheap, the cheapest. If the fruit is bruised, cut out the blemishes; if the material is damaged, patch it. Fix it, recycle it, make it usable, buy bargains, make do.

Maurice nodded off, and I slipped out for a stroll in the Parc Batignolle, whose budding shrubs signaled a false spring in winter. Crossing the park bridge, I heard a commotion of ducks, pigeons, and running children, and pictured myself as a well-cared-for child playing hide-and-seek with my cousins. My mother, seated on a bench, would be immersed in a history of *Francois Premier,* whose ordinances she catalogued, or was she rereading a life of *Henri de Navarre,* whose summer palace was erected in the town of her birth? We children reminded her it was supper time. "Your mother would come into a room, find an easy chair, open a book, and three hours later would be in the same position, utterly absorbed in her reading. She was like a statue." Maurice lowered his eyes and assumed a studious pose.

"Did she do sports in school?"

"No, she loathed competition as much as domesticity. Without me during those last days, she would have lived on boiled potatoes." We turned to the subject of my mother's capped front tooth, which I remembered clearly as being gold, the flashing bright metal riveting my attention to her parted lips.

Maurice recalled the tooth as silver. He lifted a table knife and motioned to the blade to make his point. Maybe he unconsciously transmuted her gold into silver to diminish the extremes of her physical and religious self-denial. How could I fail to note it was gold, or forget her pale mouth and the monotony of her pious words when I was a child kneeling beside her, praying in Belgium for God's mercy?

Arriving before dinner, Marcel was flushed with excitement at the prospect of our journey south. "What a beautiful woman!" He gathered my hands in his and grazed my cheek with a light kiss. Next day we would drive an hour to Dourdan, from which our eight hour trip to Nérac would begin early on the following morning.

The house in Dourdan was cheerfully crammed with books, magazines, plants, toys, and furniture in a mix of styles. My small room at the end of the hall offered a comfortable bed, firmer than the cot at rue Brochant. Maurice would wake me at dawn. We waited for Jean-Jacques, who arrived after eight, tanned, even in early winter, looking lean and fit in a blue blazer, shirt and tie that set off his blue-green eyes.

A whiskey cocktail in hand, he spoke over a cordless phone and paced in and out of the rooms, restless, a French panther. We conversed about wine and food, politics, travel, and Béate's year in Birmingham in the English midlands. Languages mingled freely as we lifted our glasses to toast *Salut, Cheers,* and *Prosit.*

Maurice had believed the Allies would lose World War II and chose to study German, which he spoke well enough, while Marcel's German was perfected in prison camp before or around the same time that Béate's parents were born.

As we began our journey, Venus, the morning star, dimly floated through rising clouds. My cousins communicated along the highways in loud voices, not always managing to hear each other clearly. "What did he say?" Marcel shouted from the back seat.

"What did *you* say?" I asked Maurice, not always distinguishing his words over the engine and road noise. A hearing disabled trio headed for Bordeaux and outlying reaches.

I enjoyed Marcel's company. He liked teasing me. We jested. He called me a handsome woman, and I called him a handsome man. He bowed courteously and we exaggerated our gestures like actors in the *Comédie Francaise.*

After passing the Garonne, the Charente, we entered Nérac and settled into a gray evening. The house was cold, and the bath's jury-rigged sprinkler-shower fixture fell apart in my hands. It was not worth bothering about, Maurice remarked. One could take a sponge bath. My portable white-sound machine, whose soothing hum normally helped lull me to sleep, had worked perfectly during my first visit. But now, its American plug no longer engaged the venerable French outlet. Cousin Marcel, my rescuer, offered me a knock-out pill he claimed would either help me sleep or kill me.

"If the latter," I retorted, "don't call a priest." Maurice later foraged in a dresser drawer and removed some of Jeanne's costume jewelry pins and rings. "Here, these are for you. Their value is purely sentimental."

"And this, too." Maurice handed me a bracelet worn by my grandmother—so old the clasp had frozen shut. Without knowing it, Maurice had given me the keepsake I long ago requested from my mother: a souvenir of *her* mother.

I woke to a local public address system broadcasting Christmas shopping bargains in town—blaring its messages outside my window every fifteen minutes, interspersed with insipid music. We were overwhelmed with noise, I complained to a sympathetic Marcel. *"Les emerdeurs sont toujours partout et parmi nous."* Roughly translated: "Jerks are everywhere among us."

I proudly wore Aunt Jeanne's pins on my coat collar and on the pocket of a long-sleeved blouse. Jeanne's spirit pervaded this house; it was she who had modernized the kitchen, brought paintings from Paris, and repaired the gallery.

Heavy rains drenched us in Poudenas as we again dined at the Relais Henri IV. Relishing the last of our wine and warmed by a fire in the hearth, we discussed the religious skepticism of the family and contemplated the origins of Marthe's strong faith. Maurice recalled that she turned to God after contracting typhoid during her last year at school in Agen. A vulnerable seventeen, isolated and dangerously ill, she feared she would succumb. Had there not been a schoolmate or a roommate who died? He speculated she then made a pact with God, promising a life of piety and devotion in exchange for survival.

Outside the town of Sos, I was brought to the rushing stream in which Maurice and Marcel fished for trout and perch when they were boys on summer holiday. They solemnly presented their catch to my grandmother, who would serve the fish that day. They debated the kilometers they walked in the hot sun. Five? Seven? And how many years? Seventy? Seventy-five?

Back in Nérac, the brothers tossed back a few shots of cognac and repaired to the salon to watch soccer on TV. A cold snap visited the region, so for warmth I ran a hot iron over my grandmother's one-hundred-year old linen sheets whose blue embroidered *D*s swirled at the hems. My sleep had been enveloped in the past, and my waking hours in family stories and visits to cemeteries where we paid homage to our ancestors.

"They were all on the list," Marcel sardonically quipped.

It was still cold for the south, but the sun wandered in and out of the clouds, warming the stone streets of Francescas, the home of

Vital, our seventeenth-century forefather. After lunch, our waitress directed us to Ligard, where we hoped to locate a Dulong cousin, the owner of the Chez Dudule bar-restaurant. Marcel explained that "Dudule" was a familiar short form of Dulong.

Chez Dudule, with its rustic atmosphere of a hunting lodge, overlooked a countryside of rolling hills. In a dark bar, we ordered beers and chatted with a handsome, middle-aged Madame Dulong, who informed us that her father-in-law, the previous proprietor, passed away last year.

"He, too, was on the list," Marcel repeated as we drove to the cemetery in Espiens. Maurice reminded me that Jeanne purchased the large tombstone through a sense of loyalty to her family, while Marthe's return home was prompted by financial need and old age. Had she the means, I was convinced, she would have chosen to stay in England for her remaining days.

My French had started to sputter and choke, and I had to force the words with a small kick to get my motor revving. I felt exhausted. I hesitated asking for another of Marcel's knock-out pills; three over three nights seemed excessive.

"You are stronger than I am, you two," I bantered with Maurice and Marcel, leaving them to occupy the hours with talk of grammar, the ablative and vocative tenses in Latin.

After a long trip slowed by weekend and holiday traffic, we returned to Dourdan. Béate, an excellent cook, had prepared a Christmas Eve dinner of quail soaked in Irish whiskey (a waste of good Jamison Scotch, I thought), roasted vegetables, and a smooth Neapolitan cake for dessert.

The brothers discussed hunting and fishing in the days of plentiful game. Jean-Jacques derided the disastrous gun culture of the United States, but noted France's romance with American Westerns, the high-noon and shoot-'em-up films of his childhood.

Tomorrow would be Maurice's birthday. My gifts to him were a camera and my illustrated book of poems, a collector's limited edition, titled *Naming the Moons.* I had also brought a copy for Marcel, but Maurice explained that at this time in Marcel's life he would have zero interest in poetry. And since he had no command of English—or translator, such as Béate, at hand—my gift would be lost on him.

I had just resigned myself to staying one more night when Maurice announced we would return to Paris, after all. I knew my hosts would feel more comfortable lighting up in my absence, and I would be spared their cigarette fumes. It was a nicotine world, one I'd inhabited until quitting the habit in the late 1970s. "Your mother also detested smoke." Maurice discovered another mother-daughter link.

I was back in my calm corner of Maurice's apartment, a bit player in the patchy gray theater of Paris in winter. Unplanned days spread out before me, and I welcomed them. Poking around the apartment, leafing through some of the thousands of books arrayed from ceiling to floor gave me pleasure and a deepened sense of family history. At lunch, Maurice repeated his reluctance to judge Marthe, but he still failed to understand why I was abandoned to the nuns, and in another country. "Why Belgium and not Nérac?"

"My mother didn't want me living in France where her secret might get out, and she would never have brought me to Nérac," I insisted. "It was not in her character to confront clicking tongues and pointing fingers. Nor could she face her own mother's disdain. Her father's warmth and tolerance wouldn't be enough to sustain her. Her sister might have pulled it off: Jeanne who stood up to the Nazis when called in for questioning, Jeanne who rode a horse bareback in Kansas without knowing how to ride."

"Perhaps so." Maurice gave me a smile that flickered under his moustache. I knew I was marking time, a pampered hostage of Paris sometimes wishing for Maurice's serenity and Jeanne's sense of entitlement. Another mild winter morning with the sun nowhere to be seen descended on Paris. Schoolchildren were off on holiday, and even the birds of Parc Batignolle had migrated to warmer provinces.

I learned that Maurice had assisted Jeanne in translating *David Copperfield* into French—with editing, spelling and syntax—although not for her translations of *Moll Flanders, Adam Bede,* and *Oliver Twist,* which he had not even proofread. It was not clear to me whether any of these works were funded privately or by the government.

Jeanne was a *directrice,* a director in the Department of Labor under President de Gaulle, with whom she dined at receptions held in his residence. Had Jeanne been my mother, I mused, she would have kept me in Paris, and showed me off to her friends. "Here's my *bébé,* my little rabbit."

I tried to imagine her as an ebullient parent urging me to take first prize for this and that contest, attending my piano recitals, escorting me to museums, the ballet, the opera. That she might be a domineering and harried working mother also occurred to me, but I preferred to spin out the fantasy of a grandly nurturing Jeanne. But as I walked the long hallway to the front rooms, it occurred to me that I had found a French mother in Maurice; it was not the first time I had made mothers of men.

The next day, up at eight-thirty, Maurice had slipped into a clean shirt; eaten a brioche and coffee; washed yesterday's dishes; and shopped for groceries, toting his carry-all net bag. Another gala lunch followed, garnished with a hearty red wine from the Tarn that eased our talk of poet Paul Verlaine, whose son, also named Maurice, became a Métro conductor in Paris.

I was startled by another family anecdote revealed by Maurice quite by chance. When visiting Paris, my grandfather met my father, the monsignor, to voice his displeasure at knowing Marthe was working long hours for a Catholic priest who offered little pay for scholarly work, without the promise of pension or promotion.

He had not educated his daughter to receive such meager returns and, indeed, had hoped she would assume a university or government post. Of course, he had no cause to suspect anything between them but a professional relationship. Certainly, even his good nature and liberal convictions would have been sorely tested by knowledge of their liaison.

Although I had finally begun to think in French, just days away from my departure, some thoughts hobbled and flopped and my lips pined for the fluent ease of English words. Not that Maurice

Marie and Alfred Dulong in their seventies

complained; on the contrary, he praised my pronunciation and clarity of speech. Mumblers distressed him.

Carrying the chipped blue English dinner plates from Stoke-on-Trent, the heavy cutlery and crystal wine glasses that belonged to Suzanne, I set the table for three.

For our farewell dinner, we would be joined by Domino, a family friend and professional chef who rented a former maid's room on the floor above; he was to keep an eye on the roast chicken and whip up a mayonnaise dressing for the chilled asparagus. We spoke of the move to Dourdan he believed would be healthy for Maurice.

"Maurice has not finished mourning for Liliane; he cannot let her die." Domino confirmed what I had long suspected. I heard more about the money cousin Paul had supposedly appropriated from Marthe from the sale of Jeanne's Croix Nivert apartment, a very large sum in U.S. dollars. He hesitated naming the exact amount.

Not one to deny herself, Jeanne had spent liberally on travel, clothes, friends, good food and wine and left few cash assets in her will. But money from the sale of the upscale apartment would have gone to Marthe, her next of kin. Left to her devices, would Marthe have willed that inheritance to the Church? No, I could not imagine her at the end of her life turning a cold shoulder to gentle Maurice and the family that attended to her in those final years.

This winter morning's cockcrow was a squalling baby somewhere in the intestines of the building. I detected its cry while sitting groggily in the WC down the hall, and less distinctly when returning to my room. Over midmorning coffee, Maurice mentioned a party held here to celebrate Jean-Jacques's birth in 1952; as a parting gift, he presented me with a note written by Albert Camus in tiny script, tendering regrets at missing the affair. How many days before Jean-Jacques's second son, Thomas, would enter the stream of Dulong men?

I left rue Brochant with images of Christmas in the mother country—difficult, tender reflections—poised for the moment as I was in the center of a small and cohesive family, a bona fide clan with all its burdens and consolations.

We took a taxi to the de Gaulle airport. "When you see me next, I'll have a new set of teeth, a hearing aid, and a wig."

He cut a dapper, quintessentially French figure in a gray raincoat and slouched hat. "And a gold earring," I added, "I will visit you again in Dourdan or Nérac."

"I am counting on it," he replied. I glanced back several times and waved. *Au revoir* Maurice.

Wisconsin Studies in Autobiography

William L. Andrews
General Editor

Robert F. Sayre
The Examined Self: Benjamin Franklin, Henry Adams, Henry James

Daniel B. Shea
Spiritual Autobiography in Early America

Lois Mark Stalvey
The Education of a WASP

Margaret Sams
Forbidden Family: A Wartime Memoir of the Philippines, 1941–1945
Edited, with an introduction, by Lynn Z. Bloom

Charlotte Perkins Gilman
The Living of Charlotte Perkins Gilman: An Autobiography
Introduction by Ann J. Lane

Mark Twain
Mark Twain's Own Autobiography: The Chapters from the North American Review
Edited, with an introduction, by Michael Kiskik

Journeys in New Worlds: Early American Women's Narratives
Edited by William L. Andrews

American Autobiography: Retrospect and Prospect
Edited by Paul John Eakin

Caroline Seabury
The Diary of Caroline Seabury, 1854–1863
Edited, with an introduction, by Suzanne L. Bunkers

Marian Anderson
My Lord, What a Morning
Introduction by Nellie Y. McKay

American Women's Autobiography: Fea(s)ts of Memory
Edited, with an introduction, by Margo Culley

Frank Marshall Davis
Livin' the Blues: Memoirs of a Black Journalist and Poet
Edited, with an introduction, by John Edgar Tidwell

Joanne Jacobson
Authority and Alliance in the Letters of Henry Adams

Cornelia Peake McDonald
A Woman's Civil War: A Diary with Reminiscences of the War, from March 1862
Edited, with an introduction, by Minrose C. Gwin

Kamau Brathwaite
The Zea Mexican Diary: 7 Sept. 1926–7 Sept. 1986
Foreword by Sandra Pouchet Paquet

Genaro M. Padilla
My History, Not Yours: The Formation of Mexican American Autobiography

Frances Smith Foster
Witnessing Slavery: The Development of Ante-bellum Slave Narratives

Native American Autobiography: An Anthology
Edited, with an introduction, by Arnold Krupat

American Lives: An Anthology of Autobiographical Writing
Edited, with an introduction, by Robert F. Sayre

Carol Holly
Intensely Family: The Inheritance of Family Shame and the Autobiographies of Henry James

People of the Book: Thirty Scholars Reflect on Their Jewish Identity
Edited by Jeffrey Rubin-Dorsky and Shelley Fisher Fishkin

G. Thomas Couser
Recovering Bodies: Illness, Disability, and Life Writing

José Angel Gutiérrez
The Making of a Chicano Militant: Lessons from Cristal

John Downton Hazlett
My Generation: Collective Autobiography and Identity Politics

William Herrick
Jumping the Line: The Adventures and Misadventures of an American Radical

Women, Autobiography, Theory: A Reader
Edited by Sidonie Smith and Julia Watson

Carson McCullers
Illumination and Night Glare: The Unfinished Autobiography of Carson McCullers
Edited by Carlos L. Dews

Marie Hall Ets
Rosa: The Life of an Italian Immigrant

Yi-Fu Tuan
Who Am I?: An Autobiography of Emotion, Mind, and Spirit

Henry Bibb
The Life and Adventures of Henry Bibb: An American Slave
With a new introduction by Charles J. Heglar

Suzanne L. Bunkers
Diaries of Girls and Women: A Midwestern American Sampler

Jim Lane
The Autobiographical Documentary in America

Sandra Pouchet Paquet
Caribbean Autobiography: Cultural Identity and Self-Representation

Mark O'Brien, with Gillian Kendall
How I Became a Human Being: A Disabled Man's Quest for Independence

Elizabeth L. Banks
Campaigns of Curiosity: Journalistic Adventures of an American Girl in Late Victorian London
With a new introduction by Mary Suzanne Schriber and Abbey L. Zink

Miriam Fuchs
The Text Is Myself: Women's Life Writing and Catastrophe

Jean M. Humez
Harriet Tubman: The Life and the Life Stories

Voices Made Flesh: Performing Women's Autobiography
Edited by Lynn C. Miller, Jacqueline Taylor, and M. Heather Carver

Loreta Janeta Velazquez
The Woman in Battle: The Civil War Narrative of Loreta Janeta Velazquez, Cuban Woman and Confederate Soldier
With a new introduction by Jesse Alemán

Cathryn Halverson
Maverick Autobiographies: Women Writers and the American West, 1900–1936

Jeffrey Brace
The Blind African Slave: Or Memoirs of Boyrereau Brinch, Nicknamed Jeffrey Brace
as told to Benjamin F. Prentiss, Esq.
Edited and with an introduction by Kari J. Winter

Colette Inez
The Secret of M. Dulong: A Memoir